REWINDING YOUR BIOLOGICAL CLOCK

REWINDING YOUR BIOLOGICAL CLOCK

MOTHERHOOD LATE IN LIFE
Options, Issues, and Emotions

Richard J. Paulson, M.D.
and Judith Sachs

W. H. Freeman and Company
New York

JUL '24 2000

To the families of past and future patients, and to my own family,
who provide me with inspiration and purpose: Lorraine,
Jessica, Jennifer, Philip, Erika, and Wolfie Paulson.
And to all parents past and future, including
my own, Paul and Hanna Paulson.

R.P.

For my mother.

J.S.

Library of Congress Cataloging-in-Publication Data
Paulson, Richard J.
    Rewinding your biological clock : motherhood late in life : options, issues,
and emotions / Richard J. Paulson and Judith Sachs.
        p.   cm.
    Includes bibliographical references and index.
    ISBN 0-7167-3303-X
    1. Childbirth in middle age. I. Sachs, Judith, 1947– . II. Title.
RG556.6.P38   1998
618.2—dc21   98-36837
                                                                                        CIP

Printed in the United States of America

First printing, 1998

And God said unto Abraham, "I will bless [your wife Sarah], and moreover, I will give thee a son of her; yea…she shall be a mother of nations; kings of people shall be of her."

Then Abraham fell upon his face, and laughed, and said in his heart, "Shall a child be born unto him that is a hundred years old? And shall Sarah, that is ninety years old, bear?"

Now Abraham and Sarah were old, and well stricken with age; it had ceased to be with Sarah after the manner of women. And Sarah laughed within herself, saying, "After I am waxed old shall I have pleasure, my lord being old also?" And the Lord said unto Abraham, "wherefore did Sarah laugh, saying 'Shall I of a surety bear a child, who am old? Is anything too hard for the Lord?'"

And the Lord remembered Sarah as he had said, and the Lord did unto Sarah as He had spoken. And Sarah conceived, and bore Abraham a son in his old age.

Genesis 17:15–17, 18:11–14, 21:1–2

CONTENTS

PREFACE

I have always felt that medicine owed an obligation to give us more than good health. That is why I became a reproductive endocrinologist.

My first love, curiously, was physics rather than biology because it represented to me the essence of science—it was precise and exact, and it let me understand the nature of things. But I also felt that science should directly relate to people, and that's what led me to medical school. I chose obstetrics and gynecology because it was the one specialty that dealt with the essence of life itself—reproduction. Delivering babies was a messy and intensely primal experience, unlike any other. Guiding the transition from the womb to the outside world, witnessing the beginning of existence—it couldn't get much more exciting.

Most of medicine was an attempt to slow the inevitable decay of the body; to stave off the illnesses and injuries that beset us as we age. But a new baby was perfect—no atherosclerosis, no cancer, no arthritis. No matter how rough life had been for the parents, their new child was a clean sheet of paper on which to write a fascinating life story. Another thing I liked about my chosen specialty was that it dealt with some of the most crucial social issues of our time—contraception, world population, teen sexuality, and sex education.

From the beginning of my residency, I saw the subspecialty of reproductive endocrinology as something that would satisfy my need for precise, exact science. This study offered an essential understanding of the way cells worked and how the very inception of life was possible. Looking under a microscope, I could see the processes responsible for the survival of our species. It was complex, and yet basic. After my four-year specialty residency, I was too curious about this field to stop, so in 1984, I began my fellowship in reproductive endocrinology and infertility at the Los Angeles County/University of Southern California Medical Center.

At this time, in vitro fertilization (IVF) was in its infancy. There were only a handful of programs in the country, and successes were few and very far between. When I started work in this field, it was not with the intention of helping infertile couples to have babies (although I was hopeful that might be important in the future), but rather to help those women who had problems with hormonal regulation, such as female athletes who had stopped menstruating. I wanted to understand how nature knew so well what was going on inside an individual that it could turn reproductive potential on and off whenever the occasion called for it.

At the beginning of my second year of fellowship, in 1985, I started a rotation in the IVF program of USC under its director at that time, Richard P. Marrs, M.D. I was mesmerized by the ease with which I could see follicular development on the ultrasound machine and along with it, egg growth, maturation, and ovulation. It was concrete, right there before my eyes—not just a set of numbers I got back from a lab after doing blood tests for my patients' hormone levels. I was amazed at the process of follicle aspiration, which was an active intervention in the act of reproduction.

But what struck me most viscerally was the sight of human eggs, sperm, and embryos in laboratory dishes. This was it! The basics of life lay in front of me. These microscopic bundles of cells were my patients; some were well, and others were ill. Some died, but many made it and achieved ultimate success—they implanted and eventually became new human beings.

So infertility, and what medical science might do about it, became my passion. I could never understand why so many people, even some in the profession, regarded the treatment of infertility as out of the mainstream. It was considered a peculiar subbranch of obstetrics and gynecology, like the study of some rare and unknown disease that appeared once a millenium in a tiny segment of the population. This seemed absurd to me. After all, almost everyone chooses to reproduce, and everyone was vulnerable to the factors that cause infertility. I felt an immediate kinship with infertile couples—I always empathized and thought, "There but for the grace of God, go I."

And yet, it was not treated as a serious condition by the medical and health communities, and this struck me as heartless. Let's take the example of a young woman who develops leukemia and needs chemotherapy to survive. After her course of treatments (which are paid for by insurance because society empathizes with cancer victims), she's very likely to have lost ovarian function and be in premature menopause. In order to have a child, she'll have to find an egg donor to help her out. But society, so sympathetic to her leukemia, now turns around and says that wanting a baby at this point is a luxury she'll have to pay for herself, just as she might pay for elective plastic surgery. This inconsistency in attitude toward illness and health drove me deeper into my specialty—now I wanted to change minds as I assisted patients.

In the early years of my practice, I saw young women who were heartbroken because they couldn't do what seemed so easy for others. Here they were in the prime of their reproductive years, unable to reproduce. Over time, the scope of infertility treatment broadened, and older women started coming into my office, women who had had first families, but who wanted to try again, as well as women who had never conceived, but were now in stable relationships and wanted a child.

The issue of pregnancies among older women gave me pause at first. I was very skeptical about the motivations of older couples who wanted babies and concerned about the children who would be born to individuals of such advanced age. But over time, the determination and dedication of the women who came to me, as well as a family friend who lost a child and was too old to conceive again finally convinced me. I realized that the profession was changing in ways that would forever alter the classic vision of motherhood.

Reproductive endocrinology is still in its infancy—we will be able to do so much more as we investigate the intricacies of this field. We will be akin to physicists seeking elementary particles and fundamental physical laws. As we uncover more of the secrets that hold the key to new life, we may be able to balance population growth, eliminate genetic disease, design the perfect contraceptive, and accomplish other reproductive feats that will take all the surprise and shock out of pregnancy at menopause.

And as we look toward the future, we hope to be able to offer every person, regardless of age or physical well-being, his or her full reproductive potential. Having a baby is a creative act; making that act possible is both a challenge and a gift.

Richard J. Paulson, M.D.

ACKNOWLEDGMENTS

We gratefully acknowledge the enormous help and advice given by many colleagues in so many fields, the recipients, the donors, the counselors and therapists, the ethicists and the medical staff personnel at USC Infertility Center and at the University office.

The women who made up the character of Sarah and those donors who told their stories will not be mentioned by name. But they are the reason for this book, and our gratitude toward them is boundless.

The insights into the psychological process were afforded by:

Elaine Gordon, Ph.D., clinical psychologist, Santa Monica, CA

Margot Weinshel, Ph.D., The Ackerman Institute for the Family, NYC

Carol LieberWilkins, Ph.D., clinical psychologist, RESOLVE, Somerville, MA

Alice Domar, Ph.D., Beth Israel/Deaconness Hospital Infertility Center

Jane Rosenthal, Ph.D., Columbia-Presbyterian Hospital Infertility Program

Andrea Braverman, Ph.D., Pennsylvania Reproductive Associates

Mary English, CRMP MSN, Pennsylvania Reproductive Associates

Linda Applegarth, Ph.D., The Cornell Medical Center
Sandra Leiblum, Ph.D., Robert Wood Johnson Hospital Infertility
    Program

The complex world of bioethics was elucidated by:

Alexander M. Capron, J.D. The Law School, University of Southern
    California
Glenn McGee, Ph.D., Center for Bioethics, Philadelphia PA
John Robertson, J.D., University of Texas at Austin
Willard Gaylin, Ph.D., Hastings Center for Bioethical Research
George J. Annas, J.D., M.P.H., Boston University School of Public
    Health
Evelyne Shuster, Ph.D., Veterans Administration Medical Center

We would also like to thank the staff of the USC Infertility Center,
without whom the work would never be done:

Agnes Cotangco, R.N., IVF and oocyte-donor coordinator
Susan Klumph, L.V.N., IVF-nurse coordinator
Donice Crist, R.N., IVF nurse coordinator
Mary Francis, B.S., Laboratory coordinator
Wel Yuan, Ph.D., Embryologist
Heidi Wescott, Secretary
Diane Sinnott, Office manager
Dr. Chun-Yeh Wang
Dr. Johnny Jain
Dr. Sandra Bello

and Diane Quan at USC, who bravely established an e-mail connection
for the two technically challenged authors.

Thanks, certainly to our agent, Al Zuckerman, at Writers House for
standing by us and to John Michel, our editor, who had so much
enthusiasm for our project.

INTRODUCTION

It used to take two, a man and a woman of a certain age, to make a baby. These days, however, our options are practically unlimited. The biological imperative to reproduce used to come to a dead halt when the body had aged sufficiently and lost its alacrity to perform the magic trick of conception. But that's not the case anymore. Even if your hormones are flagging, your egg supply is low, your sperm aren't swimming, and your physiological equipment is faulty, you can still have a baby. You can borrow sperm or an egg from someone else, living or dead, or you can enlist the aid of a gestational carrier and implant your embryo in her uterus. You can have one child from this intervention, or multiple children, and in the future, if your embryo is split and one half is frozen for later implantation, you could even have identical twins born years apart.

Indeed, we live in a brave new world that has given hope to hundreds—literally a new lease on life to those who despaired of ever playing the parent role.

What does the development of this new technology say about the human drive to reproduce? That it is stronger than our instinct for personal survival: Somehow we know that if we wish to continue as inhabitants of this planet, we have to do anything and everything to keep our species going.

It makes no difference whether we are gay or straight, well or ill, young or of advanced reproductive age. In one way or another, we've been able to bypass most of these barriers. For centuries, men have kept on keeping on, because their ability to father a child never actually vanishes, although it does decline a bit as they get older. But for women, who are robbed at menopause of sufficient hormonal stimulation and viable eggs to get pregnant, the story has changed radically in the past decade. Women no longer have to content themselves with the grandmother role when they are itching to bring forth an infant and begin the age-old process of nurturing and supporting new life. Now those who choose to can go through the process of conception, gestation, and birth by borrowing an egg or even a uterus.

Everyone deserves the chance to bear children—and perhaps older mothers are the ones who deserve it the most. Giving birth may be the most important job we do on earth, because no matter what we have accomplished as individuals, it is only as we impart our knowledge, love, and caring to another generation that we imbue civilization with a sense of history. It is in having children, of course, that we live on after death.

We are never so keenly aware of the division between life and death as when we pass into that shadowy realm called middle age. Our own parents have become dependent or have passed on, leaving us in charge. Now we are old enough and experienced enough to realize our strengths, weaknesses, fears and hopes. Perhaps it's exactly at this time of life that we know ourselves best and have the most to give. Yes, we have doubts about our own futures, but we can see clearly, looking forward and back. And that makes us capable of being flexible, sensible, interesting parents.

"Sarah," the heroine of our story, is actually a composite of several women who took this leap of faith and decided to become mothers after they were no longer physiologically capable of conceiving without assisted reproductive technologies (ART). The lives of these women have been immeasurably enriched by the excitement and promise of the children they brought into the world when they were old enough to raise them well. The honest, nuts-and-bolts information about what it takes to be a pioneer is what gives *Rewinding Your Biological Clock: Motherhood Late in Life* its drive and commitment. The inspiration of what these women have accomplished keeps our eyes on the goal: do what you have to do in life, regardless of the obstacles.

Centuries ago, Dante Aleghieri began *The Divine Comedy* by writing that the middle of life is a time of confusion, when we are "lost in a dark wood where the straight path is obscured." When we are very young, we are encouraged to dream. Our teachers and mentors and our own parents, if they're not burned out and embittered by what life has left them with, tell us that our potential is unlimited, and we have the resources within ourselves to do anything we choose. But as we age, and life hammers us down, we start to settle and compromise. Maybe we can't save the world, maybe we'll never earn a million, maybe we won't go back to school and finish the degree. So being doctor, lawyer, Indian chief, falls by the wayside.

Now just imagine what we might accomplish if we knew that our human potential was bigger than we expected. Since we have the ability to stretch our human resources, a woman could be a mother at 60, an astronaut at 70, and President at 80. Instead of extreme old age being the time of decline and deterioration as society has characterized it, our final years could be the culmination of a lifetime of achievements that only get bigger and better as we get older. We will not go gentle into that good night; we will go with a bang rather than a whimper.

Post-youth, post-natural reproduction, we have been given a gift. What does it matter if your hair is gray and you can't see the print in the phone book anymore? This is small change—we've got the big money. Women today can bear children instead of preparing for their retirement. They can profit by the new technology that allows them to stretch their lives and their dreams. The way through that dark wood is clearer now, and on the other side is new life—for us and for the next generation.

CHAPTER ONE

SARAH, A WOMAN WITH A PURPOSE

She was running smoothly, easily, when it started to rain. No problem; she'd trained in rain and it didn't phase her. But what a bummer—her first marathon, and she'd been counting on everything going smoothly. *At 48, I need all the help I can get!* Sarah slipped and felt her ankle go. She quickly righted herself and picked up her pace, but she was annoyed. Why did she decide she didn't need her ankle brace? Was she fooling herself? This wasn't going to be easy.

The girl next to her, a California type with long, tanned legs that seemed to stretch out like Gumby's, pulled ahead effortlessly. She was 20, 25 at most. Her ponytail bobbed behind her with rhythmic intensity. *Okay,* Sarah thought, *I've been on this earth at least twice as long as her—I should pass her with life experience alone.* She remembered a great bumper sticker she'd glued to her ancient Volkswagen bug: "Old age and treachery will overcome youth and stamina." Her small, compact frame felt screwed into the ground, the raindrops getting behind her contact lenses. She blinked and breathed evenly, then surged forward. She felt the drag of the big hill begin when she heard the sound of thunder in the distance.

"Oh, damn." The girl looked at the sky anxiously, and she stopped dead. Sarah sailed past her, grinning to herself. *What a wuss. Letting a little storm scare her. Kids these days, they can't take anything.* It was funny how the weather didn't really seem like an obstacle, though maybe it should have. If it were really bad, they'd call the race. She could stop and get over into the shelter of one of the buildings. A van would come by and pick everyone up.

But right now, she just didn't want to stop. She wanted to leap across the finish line, with Joe cheering her on, and her kid sister Marilyn pelting her with paper cups full of water. Anyhow, she was certain it would be over before there was serious lightning and she got zapped.

There were these little kids all over the street, running out from under their parents' umbrellas. Probably they'd come to watch their moms running. "Look at that lady!" one pigtailed six-year-old yelled, pointing toward Sarah, "she has big feet and she's so fast!"

Kids. Loud ones, shy ones, kids everywhere. Kids watching grownups play. It was kind of a nice turnabout. Sarah had no trouble picking up speed after the child's encouragement. *What if she was mine,* she thought enviously, *I'd sweep her up in my arms and run with her.* She felt just that strong.

Her shirt was clinging to her thin chest, her breath a little ragged now. This hill was always a killer—Sarah didn't have the stamina for upgrades. Her ankle ached, and she told herself to stop thinking about what was wrong and concentrate on her goal. She had this picture of herself as a kid, running up a hill with her two big brothers, trying to catch up. She never did, damn it. But now she could run circles around either of them. Steve was 50 and a couch potato with abs that were buried in rolls of fat around his middle, and A. J., 52, was glued to his computer day and night and wouldn't run a race like this if you told him a pot of gold and a way out of his heart condition was waiting at the end of it. "Pure ridiculous nonsense," this true-blue academic would say.

She ran faster.

It was six years ago—when Sarah had just turned 42—that she started running in the park. She did it to get in shape after the accident that had nearly killed her two years earlier. She'd joked to Marge, her physical therapist, that not only was she going to walk again, she would run, and Marge had laughed and said, "go for it." But it was another year before Sarah was ready to tackle "the Race for the Cure," the local community effort to help beat breast cancer. Strange symbolism—the training was a cure for what had been the matter with her life for a while. She was going to get in shape—physically and emotionally. The accident was a great teacher.

She'd been in the passenger seat when her car was hit by a drunk driver coming home one night. The driver was badly injured, but Sarah almost didn't make it. Nearly every bone in her body was broken. They took out her spleen and gave her a lot of new dental work, and she had about a year of recovery to think about the rest of her life. She had a lot of changes to make, and this seemed just the right time. Breaking up with the married man she'd been counting on for the last six years, moving back east, getting a better job—it was incredibly tough, but she did it. She stopped smoking and feeling sorry for herself because she was suddenly manless and her life was in turmoil. The breakup with her lover was more wrenching than she could have ever imagined. Sure, she now felt like a person instead of a scumbag because she wasn't aiding and abetting the dissolution of the holy state of matrimony, but on the other hand, she was mourning the loss of a very important relationship. Since Sarah's marriage had ended 13 years earlier, Sam was the only serious coupling she'd done. But it was time for both of them to move on. She knew that, even though she didn't like it.

Her mind flipped back to all that she had already overcome. After the accident, after her limbs healed, her heart started to heal, too. She began to think about what she really wanted in life: What was so vital that she couldn't go to her grave without it? The running and health food and no smokes were all good—but all external. She longed for a connection to life that she hadn't yet made. After all, she was halfway done if the statistics were right. Another 40 or so years were sitting right there on her plate, but she was determined not to live them the same way she'd done the first 40.

What Sarah longed for was a family. More than just her sister and brothers, more than her crotchety mother. She wanted a baby.

And then she met Joe at an awards dinner. She didn't like him at first—he seemed aloof, awfully stuck on himself. He was 12 years younger than Sarah and had been a freelance advertising copywriter since college. But she found out over the next few months when they collaborated on a project together, that he didn't just *say* he knew everything, he really did. His surety and attitude were based in a self-confidence that, he later confessed, came from martial arts. He was a black belt in aikido; funny, smart, rooted like a redwood. And they started hanging out together, although Sarah was very wary. After her long-term affair, she didn't want to get sucked into falling in love again. And anyway, this guy was too young. What could they possibly have in common?

Except, as it turned out, they had everything in common. They loved gourmet cooking, cool jazz, and slow blues. And children. If there was anything they hadn't tried—sex in the bathtub, making eggrolls from scratch, riding their mountain bikes in the snow—they tried it. They were very touchy-feely. It was hard to sit in the same room and not connect. After eight months, they talked about getting married. Or Joe did. Sarah wasn't thrilled with the idea.

"I want you forever," he explained one day when they were taking a walk in the park. "And I want it in writing. I want to argue about which road we took to Aunt Bea's when we got lost in the snow."

"When was that?"

"It hasn't happened yet. But it will, and then 20 years from now, we can argue about it."

"This doesn't sound like a reason to go through all that *Sturm und Drang.*" Sarah was feeling uncomfortable. She had never liked marriage much. It was filled with expectations and boredom and broken promises and secrets. But she had been married to the wrong guy, after all, and she was certainly different from the nervous young designer she'd been at 28 when she got divorced. It was conceivable that with the right man and the right Sarah, it would work.

"Think about it," Joe said. "Think hard. Because I think we both need closure, sweetheart. I'm not going anywhere and you aren't either."

She shook her head, feeling her stomach bunch up.

"I like it the way we are. We live together, sometimes work together."

"We could be more," he said.

"I'll die before you," Sarah said.

"Women in this country typically outlive their husbands by six and a half years. I'm very healthy, which means I can last at least another five beyond that, whereas you went through a major body trauma in that car crash, which undoubtedly lowered your life expectancy. We can die together. What about that?"

Sarah started crying. It was ridiculous, but there had never been a person in her life who wanted her that badly. They stopped at the playground and sat next to the swings so she could retrieve the crumpled tissue from her shorts and wipe her eyes. A whiney toddler was holding a cookie in each hand as he sank down in the sandbox. Two sunburned, fair-haired, angular five-year-olds with Band-Aids on their Raggedy Ann's knees were playing in the shade; gawky boys with holes in their socks danced in the spray of the fountain.

And the mothers. Some barely out of their teens, but many old enough to be her kid sister. Most were in their thirties, with lustrous hair that didn't need Clairol to cover the gray, and no liver spots. They watched their children's frantic play with a detachment Sarah found annoying. They seemed distracted, anxious, or overprotective. They didn't know how lucky they were—but she did.

Sarah couldn't get kids out of her head. She was certain that this was the connection she was looking for, the one that would fill in the rest of the picture. If that were her kid in the sandbox, she would get down in there with him. She'd have skinned knees and a sunburned nose and a whole armful of Band-Aids. She'd climb trees and roll in the mud and do anything that would bring her close to this new person that she'd brought into the world. And Joe would be there beside her.

"Joe?"

"Yes."

"I was married when I was too young. Now I hope I'm not too old."

"Sweetheart ..."

"I want you, and I want a baby, too."

He squinted at her. "Adopting one?"

Sarah smiled. " Maybe. Although I was thinking of homegrown."

Evidently, there was a good reason to love this man. Instead of recommending intensive psychotherapy, he smiled back and took her hand and said, "I do."

So they got married. For a few months, they had lots of sex. It was delirious and fun, and they did it in all positions and all places and joked about the kind of baby that would come from that kind of intimate erotic contact. After a while, though, Sarah started to feel like she had an ulterior motive every time they went to bed. At 42, her clock was ticking slowly, inexorably down. Each month, when she saw that red stain, she sighed.

After six months, they went in together to talk to her doctor, and explained that they'd been having unprotected sex, with no results. The doctor explained that Sarah probably wasn't ovulating anymore, at least not regularly. The monthly bleeding was simply the sloughing off of the lining of her uterus under the stimulation of the hormones she was still producing. But her eggs were old, and not cooperating. She did say, though, that it was possible that there was one great egg left in one of her ovaries, just waiting to get goosed a little. She thought that they might start with some of the more conservative protocols before trying IVF, or in vitro fertilization.

They stimulated her ovaries with fertility drugs, but when nothing happened and she was about to celebrate her 43rd birthday, they moved on to IVF.

In vitro fertilization involved taking several ripe eggs from Sarah's ovary that had been stimulated to grow with supplemental hormones, and fertilizing them with Joe's sperm in a petri dish. The resulting embryos were then replaced in Sarah's uterus with the hope that one or two of them might implant.

The drugs she took made her moody and gave her headaches, and having Joe give her injections was not the nicest thing in the world, but she endured it, along with the repeated ultrasounds and blood tests. But she was encouraged; they told her she was a "good responder." That meant the medication was working.

On the day when her follicles were ripe and juicy, she was given drugs to make her relax and kill the pain, and the doctor harvested 12 eggs from the follicles in both of her ovaries. And then Joe went in a back room and masturbated into a specimen jar and they waited two days while the ingredients "cooked" in the petri dish and eggs and sperm cleaved together and went through cell divisions and turned into embryos.

"I feel like a little laboratory," she told Joe the morning they went to have the embryos placed in Sarah's uterus. "All these scientists are puttering around, doing experiments, pouring chemicals into test tubes. And now for the coup de grace. I'm nervous."

Was it nerves, or the failure of the eggs themselves, or just their rotten luck? Two IVF cycles later, nothing had happened, and Sarah was nearing her 44th birthday. She was heartbroken. "It should be so easy to make a baby," she moaned. "Everybody does it."

They tried another cycle. Their timing, they thought, was impeccable, but evidently Mother Nature didn't agree. About three weeks into her next cycle, Sarah was miserable, grouching at Joe, distracted at her job, unable to stop crying. It was time to call it quits.

"Listen, darling," she said to her husband that night in bed. "We gave it our best shot. I have to believe it's not in our cards to be parents. Maybe, after my untimely demise, when you've done your mourning, you'll take a real young bride and make plenty of babies, but ..."

He put a hand over her mouth. "That's not funny."

"Yeah, well, neither is this! My whole goddamn life has been consumed with drugs and blood and eggs and programmed sex. I've had friends go through years of banging their heads against walls, Joe. They've lost sleep and self-esteem and any hope they ever had. The stress, the expectation, whatever you want to call it, can destroy marriages. I don't want to get up at five so we can run to the doctor one more time for one more shot or one more test. It's absurd. Let's move on."

They went away for the weekend and didn't have sex. It was nice just cuddling.

Right foot. Left foot. Right foot. Funny, the kinds of thoughts that run through your head when you're so exhausted you can't move. The marathon was nearly over, but Sarah's legs were numb. For some reason, she kept flipping back to the baby they'd never had. Could never have.

The hill was way behind her, but Sarah was getting tired even on the flats. About half a mile to go. The rain pelted her back, her arms, her head. She watched other, sprightlier runners dashing beyond her. Was she too old to do this right? As she turned the corner of Laning Drive, she skidded and fell. She felt a burning sensation in her knee where she had scraped it.

There is a moment just before you complete a task when you doubt yourself, when you have a momentary urge to let it go, to give up before it becomes too much. She was really gone, but there had to be some way to get home. Looking up, she could see the banner across the finish line before her. Other runners were pouring on the juice, getting way ahead.

"Get up, Sarah! Don't just sit there, for God's sake!" She heard Marilyn screaming from the sidelines.

Oh, all right, she thought. *I have to do this or I'll hate myself for the rest of my life.* She choked back hot tears and dragged herself up from the pavement, feeling the rain push her on. She melded into the crowd around her, trying not to think about everyone ahead of her. She wasn't competing against them. It was just Sarah against Sarah. All she had to do was finish. A shirtless boy about three years old was waving a balloon at her, jumping up and down, really excited.

She put on some speed, breathing the way she was supposed to, from her diaphragm. Her heart beat a strong tattoo, and when she glanced down, she could see those muscles rippling up her thighs. *Nice legs for a 48-year-old,* was what Joe always said. *Push from your feet; let the body move as one unit.* He was her coach, her pain-in-the-ass prod, her one true love. And he knew what to say to get her revved up enough to conquer her fears.

Out of nowhere, Sarah's strength returned. This was it, better than sex, more satisfying than a double hot fudge sundae. *I'm flying. I'm better than I've ever been. I'm across the line.*

Then she saw Joe's face. He was waving a soggy bunch of daisies from a few yards away. She staggered, dripping, into his arms. "You done good, kid."

"What's my time?" Her breathing was ragged; a burning sensation right down her throat to her stomach.

"God, who knows? Who cares? Just enjoy the sensation of being here. Come to think of it, the sensation is pretty wet. Let's get out of here."

But she couldn't rest until Marilyn caught up to them wearing a Polaroid she'd taken of Sarah crossing the finish line. She'd stuck her wrist into the shot so that her watch was visible. She'd done it in 3 hours, 37 minutes, 12 seconds. Her own personal best. Sarah was glowing.

She sat on the leather couch in the living room that night, munching a half-sour pickle, ogling the food layouts in old *Gourmet* magazines, and remembering how far she'd come. She thought about what she'd been like right after the accident, angry and scared that she'd never be whole again, sitting uncomfortably in a chair with a wired jaw. She thought about herself two years later, limping along in the park every morning, doing her painful two miles at a slow jog. She thought about their wedding, and everything she and Joe had done together over the years. Only one thing they hadn't done.

"Sweetheart," Joe said quietly, mincing parsley, "I was reading about this woman in Italy, older than Sophia Loren, who had a baby."

"Oh, yeah?" Sarah rubbed her feet. They always thought of the same thing at the same time. It was getting boring.

"Ever heard of egg donation?"

She felt a pang at the pit of her stomach. "Yeah, it's a charity thing for Easter, right?"

"You are such a brat. You know what I mean. She got an egg from a younger woman and it got fertilized with her husband's sperm. Like our IVFs but with two women instead of one. Get it?"

A baby at 48. Was he nuts? They had a good marriage; they shared everything. She'd long since forgotten the IVF disasters. Well, not forgotten, but forgiven.

"Do you still want a child?"

"Of course I do. I think there's room in our life for something else, someone else. But I don't want the misery connected with getting one. I just don't want the process to take over our lives."

"I hear they have high success rates. I'd be willing to try," he said, "but only if you really want to. Think about it."

Years ago, after the accident, Sarah had spent a lot of time in therapy with a wonderful woman, Lolly Ford, who never directed her but simply let her explore some of the deeper issues in the recesses of her mind and soul. She called and made an appointment to see Lolly. Her therapist's hair had turned white, and she looked a lot shorter (although it was hard to tell sitting down across from each other). But she still wore what Sarah used to call her "hippy-dippy" print tunics and sandals to the office. She welcomed Sarah in, and it was like coming home. She'd always loved that room with its double doors (for perfect sound baffling in case you were crying hysterically) and the Native American masks, souvenirs of Lolly's residency on a reservation in New Mexico.

"What brings you here?" she asked when Sarah was silent after the hello.

"I'm on the edge of a big thought," Sarah said. "How much did I used to talk about my feelings about having another child?"

"Some. A lot, actually. But you said it was impossible."

"I guess because it was something I couldn't see doing alone. I was sure my mother wouldn't like it."

"Your mother doesn't like much of anything, as I recall."

"She'd be jealous that I'd spend more time with my child than her."

"I should hope. That's what you're supposed to do with babies. Mothers should be able to take care of themselves."

Sarah stretched out her legs. There was another long silence. "I'm married. I think you'd like him."

"Do you like him?"

Sarah laughed appreciatively. "I'm nuts about him. He's a mensch. My mother isn't thrilled. She actually asked me, 'how can you want to take care of a man when you have a mother as dependent as I am?'"

"Such a grownup," Lolly nodded. "It would be worse if you had a baby. You'll have to do a lot of ignoring. Your mother clearly still means a lot, maybe too much, to you."

"I'd love my child more than her. I already love Joe more than her. Yeah, I do think about her a lot." Sarah fiddled with her fingers, reaching for an imaginary cigarette. She had always smoked in therapy. "But I don't feel guilty. It's taken me all these decades to realize that being selfish is okay."

"Why do you think giving love is selfish?"

"Not selfish. Self-filled. Isn't that one of those jargony, self-help phrases you shrinks came up with to make the client feel okay? Ah. Yes. It's that when people are needy and clingy and demand me that I turn off. When they just open in my arms, then I learn how to care and love."

"I guess you're happy with Joe." It was a statement rather than a question.

"He's it. He never goes away and just gets bigger and better. It's so neat how we click in, like Legos. I remember when I was in high school, I had this friend named Katie—the first of us to have a real boyfriend. And she said to me that she had 'baby in the eye' when she looked at him—as though she could actually visualize the child that would come out of both of them. God help her, she dropped out to have that kid, and you can imagine, none of us were supposed to mention this scandalous event ever again. But I keep thinking about what she said before she consciously had a child with this boy. She was driven by something, and because she was so young and stupid, she didn't know how to control it.

"I feel just like that when I look at Joe. We would make a very good baby together. We tried and failed before. But this time, it could work."

"Pardon me for asking, but is there a piece of this you haven't told me? Are you still menstruating? Are you like one of those Georgians in Russia who eat yogurt and surpass all records for human development and longevity?"

Sarah started to laugh. "Lolly, we're going to use an egg from some young woman who'll donate to us."

"Such a brave new world. When I was young, I thought babies came from the stork."

"Well, you were very dumb. I'm glad you've learned so much in the last few years." They grinned at each other.

"Joe's with you on this?"

"He seems to be. I know I've got a few years on him, but he's never been married before, and seems to feel like he has all the time in the world."

"That's a problem of your generation," Lolly nodded. "You've always gotten whatever you wanted when you wanted it—the good job, the nice car, the 7-11 in the middle of the night in case you absolutely have to have a Twinkie. You guys don't know the meaning of 'can't.'" She sighed and scratched her nose. "So I suppose you came to have me give you my blessing."

Sarah got up and went to the window. "I have to tell you I'm really scared. I've lived lots of decades, kind of sleepwalking through my life. I got into that affair with Sam never wondering if he'd really leave his wife, and all those years passed, and it was nice, but it didn't gain me anything except some good sex. He and I talked about a child then, but some little voice inside me said it wouldn't have been right. I just wish the voice had talked to me sooner. And I stayed at one job forever assuming I'd be made head of the department. It never happened. And then the car crash."

"Have you talked to Alison about this?"

Sarah's face froze. "No."

"Did she come to your wedding?"

"No, it was just me and Joe and a couple of friends. She was too far away." Lolly just had to twist the knife—of course that's what a good shrink does.

"Are you going to call her, Sarah?"

"I will. Don't nag."

"I think that might be a good idea. How long has it been now?"

She took a breath that rattled in her throat. "Almost four years."

"Time to get your *whole* life in order."

Sarah's eyes were wet. "I want ... I'm so tied in knots whenever I think about her."

"She wasn't trying to kill you that night, it was the drunk driver. We've been through all this."

"Of course."

"Babies grow into children, Sarah. And children grow into adults. They always have and they always will."

Sarah couldn't answer that one. When her allotted 45-minute hour was over; she wondered why she'd come. She was angry, and walked the 30 blocks home with a rigid face and hard eyes.

Joe was making a soufflé when she walked in and threw herself on the couch.

"How about a salad? Would you wash some lettuce? Hey, what's with the puss? Sweetheart, what's wrong? What happened with Lolly?"

Sarah chewed her lower lip for a moment. "I spent some time this afternoon thinking of ad campaigns. Great deals for elderly moms—the new mother gets a box of Depends and the Huggies are half-price. Or how about she buys the Anbesol for teething and she can use it on her dentures too? Isn't that great? Joe, there will be combos of product lines we never dreamed of—wheelchair manufacturers will throw in a pair of rollerblades; Medicare will be prevailed upon to pay for orthodonture. I mean, the advertising industry will go berserk."

He sat down and took her hand. "Second thoughts?"

"And third and fourth ones. I'm having a hot flash right now and contemplating pregnancy. I must be certifiable. But, and this is the weirdest thing, I'm acting like I want to turn back, but I feel this is so important I can't. Every time I think of a hurdle, I think of how to get around it. I just, really, more than anything else I've ever accomplished, think that being a mother now at this time in my life, would be exactly right."

"I want to do this with you, sweetheart. But I'm very well aware that I get to stand by and watch and you have to go through this whole thing. Motherhood could fall heavily on your shoulders. It's not like you're the most easygoing person in the world."

"So, where do we begin?" Sarah's soft brown eyes took in the room, the view out the dining room window to the park beyond. She looked down at her long hands and big feet sticking out of her long rayon skirt and her husband's leg touching hers. Very substantial, that's how she felt. There was something to this new turn of events. She'd begin with a phone call to the doctor. She'd need a specialist. She'd need all kinds of tests. Probably an evaluation by a psychiatrist. There had to be lots of other women who'd done this before—she could talk to them.

She got up to make the salad. She'd worry about everything else tomorrow.

CHAPTER TWO

MOTHERS AND BABIES
OF A NEW AGE

Motherhood is a sticky issue. There is probably no concept more integral to our lives than "mother." The word is worn on the arms of sailors, talked about in church, celebrated by Hallmark, used as a down-and-dirty curse on the streets. A mother soothes away the cries and tears of the infant in her arms as she rocks with a rhythm so old it can't be dated. She bares her breast and encourages that little mouth to latch on, so that the nourishing flow of her milk can sustain the life she has engendered. Mother is the voice in the dark that banishes the monsters; she is the one we call when we're down and out. Mother prods and pokes us to be better than we are, to overcome obstacles and make our way in the world. You think about mother, you think about your roots—what you are and where you came from.

Who should be a mother? It has to be someone who can perform the procreative act and bear children, right? Except that many wonderful mothers aren't able to conceive and gestate a child. Many terrific mothers have adopted kids.

One other idea we have about mothers is that they're young. But among the extremely longevous Tarahumara Indians of northern Mexico, in select communities in the Russian Caucasus, and in certain mainland Chinese villages, there are women for whom menopause doesn't occur until their late fifties. These women routinely bear children at what we would consider an advanced reproductive age. And in our own society, there are grandmothers of 80 who take over the mothering role after their own children have died, gone to jail, or moved out. So a mother can be pretty old.

Maybe a mother who gives birth to her own children has to be anatomically and physiologically able to bring forth new life. Her body has to conform to certain biological and chemical criteria.

But maybe not.

In Biblical times, having a baby at 90 was a miracle. Today, we may call it miraculous, but it could be possible, since science has mastered a lot of miracles. Perhaps 90 is stretching it a bit, but a modern-day Sarah, several decades younger than her ancient sister, can achieve a pregnancy and deliver a child decades after she loses her own reproductive ability.

The advent of *assisted reproductive technology (ART)*, where an egg and a sperm can be removed from the human body, joined together in a biological marriage, and replaced in a uterus (the mother's or another woman's), has greatly expanded the scope of human reproduction. The question is, Just because the mountain is there, do we have to climb it? Just because we can manipulate life, should we do it? And how do we select—or do we?—the suitable candidates from the unsuitable ones?

What Can We Gain from the Science and Art of Medicine?

Babies with serious medical problems used to die in utero; today, we can operate on them while they are inside their mother. When coronary bypass surgery was first developed, it was a temporary slap in the face of death, providing a few more brief years after a heart attack. Today, this surgery may afford several decades more of life *before* an infarction strikes, to someone whose heart is *likely* to break down. Diseased livers, lungs, and kidneys used to lead inevitably to the end of life; today, organ transplant offers a second chance to those who might not even have had a first. Our society thrives on technological advances—at first, they are used only in emergency situations, then, as methods become more efficient, they are weaned into the lexicon of possible treatments. And finally, as society starts to accept the advent of a new order, these advances can be used to improve the quality of everyone's life.

Of course, these innovations I've just described *save* lives. Is medicine valuable only in its ability to cure disease and to repair abnormalities? Or is it worth more? *Isn't creating a new life as valuable as saving an existing one?* If there were to be a deadly plague that swept the world, our species would vanish and the only remaining legacy of our civilization would be a junkpile of cars, computers, and compact discs. A germ that was able to wipe out human reproductive ability would have the same result, albeit delayed. If you imagine the earth five decades after such an infection, the population comprised only of people over 50, then the significance of ongoing reproduction takes on a lot more weight. Something vital is at stake here.

The desire to reproduce is one of the strongest human drives, second only to survival itself. If none of us passed on our DNA and undertook to parent the next generation, life would end with us. And though there are those who never feel the pang of their own mortality, most of us feel that we can continue in some form after our own deaths by perpetuating our line across time and space. We are here, then we're not here, but the children who live after us preserve our memory and our experience—and pass along our legacy to their own children. This is what makes history.

There are, of course, many arguments against using ART to help older women. Some denounce egg donation as selfish, stating that midlife women had their chance and squandered it. They wasted years on building careers, traveling abroad, and moving from one relationship to the next before finding the "perfect" one. And now, after they've passed the finish line, they want another chance to run the race. Some say such reproduction is unnatural, that women were biologically equipped to be fertile for a limited time only—so we should keep it that way.

People say it's unfair to the child—that each individual born on earth deserves to have a mother up to and even through their maturity.

People say it's an inappropriate application of science and technology—that high-tech medicine should cure rather than enhance. *Oocyte,* or egg, donation was developed for young women who had gone through premature ovarian failure, or who had lost their ovaries through surgery or radiation, but more recently, it has been applied to women of all ages who desire a baby.

People say it's coercive, that the monies given to donors and the impassioned pleas leveled at young family members put an unfair pressure on women who might otherwise hold onto their eggs. There are ethical arguments around familial donation—that daughter-to-mother egg donation as well as father-to-son sperm donation should be prohibited because of the confused kinship arrangements that might result.

There is the problem of disclosure: Do you tell your child, and if so, when? If you don't tell, do you set up a series of family secrets that may one day explode in your face? If you do tell, are you saddling your child with information that may stigmatize him or her throughout life?

There's the religious argument: God didn't intend for babies to be born this way, and to take over God's job is beyond the scope of the human ego. One feminist argument maintains that high-tech fertility is all an elaborate plot on the part of a male-dominated society to keep women barefoot and pregnant until the day they die.

Some of these may be legitimate concerns, but do they really justify withholding treatment from those who would benefit from it? Isn't it a woman's right to bear children if and when she wants to, regardless of whether she needs technological assistance to do it? If we are really pro-choice, we should be champions for the inception of life as well as control of reproduction by contraception, and for the option of terminating unwanted pregnancy. Why not allow women to become pregnant in their forties and fifties when their maturity renders them able to be nurturing mothers who love and give of themselves entirely?

If you are physically capable of having a baby, and happen to do so, no one squawks. But if you are slightly unconventional—if you're single, a lesbian, or over 50—your desire to become a parent suddenly gets put under the spotlight. You are immediately suspect for longing to complete the part of your life plan that is a given for others. Some women would be great mothers at 55, others would be terrible mothers at 25, and vice versa. As a society, is it really in our best interest to try to regulate who can parent and who can't or when they should do it? Think of the arbitrary limits that would be set: premenopausal, with a clean bill of health, a strong constitution, an IQ of 120, and a predilection for someone with a set of genitals different than yours.

This is nonsense. The people who will be the best parents are those who are committed, motivated, caring, and loving. They are the ones who are most likely to put in the time, money, and emotional output necessary to buoy up the next generation. And if they choose not to adopt an already existing child, but wish to add something of themselves to the collective gene pool, why not let them do so?

Postmenopausal pregnancy is simply a new way of respecting individual choice. Life and science are not always in sync—one usually has to play catch-up with the other. We are all born with a vast potential that we never tap, but thankfully, as technology provides us with new keys for old locks, we become freer. Within the bounds of safety and moral and ethical appropriateness, we should allow every woman, every couple access to the full range of reproductive innovation. As our society ages, and what used to be considered "midlife" becomes "youthful plus 10 or 20," it is imperative to endow those most mature, most experienced, and most resourceful to participate fully in every aspect of social and cultural activity. Isn't it about time we stretched the stages of human development to match our own shifting capabilities?

THE STAGES OF LIFE

In the Middle Ages, childhood ended at six or seven, when the now small adult was put to work to help keep the family going. Today, young people may be supported by their families well into their twenties (and we all know several 40-year-olds who never left home and are *still* hanging onto mom and dad).

Puberty used to be the dividing line between infancy and maturity. Today, it is a jump-off point for a life well lived or squandered. Teens can go wild and stay wild, or use these years to explore independence and question authority.

Then we come to the reproductive years. In centuries past, this stage coincided with puberty since life was short and at age 12 or 13 it was high time to start on the next generation. The Industrial Revolution and mandatory public education changed all that, and women finished grammar school and then went to work to help support a family. In this era, they generally didn't start getting pregnant until they were in their late teens or early twenties. As more women opted for high school and higher education, even more time elapsed before the first pregnancy. Up through the 1950s, women traditionally waited until graduation, and then bore children up to their early thirties. It was unusual for a woman to be adding to her family after she was 35.

But in the past four decades, there has been a radical swing in the childbearing years. Teen pregnancy has become a watermark of the permissiveness of our society gone to extremes. Young kids have babies because they can. If they've thought about their action at all, they may rationalize that they can get unconditional love from this little creature (unlike the very iffy type of love they get from their parents). In the worst-case scenario, they discover they are incapable of this huge responsibility, and disaster may strike in the form of neglect, abandonment, or abuse—even infanticide.

At the other end of the spectrum, the twentieth century has seen a much older group of mothers. Working women have opted to have their families later, after their careers are established. They may have had a first family, then gone to work, and years later, married again. Many older women who have finally settled into life, at last comfortable with a partner they love, and resources of their own to bring to the relationship, want a new family. Like Sarah, they see the future clearly and know they are finally capable of sharing what they bring from their past and what they can do now in the present.

So when is the right time to have children? If only we knew. What's clear is that being a parent, at any age, is about the most important job we do throughout our lives. If no one were willing to be a parent, every generation would have to start from scratch. Each person born on earth would have the lonely chore of learning the pain and problems of dealing with the world. Parents exist to nudge and prod and guide and discipline and encourage and supervise so that children can be sheltered during their growing years, and make mistakes safely, knowing that they can pick themselves up and try again. The good thing about having parents is that they let us fall, but not too far. We can learn something without taking too many risks.

It's one thing to make a new life, but quite another to stick out the next few decades to parent the next generation. At 18, a woman has attained her full hormonal potential, but she is also busy creating her own persona, her circle of friends, her intimate relationship, her career path. She may be perfectly capable of having a child, but developmentally, she is barely out of childhood herself, and therefore will find it very difficult to give unselfishly of her time and energies without stifling her own growth. And that's where the older parent comes in.

When you've been on earth for a while, you have your priorities in order. You can go out and party but still be aware of your responsibility to feed and change the baby in the middle of the night and get up in the morning and go to work. You can enjoy a rich sex life within your commitment to one person so that your child will be secure in the love of his family. You can take care of your aging parents and your child at the same time if you have to without giving up on one or the other, no matter how overwhelmed you may feel. You can take care of yourself—physically, mentally, emotionally, and spiritually. And you can marvel at how much you grow as you watch your small son or daughter discover their fingers, take their first steps, and eat their first ice cream cone. You don't relive that stage with them, but instead, you are able to view your own childhood through the lenses of your maturity and overlay of all you've experienced since those long-ago days.

Having a child late in life isn't easy. But it may be the best thing for the child because you have waited so long and worked so hard to arrive at this stage.

MEN, WOMEN, AND SEX

As we know, the deck is not stacked evenly. It is perfectly "natural" for a man to produce children when he's 80, and no one says boo about it. Why should men be able to father children forever while women are time limited? A man, who manufactures sperm throughout his lifespan, can make babies (barring congenital defects, disease, or trauma to his reproductive organs) until the day he dies. A woman, who is given just so many eggs at birth and no more, has only a few decades in which to conceive.

Throughout the centuries, old men have married young women so that they can feel vigorous and potent, and also so that they can add heirs to their line. In our century, Pablo Picasso, Pablo Casals, Tony Randall, and Strom Thurmond were all in their seventies or eighties when they gave out cigars and everyone congratulated them with winks and smiles. It's an accolade for a man to be that virile at any age, but when he's really old, and has succeeded in giving his young bride a baby, he is Super-Stud. His plumbing works just fine, thanks, and the one sperm that found its way to the desired destination was motile, viable, and had no chromosomal abnormalities. Pretty darned good for an old guy.

Remember, too, that if any of these fellows had had a problem with the mechanical end of things (trouble with the hydraulics of the penis that must launch those swimming sperm), medical science would have been right there, ready to assist. An injection or a vacuum pump might have helped him keep his erection, or, if an external aid was not sufficient, an implanted pump could have produced an erection for him any time he pressed a button. And now, thanks to a fluke in pharmaceutical experimentation, keeping it up is as easy as downing a little blue pill.

But society, up to now, has not felt the same about female fertility. After menopause, hormonal levels decline dramatically, and the few, if any, existing eggs left in the two ovaries are not viable. At this point, a woman's connection with reproduction is severed. She can be a grandmother, and care for other women's children, but up until about 10 years ago, she could not be a mother. And if *she* experienced sexual difficulties, there were fewer options available to her than to her male colleague. She could get a prescription for vaginal estrogen, or use a water-based lubricant, but if she was in extreme discomfort, she might just stop having sex. Too soon to give up on this wonderful activity, but many postmenopausal women aren't given the encouragement—even by their doctors—to go on.

To see a woman of 50 pregnant is a shock. It's not unusual to see a middle-aged woman with a child she's adopted—but it's not usual either. There are those who don't think anyone in middle age has enough get-up-and-go to chase a toddler, let alone last long enough to attend that child's college graduation. Society says that this is stretching legitimate parenthood a bit. But what about a 50-year-old who pulls out all the stops? To see her with a big belly of which she is justly proud, or to see her nursing her child in a public place, well, it turns heads. Some people say it's "distasteful," "unseemly," or even "repugnant" to be reminded that a woman past menopause can also consummate The Act. Just when we think we know what men and women are all about, those menopausal matrons go and act like they were 20—young and perky again.

We have trouble with a 50-year-old woman who proclaims to the world that she is still vibrant and sexy. Yes, sex was ever the culprit in the motherhood drama, and the remnants of our puritan heritage trump our interest in new technology . (Technically speaking, of course, a woman having a baby through egg donation does not have to have sex. It's our image of her getting "knocked up" that's the problem.)

We do not castigate men in the same way for the same action. Imagine for a minute: Henry Kissinger, George Steinbrenner, or Milton Berle holding his new baby in his arms. Certainly possible. Now wipe away that image and replace it with Margaret Thatcher, Barbara Bush, and Dr. Ruth.

Does not compute.

There is no reason to think these women could not become mothers today. But most individuals would severely disapprove. For a woman, there have always been limits, and society likes to keep it that way. We should consider how narrow-minded that seems in today's world. Women baby boomers are hurtling past menopause. They are actively involved in every facet of human endeavor, including the most hazardous or physically taxing—they work in fire and police departments, they rock-climb, they do white-water rafting. Why not let them do something essential: have babies?

THE INFERTILITY EPIDEMIC

The only way that the species continues is by reproducing itself. And from earliest times, men and women have called upon their particular deities requesting that they be allowed to bear children. If you look at the statuary of every ancient civilization, you will see fertility icons—the short, squat, full-bellied, full-breasted females of South America and India; the long, tall females with jutting breasts and a surprise stomach from Africa and Hawaii. The power of these goddesses was considerable in societies that were anxious about the perpetuation of their race.

There were also communities where infertility was grounds for divorce. In some African tribes, a woman was encouraged to commit adultery if her husband was impotent, and the husband was urged to do the same if his wife was barren. In one Nuer tribe in the Sudan, a new wife would not even move into her husband's home until her first baby was weaned—if the child did not survive, the marriage would be null and void and she would have had to move back to her parents' house anyway. This is not an archaic tradition. In twentieth-century California, an Italian-American man was overheard telling his son-in-law to consider divorcing his wife, because after three years of marriage, she hadn't yet borne him children. It was obvious to the father that his daughter was worthless. In today's Beverly Hills, some Arabic fathers demand semen analyses of their daughters' fiancés prior to consenting to the marriage, lest their daughter be blamed for future infertility.

Fortunately for family solidarity, throughout most of the world, infertility is currently regarded as a medical problem that can be solved in many cases. But for some women alone and many couples, all the IVF treatments in the world won't help. Whether a woman is 28, and has just lost ovarian function because of a course of chemotherapy for leukemia, or she's 40, and has just learned she has Huntington's chorea, a condition she would not willingly pass onto the next generation, if she truly desires a child, she may walk through fire many times to get one.

Fertility counts. It counts a lot. Infertility can ruin your sex life, your relationship with your friends and relatives, and most important, it can destroy the delicate fabric of a marriage. Even if you are not infertile, but of advanced reproductive age, you may spend countless days and nights longing for that which you've been denied. Nature has gone out of her way to keep our species going, but she cares nothing for the individual. And so, if we have trouble conceiving, we go back to the totems—we don't just rub the belly of a pregnant goddess, we also go to the reproductive endocrinologist for a full workup. We will pray that one of the treatments or technological advances will do for us what we could not accomplish naturally. Reproduction is the essence of life; it's what makes us more like a tree than a rock, putting out new shoots and spreading seeds that will grow into new trees. And if we can reverse a fertility problem, we will.

By the year 2000, nineteen million women in this country will have stopped menstruating—and many of them deeply regret the fact that they will no longer be able to conceive. Although fertility rates drop sharply after the age of 35, and it's practically impossible to get pregnant without assistance after 45, there are plenty of women out there who try. And try.

What happened to the fear you had in high school that the first time you had unprotected sex, you would instantly and irrevocably become a parent? Funny how what seemed as easy as breaking a condom became the biggest chore of your later years. As the years pass, the likelihood of natural conception lowers, until by midlife, it is incredibly difficult, maybe impossible.

In 1800, in America, most women bore seven children, of whom, on average, five survived infancy (many did not live to reproductive age). By 1880, the average number of live births per woman was just over four, and by 1900, it had dropped to three and a half. Margaret Sanger was busy educating America about birth control and getting thrown into jail repeatedly for her efforts, and Teddy Roosevelt was vehemently against limiting family size. He blasted small families as "decadent," and denounced women who didn't want children as "criminal against the race ... the object of contemptuous abhorrence by healthy people." But his admonitions fell on deaf ears, and 50 years later, when most baby boomers were toddling around, there were only 2.5 children in each typical American family—primarily by choice but also, perhaps, because of increased difficulty conceiving as women had their families later in life. There is a statistic that says that as the mean age of childbearing rises, fertility rates inevitably drop. Of course, this is as much a sociological as a biological statistic; naturally, fewer women over the age of 40 will *want* four children, regardless of whether or not they can have them. According to surveys from the National Center for Health, in 1979, about 40,000 American women waited until they were over 30 to have their first child. Just one year later, that number had increased by 250 percent, which coincided with a doubling in the reported incidence of infertility.

Since more couples postpone having families these days, and divorce and remarriage cause older couples to attempt second or even third families, our chances for hitting the bull's-eye whenever we want get worse as time passes.

HELP FOR INFERTILE COUPLES AND SINGLES—ASSISTED REPRODUCTIVE TECHNOLOGY

Helping couples to achieve pregnancy may be as simple as pointing out how reproduction works and when a woman's ovulation occurs. But most couples who come to the fertility specialist end up requiring more substantial assistance, and happily, there's a large menu of techniques available today. The first and simplest intervention is the use of fertility medications, to induce ovulation in women who do not regularly release an egg from their ovaries. Next, we might try *intrauterine insemination (IUI)* in which sperm (from a partner or a donor) are concentrated in a centrifuge and inserted back into the female reproductive tract. The more technically sophisticated techniques involve collecting both eggs and sperm, combining them in the laboratory, and then replacing them at a specific time in the female reproductive tract. The *assisted reproductive techniques (ARTs)* range from the relatively simple *gamete intra-fallopian transfer (GIFT)* to the more complex *tubal embryo transfer (TET)*.

All of the ARTs represent attempts to refine and improve the original technology of *in vitro fertilization (IVF)*. In this procedure, the ovaries are stimulated with supplemental hormones so that they will produce multiple follicles (each one containing an egg). The eggs are collected from the ovaries just prior to ovulation, and are then placed in a petri dish with the sperm where they can be fertilized. The resulting embryos are then put back into the female reproductive tract where hopefully, one or several will implant. The methods of egg retrieval have changed, the techniques of ovarian stimulation have been refined, and laboratory methods have taken several quantum leaps ahead, but the process has remained essentially unaltered from its development some 20 years ago.

In order to understand egg donation, which is reproduction using multiple individuals' gametes, we must first understand IVF. So let's go back to the beginning of the story. It all started with an animal geneticist in Yorkshire, England.

THE HISTORY OF IVF

Robert Edwards was fascinated by superovulation, the process by which he could cause many eggs, rather than one egg at a time, to blossom from a mouse ovary. As a laboratory scientist in the 1950s, he needed large numbers of mice, so he stimulated them with hormones and was delighted to be able to harvest hundreds of eggs from them. His fascination with fertility persisted through the next decade, when he began experimenting with human eggs, sperm, and embryos, but it wasn't until 1967, when he met up with gynecologist Patrick Steptoe, that his ideas came to fruition.

Steptoe had been excited by a new procedure called *laparoscopy*, where you could perform surgery without opening the entire abdomen, using only two tiny incisions. This caused a lot less trauma to the patient, and recovery time was brief.

Edwards, at this point, was considering using medication to help women with infertility due to ovarian failure, but he desperately wanted to look inside the body and see the ovaries he was treating with superovulation drugs. At a meeting of the Royal Society of Medicine in London, he made the acquaintance of Patrick Steptoe. The marriage of laparoscope and superovulated ovaries was destined to occur.

By 1968, the two men had developed most of the techniques that made IVF possible, and over the next few years, they perfected the harvesting of superovulated eggs beneath the view of the laparoscope. Working to get as many ripe follicles as possible, they gave the volunteer women in the program hormones known as *human menopausal gonadotropins (hMG)* three times between the third and ninth days of their menstrual cycle. Then, between days 9 and 11, they administered one dose of *human chorionic gonadotropin (hCG)*, the hormone that would trigger ovulation. They waited 30 hours after the injection, then put their patients to sleep and performed the laparoscopy. Carbon dioxide was pumped into the abdominal cavity of the patient, making it easy to see the various organs inside.

Using a delicate needle, Steptoe was able to retrieve many mature eggs from their follicles with very little effort. These eggs were then inseminated in the laboratory. By 1971, Steptoe and Edwards were able to grow embryos in a culture medium to the 8- or 16-cell stage. The problem was getting the embryos to implant and grow properly when returned to the human body. And an even larger problem was that this experimental work with the building blocks of human life was roundly denounced by many physicians, lawyers, ethicists, and theologians. The idea of manipulating eggs and embryos in this way was heresy: Suppose the resulting children were deformed or even monstrous? The possible risk to the unborn child was considered unwarranted. But as other researchers began delving into the murky waters of assisted reproduction, the procedures Steptoe and Edwards espoused were tolerated, if not applauded.

In 1975, after five years of trial and error, the researchers were over-joyed to achieve their first pregnancy through IVF. It seemed to be going well until somewhere around the twelfth week, when the patient's increasing abdominal pain forced Steptoe to operate. The pregnancy was growing in her fallopian tube (an *ectopic gestation*), and could have caused internal hemorrhage which would have endangered her life.

Steptoe and Edwards went back to the drawing board. What were they doing wrong? They decided—incorrectly, as it turned out—that the problem lay in using fertility drugs which had upset the patient's hormonal balance. So with their next group of patients, they decided to rely on the natural cycle—no drugs at all. They would risk having only one egg to work with. After many attempts, fate brought them Lesley Brown, a 30-year-old woman from Manchester who was desperate to have a baby. As Brown's time of ovulation approached, they removed the egg from her ovary by laparoscopy and housed it in a laboratory dish. Taking a semen sample from her husband, the hopeful doctors then mated egg and sperm in the laboratory.

Following a hunch that Lesley's body rhythms would be best for implantation a precise number of hours later, they waited two and a half days and prepared an operating room in the hospital at midnight. With steady hands, holding the catheter, Steptoe transferred the embryo through Lesley's cervix and into her uterus.

It worked. The first IVF and embryo transfer baby was on its way, and on July 25, 1978, Louise Brown was born.

The world was not too sure what to make of this brave step forward. There were hundreds of desperate women, of course, who barraged Steptoe and Edwards with letters, requesting assistance with their own pregnancies. But at the same time, there were denunciations right and left—that the whole thing was a hoax, or that the Steptoe/Edwards team and others that were springing up around the world were playing fast and loose with people's hopes and dreams, exploiting them so that they could continue their devious reproductive experimentation. England and Australia leapt to the forefront of embryo transfer research, but there were stirrings in America as well.

America's first IVF baby, Emily Carr, was born in 1981. Soon afterward, the Jones Institute in Virginia began registering successful IVF procedures. Howard Jones was quick to defend assisted reproductive technologies against their detractors who were concerned about the element of "playing God" in the conception of human life. Jones argued that there was not simply one moment in time when life began; instead, generation was actually an ongoing continuum. Consider it this way, he said: Two bits of tissue—two *gametes*—have existed since the individuals carrying them have existed. Sperm and eggs, of course, are gametes, not people. So when you combine them to make an embryo, you can safely say that you are just continuing the process that began (without your intervention) many years ago.

The History of Egg Donation

By the early 1980s, stories of successful IVF births were becoming commonplace. It was apparent that this technology in which fertilization was accomplished outside the body wasn't going to vanish, and as a matter of fact, it would undoubtedly become a mainstream option. Although just a few years earlier, physicians laughed when the subject of egg donation for women who had lost ovaries to cancer or infection came up, now we began to think seriously that third-party reproduction might be the solution for women who couldn't use their own eggs.

This was already commonplace for sperm, of course. Sperm donation has probably been going on since the dawn of man, and we have documentation that it's been used for the last hundred years. You can go to a commercial sperm bank anywhere in the world and find the same setup: The sperm are stored in vials submerged in liquid nitrogen at −196 degrees Celsius, a technique known as *cryopreservation*. At this extremely low temperature, there is no biological activity, and it appears that sperm—or any other cryopreserved tissue—can be stored indefinitely. In most sperm banks, samples from anonymous donors are held for six months in the storage facility after donation until the donor has been proved negative for any infectious disease. When the sperm are needed, they are thawed just prior to insemination.

Sperm is not only plentiful, it's easy to get and easy to give. Eggs, on the other hand, are a lot more difficult to get hold of. Pregnancy by egg donation requires the manipulation of eggs and embryos outside the human body, although they were never designed to live anywhere other than the reproductive tract. But when we started using IVF, we realized that this was what would have to happen. Once you were in the laboratory staring at eggs in one dish, sperm in another, and embryos in a third, it didn't take a great leap of imagination to think about replacing the eggs of the infertile woman with those of a fertile donor.

Eggs would be retrieved from the egg donor just as they were from IVF patients. They'd be mixed with sperm in the laboratory, and the resulting embryos would then be placed into the recipient. But in the early 1980s, when the new technology was just blossoming, egg retrieval was a clumsy process. We had to perform surgery—the "belly-button operation," or laparoscopy—and the patient had to be given general anesthesia. We really didn't know where we were going to get donors and how we'd compensate them. Consequently, work in this area progressed slowly.

During this time, a novel technology which used a more "natural" approach to egg donation made a brief appearance. Dr. John Buster and his colleagues, who were working at the institution where I happened to be a resident in obstetrics and gynecology, borrowed this innovative technique, known as "ovum transfer," from the animal husbandry industry. The process was designed as an alternative to other forms of high-tech infertility treatments, rather than a way to overcome defects in egg quality.

What happened was this: The egg donor was matched with an infertile woman who happened to be on the same cycle—both women were due to ovulate at the same time. The donor was then inseminated with the sperm of the infertile woman's husband, fertilization took place naturally inside her reproductive tract, and, four or five days later, we'd use a *culture medium* to flush the embryo from the donor's uterus. Using a double catheter system (one tube pumping the medium in, one sucking the medium and the embryo out), we would retrieve the new little life that had just begun before implantation could take place. The embryo was then placed into the uterus of the infertile woman, and the pregnancy proceeded, hopefully to term. The first success with this technique was reported in 1983.

The nice thing about ovum transfer was that you had an almost 50 percent implantation rate in the recipient when the embryo was retrieved at the blastocyst stage (the last stage of a fertilized egg prior to its natural implantation in the uterus). The trouble was, getting a blastocyst was not so easy. Most of the time, nothing came out of the donor's uterus when you flushed it, and at other times, you'd get an unfertilized egg or a degenerating embryo. The program floundered because the overall rate of pregnancies per attempt was exceedingly low.

There were other problems, too. During this period of time, reproductive technology was in its infancy, and no federal research funding was available. Where other researchers had simply passed along the cost of care to the patients who were willing to pay out of pocket for new technologies, the researchers in the ovum transfer program chose to obtain funding from a private corporation. Unfortunately, the funding came with strings attached—the corporation wanted a return on its investment, and to that end, the process of ovum transfer was patented.

There was an immediate outcry from the medical community: If medical procedures could be patented, what would this mean to future research? Would it prevent innovative medical technologies from becoming available to those who wanted and needed them? Would doctors be able to provide them on demand? And another grave concern, in this era when the HIV virus had first raised its ugly head, was the transmission of infectious disease. How could we be completely certain that the husband of the infertile woman had not passed along some disease to the donor?

In 1987, John Buster accepted another academic position in Tennessee and the program in Southern California closed its doors. By now, I was Director of the IVF Program at University of Southern California. As John Buster's team dispersed, we were to recruit its youngest member—Dr. Mark Sauer—with whom I was destined to collaborate for the next eight years.

Mark brought three vital elements into our program: He had lots of experience synchronizing donors and recipients, he was an expert with uterine flushing, and most importantly, he provided us with 12 young fertile women willing to be egg donors. Initially, we had attempted to improve the uterine flushing technology by giving the donors fertility medications, which would create multiple follicles containing lots of eggs during each cycle. As predicted, we could identify many follicles by ultrasound, but, for reasons that are still not clear to this day, we could do nothing to improve the efficiency of retrieving embryos from the uterus.

And we ran into new complications—several of the donors retained their pregnancies. We convinced ourselves that the first one had been a fluke, a failure of the apparatus. We worked on the technique some more and forged ahead. But after seven attempts, none of our recipients were pregnant, we got a second retained pregnancy in one of our donors, and had retrieved only a few miserable-looking embryos. It was time to abandon uterine flushing.

At around this time, we started looking into the possibilities of in vitro fertilization. The process wasn't new; the first pregnancy in a woman without ovaries had been achieved through egg donation back in 1984. But now we felt that standard IVF technology was the way to go. We were doing so well with IVF for infertile couples that we had reasonable confidence about adding egg donation to the IVF formula.

The advent of **ultrasound-directed follicle aspiration** could not have come at a better time for us. This technique allowed us to visualize follicles on an **ultrasound** screen, then retrieve them from the ovary using a needle passed through the vaginal wall. It would have been difficult to ask potential donors who were doing this out of the goodness of their hearts to subject themselves to laparoscopies just to retrieve their eggs. But now, we could do the procedures in the office, using local anesthesia and intravenous sedation, a far safer and more palatable alternative.

Our program differed from all the rest in that we had designated egg donors, in other words, fertile women who were willing to donate eggs. The other programs were still mixing and matching eggs from IVF candidates. One infertile woman would donate an egg to another infertile woman, which might actually "take" when combined with another man's sperm. Thanks to the myriad differences in body chemistry and the way one egg reacts to one sperm, female infertility is not an absolute.

Still, our chances of achieving a pregnancy were much higher using eggs from fertile women, like our candidates. Not only were we more likely to get eggs of high quality, but we also had a unique opportunity to compare and contrast our method to the current industry standard.

Our initial success was astounding. Coming as it did right after our failures with uterine flushing, we could hardly believe it when our first three patients became pregnant on their first attempt. By the end of two years, we had completed 26 transfer cycles and achieved 16 clinical pregnancies—for a then-unheard-of total success rate of 62 percent.

Our multiple-pregnancy rate of 42 percent meant that we had also boosted our implantation rate—and the likelihood of any one embryo implanting was astonishingly high.

These statistics were much higher than those in our regular IVF program, and two factors stood out as the cause: First, we had high-quality, healthy young eggs; second, our method of stimulating the uterus of the recipient artificially with estrogen and progesterone allowed implantation to occur much more easily and frequently than it would have if the uterus were untreated.

Our USC program had been ongoing now for quite a few years, and several women who had started with our infertility program when they were in their thirties had now passed their fortieth birthday. We felt it would be unfair to exclude the women who came to us for egg donation if they, too were over 40. We were uncertain at first as to what our chances were, but as it happened, we experienced the same high success rate in the older group as we had previously with younger recipients. So although it had been common knowledge for many years that pregnancy rates of women over 40 were lower regardless of the type of fertility treatment that they were given, egg donation wiped the slate clean. As long as we stimulated the endometrium properly, they had the same chance of conception. In 1990, we published the results of our initial series of women over 40 and suggested that there might not be an upper physiologic age limit beyond which women could not bear children.

We gradually increased our admission criteria to our program, and in 1993, we published results on our first series of women over 50. Although we had had a lot of negative press with our first results, just three years later there was less objection. Society seemed to be coming around to an acceptance of older mothers. And then a woman named Arceli Keh came to our program for treatment.

She and her husband were appropriate candidates for egg donation. They stated that she was 50 and he was 57, and they had been trying to get pregnant for the past 13 years. Mrs. Keh passed all the necessary screening tests, and in 1996 she conceived. According to our records, she was 53. We observed her carefully through her first trimester, since obviously, at 53, she was considered a "high-risk" first-time mother, but by the time we sent her to her obstetrician, I had no doubts that her pregnancy would come to term.

My shock was palpable when her doctor called me a week later to inform me that Mrs. Keh was actually 10 years older than she had first admitted. She was 63 years old. Fortunately, the pregnancy continued without event, and she delivered a healthy baby girl in November of 1996. I felt quite certain that Mrs. Keh was the oldest woman who had ever given birth in the United States. We said nothing to the press, nor did anyone on the obstetrical team, respecting Mrs. Keh's wishes to avoid publicity. But after the delivery, I became convinced that, sooner or later, the story was bound to come out. It was better to go public, lest our silence be misconstrued as a desire to cover up the story. After much soul-searching and intense discussion with the IVF team, we wrote up Mrs. Keh's case history for the medical literature, and the article was published in *Fertility and Sterility*. As part of the background research, I contacted Dr. Severino Antinori in Italy, who had previously reported his success with a pregnancy in a 63-year-old woman. But after we corresponded, it appeared that he had made an error—his patient had been only 62 when she delivered. That meant that Mrs. Keh was in fact the oldest woman in the world ever to deliver a live born child.

Mrs. Keh's situation was extremely unusual, and I am not sure that I would have proceeded if I had known how old she really was. It's hard to say whether we should have expected her good outcome, or whether it was simply due to luck, since there are only three deliveries in women over the age of 60 documented in the medical literature. Despite some minor complications, she had a relatively uneventful pregnancy. Clearly, I'm not advising that anyone wait until she's ready to collect social security to have a child, but it's not that difficult to give birth at 50 or even 55 with an embryo from a donated egg.[1]

Currently, there are fewer than two hundred women older than 50 worldwide who have given birth to children through egg donation, but there has been a steady growth in the number of programs offering this

---

[1]There are rare cases of natural conception in women who thought they were post-menopausal—a 57-year-old from Southern California gave birth in 1997. Moreover, a recent study suggests that women of advanced reproductive age who can reproduce naturally have a slower aging process in general, and are more likely to live beyond their hundredth birthdays.

treatment. The American Society for Reproductive Medicine estimates that in 1997 there are just over two hundred infertility clinics around the United States that run egg donation programs—up from 163 in 1994. This means that more women accept the idea of giving up their genetic endowment if it means they can have a child.

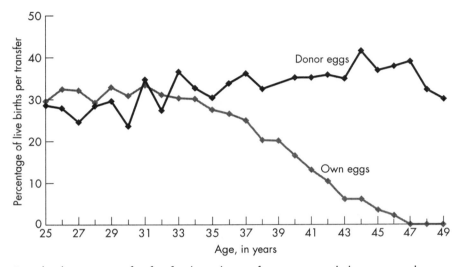

Live births per transfer for fresh embryos from own and donor eggs by age of recipient, 1995.

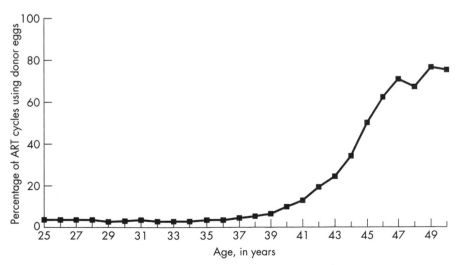

Percentage of ART cycles using donor eggs, by age of recipient, 1995.

KEEPING THE FAMILY LINE GOING: PASSING ON YOUR GENES

No matter how much a woman or a couple wants a child, using a donor can be a tricky emotional issue. One reason that human beings opt to reproduce is that they wish to combine their DNA, and that of their family, with the DNA of the one they love. Kinship ties are about as tight as any we have on earth—that old "blood is thicker than water," might be modified to read, "*our* blood is thicker than *their* blood." If you think it's tough for society to contemplate a 50-year-old in maternity clothes, think how much tougher the choice is for the 50-year-old. Naturally, this new beloved individual will represent her husband, but the child will not be her biological offspring.

Relying on another individual's vital essence to help create your child means that you give up on your own genes, and it's an issue that causes many couples a lot of sleepless nights. The problem is doubly compounded by a certain amount of jealousy for the partner whose genes will be included in the intricate makeup that becomes your baby. What we all crave, consciously or not, is a child who resembles us in some way—if it's not our looks, then perhaps our musical talent or that funny squint we make when we smile. We love it when people say, "Little Susie is the spitting image of her mom." We like the idea of a copy—not a carbon copy, but a template that includes a couple of good traits that we don't want lost forever when we go.

Giving up on your gene pool is something that most people take very seriously, and they avoid it if they can. But the desire to bring new life into the world may be greater than the ego-trip of being represented in your kids' eyes or hair or hiccup. One of the most interesting phenomena about older mothers having babies through oocyte donation is the almost universal comment that their child looks or acts just like them. The truth of the matter is that the environment of the womb itself—the stress hormones in the mother's blood, the amount of protein in her diet, the exercise she does, and the music she listens to while she's pregnant—may make a considerable difference in the child that emerges from her nine months later. And nurture, rather than nature, is the key ingredient in careful parenting anyway. If you want to raise a child more than anything, it probably doesn't matter which genes she's wearing when she makes her appearance in the world.

Candidates for Egg Donation

Most women who opt for egg donation still have eggs left in their ovaries, but they're of such poor quality that achieving a pregnancy is extremely unlikely. It's harder to see this in an egg than it is with sperm, whose defects—a bizarre shape or lack of movement—are more readily apparent under a microscope. Poor-quality or old eggs may look completely normal, may fertilize normally, and may undergo initial embryo cleavage just like young, healthy eggs. But implantation rarely, if ever, occurs. And so the demand has grown in recent years for young, healthy donors who can turn the corner for women who are willing to give up their genetic input in order to have a child.

There are also women who have no viable eggs at all. They may have had their ovaries removed due to cancer or severe pelvic infection; they might have gone through premature menopause (approximately 1 percent of women lose hormonal response and run out of eggs prior to age 35); they might have Turner's syndrome, in which menopause occurs before the menses ever begin; or they might have just gone through their natural menopause. In all of these instances, the patient would need eggs from a donor as well as artificial stimulation of her uterus with the hormones which would normally have been produced by her ovaries.

Making Hard Decisions

Women who have tried but not succeeded with other methods of ART using their own eggs have two choices: They can either adopt (and this option is far more difficult when you're older) or have a child with a donor egg. Of course there are couples who have only come together after the time for natural conception has past. If you're just starting on the road to pregnancy in your late forties or early fifties, your chances of conception with your own eggs is miniscule—perhaps as small as 1 in 10,000. No amount of ovarian stimulation or manipulation by ART can overcome the intrinsic deficit in egg quality. There has never been a pregnancy reported in a woman over the age of 46 with any assisted reproductive technology using her own eggs. Remarkably, however, in this same age group, ART with a donor egg produces the highest pregnancy rates of any of the ARTs as compared with rates of women using their own eggs, regardless of age.

If you decide to take this course, yours will be considered a high-risk pregnancy. You will have a 60 percent chance of developing one or more obstetrical complications, although most of these are not serious and are easily managed. You will have a better than 50 percent chance of delivering by caesarian section, but your chances for a healthy child are also very high.

If you have the stamina and desire, as Sarah does, you don't need to despair. True, you will have to make peace with the fact that you will have no genetic connection to your child, but you do have a viable option—you *can* have a child. It's still not an easy choice, but the best and most important things in life take careful consideration, debate, negotiation, and heartfelt introspection. Intuition also comes into play. Sometimes the toughest decisions are made because finally, after all those years, it just feels right.

For those women and couples who truly desire to become parents in midlife, the door is now wide open.

CHAPTER THREE

Sarah's Quest

The subway was fairly empty on Saturday morning when Sarah put her token in the machine and rode to Grand Central to change for the Queens line. She and her sister Marilyn were going to help their mother, Lillian, clean out her apartment so she could move, fairly unencumbered by a lifetime of possessions, to one of those senior citizen complexes where they want you to sign over everything except your hearing aids.

But all Sarah could think about on the ride to Astoria was asking her sister to help her to have a baby. *Hey, Marilyn, would you lend me an egg? Look, it's really not a terrible procedure, you only have to take these lousy drugs that make you feel like you're jumping out of your skin for a few weeks, and then the doctor just goes in and pops those follicles so I can get what I need. Easy!*

Okay, so she could be less flip about it, of course, but it all boiled down to the same thing—are you with me or against me? And then, too, how would Marilyn feel about having her egg fertilized with Joe's sperm? Technically, it was just bits of tissue in a dish. But emotionally, it would pack a wallop.

She couldn't imagine how her sister would react. Marilyn was 13 years younger than Sarah, unmarried, basically interested in her antiques, her opera subscription, her summers on Fire Island, and her friends from the health club. To ask Marilyn to think about marriage and family life was as absurd as suggesting that she join a nomad tribe in Afghanistan. Come to think of it, she'd pick the second option first. She'd probably corner the market on Afghani rugs and bring them back to America to sell for a great price.

"Hi, darling!" Sarah realized she had already pushed the buzzer on her mother's door. Lillian was standing before her in a housedress, holding a cigarette with a long ash trailing. Sarah looked into her mother's wrinkled face and marveled at the fact that she could still see herself in the angle of the chin, the wide forehead, the rich brown eyes. Wasn't DNA grand? She smiled at her mother.

"Well don't just stand there, Sarah," Lillian said gruffly. "Come on in and get to work. Your sister beat you here." Lillian Gold's deep, raspy voice never failed to make Sarah think of Bette Davis. They linked arms and walked into the living room together.

Her mother was frail, now, stooped from osteoporosis. And as Sarah hugged Lillian's thin ribs, she flashed ahead to a scene when her own yet-to-be-born daughter, much younger than she, might have to pitch in and help her out. What if she came down with a terminal illness and had to be put into a nursing home? It was conceivable, although she was incredibly healthy right now. Was that completely unfair to this unborn child she wanted so desperately?

"This is what we've done so far," Lillian waved her cigarette around, dropping ash on the carpet. "I'm getting out, and I'm ditching all this junk."

The living room looked as though a band of gypsies had encamped, and then *de*camped. Sarah and Marilyn's mom was beyond eccentric, and at 77, she was probably entitled to do whatever the hell she pleased. She had never put things where other people might put them, and over the years, Marilyn had found jewelry hidden in saucepans and important documents—like the living will—stuck behind a pile of magazines from 1983.

"Hey, Sar, look at these!" Marilyn, knee-deep in boxes, produced a tarnished silver acorn with a blue Depression glass cap. There were eight individual sets, and the glass was broken on only one of them.

"I'm going upstairs to rest," Lillian said, leaving the cigarette in a glass on the counter and rubbing her arthritic hands. "You two call me when you've got something to show."

Sarah thought she remembered where her mother kept the family album. She needed to see everyone she belonged to, to feel part of a group, the family who had nurtured and sheltered her. She moved aside a bunch of the hundred or so shopping bags that lined the walls and opened the guest closet, ducking to avoid the avalanche that crashed down from the top shelf. "Oh, Lynnie, this was what I wanted to find. Look at this old album!"

Marilyn sighed and stretched her hands overhead. Her cobalt silk shirt made a shushing sound as she got to her feet and joined her sister in the puddle of books and papers. They sat together side by side, jockeying for position as they scanned the pictures.

The sisters saw each other a lot these days, since they'd both moved to New York, and there was a new affection growing. But Sarah was still apprehensive about bringing up The Subject. She opened the album and flipped to the first picture of their mother.

"Jeez, look at Lillian—she must be thirty in this picture. Would you ever have known she had this gorgeous red hair?"

"Marilyn, doll, she's been dying it that color for decades."

"Yeah, but this was her *real* color. She was so great looking, with that strong forehead and those big, big chocolate eyes. Actually, you resemble her a lot. Oh, that has to be Uncle Pete untying the sailboat. God, was he *fat!* I don't ever remember him when he wasn't totally wasted from the emphysema."

Sarah nodded. "Well, their father was huge, and never would go on a diet—and I remember Mom saying she was pretty chubby when she was young. She doesn't look it here, though." She wouldn't have to worry about "fat genes" coming from her side—that was a good thing. Sarah turned to the middle of the album, to the pictures of her and Marilyn as kids. It was important to her to see her beginnings.

"You were cute," Sarah sighed, looking at a photo of her sister doing battle with the hose, trying to get the garden wet but only succeeding in drenching herself. "Look at your tiny hands and all that fluffy almost-white hair. You looked like a little angel. Even though I wanted to throw you out the window most days."

"Yeah, well, here's you siccing the dog on me. I guess you didn't repress those feelings."

Sarah smacked her sister lightly on the head. She turned another page. "Oh, Lynnie, is that Angelo? The exchange student you brought home from Italy your junior year? God, he was gorgeous! You should have married him."

"Nah, it wouldn't have been as much fun if I'd been thinking of marriage." Marilyn said ruefully.

"You're prejudiced."

"You're a hopeless romantic. To step into the same hole twice—God! Although this time, I'll admit you got the best man around. Even though you had to rob the cradle to do it."

It was true that Marilyn would never have a baby herself, but she wouldn't get married either and still approved of it for Sarah. So maybe she'd think the idea of egg donation was a real kick—something trendy and so *New York* magazine. It would be a stretch. She might truly hate the idea. But the two of them had often gone beyond agreement and disagreement over lots of important things in the past. There was Sarah's affair with Sam (Marilyn insisted she was a dedicated masochist to stick to that man so long) and there was Marilyn's purchase of one hundred acres in the Berkshires of Massachusetts (Sarah had reminded her sister that she didn't even like the woods, but it did no good). So she had to discuss this with her, regardless of the reaction she got.

"You know Joe and I want a baby," she blurted out without preliminaries.

"Well, that's nothing new. You tried and failed. " Marilyn shrugged. "I guess it just wasn't in the cards for you two."

Sarah had it on the tip of her tongue—*we're thinking about an egg baby*—but what came out when she opened her mouth was, "We were thinking about adopting."

"You!? You're incredibly old to start a new family, Sarie." Marilyn's face had that sour look she got whenever she was told the price of an antique was twice as high as she wanted to spend.

"You're so kind. May I remind you that I just completed a marathon with a time better than women half my age, and my husband is practically young enough to be . . . *your* husband."

"Yeah, but adopting is just a can of worms. No respectable agency is going to take you once they see your birth certificate. So what are you going to do? Go to China or Russia or South America and wait around some filthy orphanage to be shown into a back room where your intended has been lying around, undernourished and underloved for the last year or two? You never know what you're going to get. My friends Claire and Jim got these twins from Columbia, and one of them's clearly got some kind of retardation. And Sandy and Mark had this horrible experience—they found some poor white trash girl down in Mississippi who was pregnant and living with her boyfriend, and they offered to pay her prenatal expenses and everything. And it turns out these two are drug dealers who had scammed other couples before, and they ran off with about $10,000 of my friends' dollars. The black market for babies is just repulsive."

"Marilyn, I've heard all those stories, too, but they're not the norm. You hear about them because they're sensational. But there are plenty of people who have plain old routine adoptions. Not everybody goes through hell to get a child." This was worse than she'd anticipated. Marilyn didn't even think she should adopt.

She put the photo album down and walked to the window. There were these two guys about to get out of their cars and argue over a parking space. She could see the tension in their necks all the way up here. Or maybe she was just identifying with them.

She took a breath. "Joe and I actually had another idea about this baby thing. Do you want a cup of tea? We should take a break." Sarah talked nervously over her shoulder as she went into the kitchen. "What kind do you want?"

"Mom has nothing but Lipton and some god-awful herb mixture. I'll take the plain American swill, thanks." Marilyn started examining her newly acquired salt-and-pepper shakers in the light, one by one.

Sarah watched her sister's capable, long, polished fingernails lovingly stroke each acorn. She felt a knot in her stomach as she put the kettle on to boil.

"So our idea is," Sarah said as casually as she could, "we're going to try to have a baby ourselves by taking an egg from a younger woman and fertilizing it with Joe's sperm and implanting it in me."

Marilyn smiled and made a little sound that could have been a laugh. "Are you staying for dinner? Maybe we should take Mom out for a change."

"Did you hear what I said?" This was really going badly. Her sister was going to ignore her, or belittle her, or tell her she was getting senile.

"Yes, I heard. I don't know what to say. I mean, you'll end up doing what you want to do, Sarah."

Marilyn had this cool, detached side that Sarah detested. Years ago, when Sarah was an adult taking care of her family and Marilyn was a surly teenager, they could barely talk to each other. It was like they came from two different planets. Marilyn's ice shield was still her easy out, her way of not confronting or being challenged. "Well, what do you think about that?"

"Not much. I don't know a thing about it, Sarah."

"Okay. Then I guess it's out of the question asking you for one of your eggs."

Her sister put down the pepper shaker she was holding and opened the refrigerator. She looked inside for a moment, and then, closed the door.

Sarah wasn't about to let her off the hook. "As sisters, we share a lot of genes. If you were okay about this . . . see, the doctor says that . . ."

"I don't care what your goddamn doctor says." Marilyn's jaw was set in a straight line. "Sarah, I was the child of an older mother. You will recall, I think, that you and Al and Steve were teenagers before I came along. Me, the big mistake. Mom was 42—well past the age to be any sort of mother. I mean, she was probably not your Betty Crocker type at any point in her life, but when she was menopausal, well, the whole thing was just too sad."

"My friends didn't want to come over after school, do you know that? My boyfriends used to ask why I lived with my grandmother. And you're 48! Jesus, I think it's weird. I think it's bizarre that you want to have a child right now, and bizarre that you think you could borrow an egg like you were going to bake a cake or something. And I really feel put out that you would ask me. And that is what I think." She walked briskly to the staircase.

"Mom, you want to go out to dinner tonight?" she called. Her voice shook a little.

"Don't you turn away from me!" Sarah sped after Marilyn and grabbed her by the shoulder.

"Hush. Don't get Mom into a state. I don't want you discussing it in front of her. If you're so anxious for a nice young egg, why don't you ask Alison? For God's sake, your daughter's 28—that must be a perfect age. What do they do, anyway? Ask you to sit on a nest and hatch one?"

They heard their mother coming down the stairs and the conversation came to a halt. Sarah was shaking, and Marilyn's back was rigid.

"What'd you get rid of? Where are all the garbage bags, girls?" Lillian was all bent over, but she moved quickly, touching all the items the girls had dragged out of the closets. "This place is a mess," she said gleefully. "I think we should just leave it like it is, just abandon the wreck with all the junk laid out like this. That'll serve 'em right for taking $20,000 off the selling price."

"We'll clean up, Mom," Sarah said quietly. "It's just taking a little longer than we thought. Can I have this album?" She clutched the leather binder to her as though it were another limb. It might be the only evidence that she had ever come from a family some day. Her mother's auburn hair, her grandfather's fat cells, her own huge feet—if Alison chose not to have a child, all those things would vanish because there would be no one to pass them on.

And what about Alison? Could she even ask her for something like this? They had barely spoken in years. Then again, she couldn't have had a worse response from Marilyn, and she had kind of counted on Marilyn. Big sisters usually command so much respect. Well, not anymore.

Lolly was right; she had to call her daughter.

"Why don't you two go out alone tonight?" Lillian looked tired. The move was taking it out of her, and she wasn't at all certain she wanted to live in the extended-care retirement community in Yonkers to which she'd signed over everything but her dentures. "I'm pooped. Do I look pooped?"

"You look *mahvelous*, darling," Marilyn told her. It was supposed to sound breezy and funny, but it came out stilted.

"Actually, I have to get back to town. I promised Joe I'd ..." Sarah's voice trailed off as she looked at her sister's retreating back.

"Okay, all right, leave me in the middle of this *dreck*. No, don't feel guilty—this is the way my place always looks. I'll probably die of the dust inhalation before I ever get to make the move." Lillian shooed them toward the door. "Tomorrow—you come back and finish this, you understand? I'm not going to touch a thing."

"Sure, Mom." Marilyn's car was parked right outside, but she didn't offer her sister a lift. Sarah felt incredibly angry and abandoned. As unrealistic as it might have been, she had managed to fantasize about her sister giving her exactly what she wanted. Instead, all she got was hostility.

"So will I see you in the morning?" Sarah asked. Marilyn put her key in the ignition.

"I can't. Why don't you bring Joe and get the job done? Must be something you can do without a proxy."

The stinging remark hurt through the evening, and into the next day when Sarah and Joe were scheduled for their first appointment with Dr. John Leverton. He had been referred by Nancy Lacosta, their endocrinologist, as soon as Sarah had mentioned that she was interested in stopping the IVF cycles and trying egg donation. This was the man to see on the East Coast if you were old enough to have owned saddle shoes and still wanted a baby.

"Marilyn wasn't enthusiastic, I take it," Joe said as they filled out their medical history forms in the sunny office on the Upper West Side.

"She'd rather take poison. Let's forget it, Joe."

"But you're not going to forget it." He put a hand on her knee, and she melted. There was something in his touch—some kind of chemical that had a direct effect on her brain. She was calmer at once.

"Look, we don't need her. It's probably better to use a donor we don't know."

A door opened across the room, and a couple in their late forties walked out, his arm around her shoulder. The woman was crying softly, and her partner wore a grim expression. They didn't stop at the front desk, but just continued out the office door, which slammed rudely behind them.

"Like a death, isn't it?" Sarah murmured. "Do you think they lost a baby? or they just can't have one?"

"That's them. This is *us*. I feel really good about this, sweetheart, and I hope you do." Joe smoothed his tousled brown hair self-consciously, as though he were concerned about what the doctor would think of him. Sarah had always felt he looked like one of those British schoolboys in the postwar movies, with his shiny, scrubbed cheeks and eyes set a little too close together. She wished he'd take a rest—it was exhausting keeping up with someone so positive.

"Mr. and Mrs. Girard?" The nurse, Sarah was happy to see, was about as old as she was. "Come on back to the consultation room."

They were led down the hall lined with dozens of baby pictures. White and black and Asian ones—plenty of twins and a few triplets, too. They were mostly newborns, but some were toddlers, precipitously teetering on slides or poised with arms uplifted, ready to be picked up by a doting parent. *That's what we want*, Sarah thought. *A little security, just the knowledge that someone's there to catch us when we're falling.* She had never felt so vulnerable. It suddenly hit her that this was her last chance.

They were seated across from the doctor's desk in plush maroon chairs, and the door closed after them.

"Plenty of diplomas," Joe commented.

"These guys always hang up everything they ever won. Look, he used to be a ski instructor in the 1970s, for heaven's sake. And he has his helicopter pilot's license. When does the guy ever have time to make babies?" she grumbled.

The door opened again, and a brisk, small, balding man in green surgical scrubs walked through the door. He held himself gracefully, like a dancer or an athlete, and he took over the room like a much larger man, invading its corners with his presence. He went right to Sarah and took her hands in both of his; his smile was warm but no-nonsense. She glanced down at his hands—small, well-manicured, almost hairless. His eyes were a brilliant blue, clear and steady as they gazed into hers. He held her hand, sizing her up, then went onto Joe and shook his hand briefly.

"Hi, good to meet you both. I'm Dr. Leverton. I've heard a great deal about you from Nancy." He scanned the file in front of him and then closed it, paying close attention to the two of them. "So you would like to be pregnant?"

"Is that an unreasonable hope?" Joe asked.

"Absolutely not. Our pregnancy rates for women of your age using donor eggs are excellent—we're nearly at 50 percent per attempt. Actually, there are not that many women who are eager for the procedure once they've passed menopause, but I'd be delighted to increase the number in the world by one or two. So, let's talk a little. What's convinced you that *this* is the time to have kids?"

Sarah had a good feeling about him. He wasn't flashy or egocentric, but he did seem sure of himself and what he did. She cleared her throat. "We've been together for a long time, and we've wanted a baby ever since we met—someone who's part of us. And all the disappointment we went through over the years with the in vitros hasn't dulled the feeling, so we figure our commitment is real. Either that, or we're both totally obsessive because we refuse to let go of the idea." She laughed as Joe playfully punched her arm.

"No, really," she went on, "it's only now that we finally feel we have something to pass on. I have a daughter from another marriage—it's not like I don't know what it means to raise a child—but I've never had a partner like I do now. This is right. It would be kind of selfish to go on just being a couple, going to work, saving for our golden years. We love kids and we want to give back some of what makes us happy to get up each morning."

The doctor looked at Joe. "How do you feel about that?"

Joe was quiet for a moment, not jumping in with a prepared speech like he usually did. He had obviously given this a great deal of thought. "Sarah and I love to play," he said finally. "I can't see not sharing that with a kid. And we're good listeners, and we think a lot about what the world will be like when we're not here anymore. And I know there are plenty of children out there who would love to be adopted, but I guess I have this thing about it being really my own—from me." He took Sarah's hand. "She's real brave to be giving that up. We've talked about it a lot."

The doctor put one finger to the side of his eye, concentrating hard. "All right. That's a lot of good reasons. I'm delighted to see you're such thoughtful people, because this is not an easy choice. I'm sure you're aware of that. Now let me tell you a little about egg donation. First, we need the two of you to have a workup. My assistant Michelle will give you a rundown of the tests you'll have to have. Then you have to make some kind of decision about donors. Would you be using someone you know? a friend or a family member? or would you prefer one of our donors?" He looked at each of them in turn.

Sarah said, "Someone we don't know," and Joe said, "Probably one of yours," at the same time.

"Okay, I guess you're in agreement on that," the doctor smiled. "The women who donate to our program, most of them, have been helping us for a while. Some have families of their own, some haven't started yet, but they're all committed to assisting couples like you. They're paid a fee—in our program, it's $2500—not for the eggs themselves, but for their time and inconvenience."

"What, exactly, is all this going to cost?" Sarah asked.

"Michelle will go over that with you, and then you'll see our insurance advisor before you leave today."

"When we were doing IVF cycles, we built our infertility treatments into our budget," Joe told the doctor. "It was a little like knowing you have to get the car serviced, or buying milk and bread. These are just the necessities of life," he grinned.

The doctor raised his eyebrows a bit. Sarah wondered if he thought they were too cavalier about spending, but this was no time to worry about her bank account.

"Now I know you don't need the standard lecture on reproduction. I see from your chart you had quite a course on this the last time you went through it," Leverton joked.

"Yeah, at that time, we could probably have hung out a shingle in reproductive medicine," Sarah smiled. "But it was about five years ago. I'm a little fuzzy."

"I could do with a brushup myself," Joe admitted.

"Well, that's fine," said Leverton, "because I'd like to review the assisted reproductive treatments you had before we discuss egg donation. I think it's helpful to go over where you were then so you can see more clearly where you are now."

Joe and Sarah nodded.

"You started with IUI, that's intrauterine insemination, the simplest ART, or assisted reproductive technology. It's the easiest way to get the sperm closer to the egg." Leverton picked up a pair of reading glasses from the desk and scanned the Girards' chart. "I was wondering why your physician wouldn't have started Sarah off on fertility drugs at the same time—it does have a higher statistical chance of working— but I see you had a very regular cycle."

"You could set your watch by it," Sarah agreed.

"Okay. So your doctor decided not to hyperstimulate your ovaries because she figured you'd ovulate by yourself on a predictable schedule. And I also see here that there was nothing wrong with Joe's semen analysis when it was performed in 1993."

"Oh God, don't remind me!" Sarah shook her head. "He was uncontrollable for weeks, nearly busting a gut over how virile he was. He had a sperm count of—what was it?—nearly ninety million, which meant that he could probably fertilize the entire state of New York."

"Yeah, lot of good *that* did." Joe sounded frustrated.

Leverton smiled. "Well, as you know, the only thing you care about with sperm is whether they have the capacity to fertilize. Having a high count doesn't necessarily mean that the sperm are any better—just that there's less chance that you'll have a problem. What's actually more important in predicting fertilization is a history of prior pregnancy, which I see you had."

"Yeah," Joe nodded. "That was back in college—the sponge didn't work, and she decided on an abortion." His face clouded for a second, and Sarah saw him thinking back to that old flame, and that old mistake.

"But that tells us that your sperm worked at least once," the doctor said. "So. Back to what was going on with you two. What happened was, Sarah, you just went through your regular cycle, and that was monitored with ultrasound and blood tests so that your physician could be sure when you were ovulating. And then, Joe, you gave a sperm sample, which got washed and sorted, and the resulting mix was put into a catheter and inserted up through Sarah's cervix, to give the sperm a boost into the uterine cavity."

"But it didn't work."

"Right. So the next time, your doctor tried a stimulated cycle. Sarah, this meant you took some injections of a fertility medication . . ."

"Pergonal. I remember it well," Sarah interjected.

"Yes, Pergonal to stimulate your ovaries to produce multiple follicles." He took out a pad of paper with preprinted diagrams of the reproductive tract and started to scribble on them. He turned the paper around so that they could see. "Normally, the pituitary gland located just under the brain sends hormonal messages to the ovary, telling it when to start producing estrogen. The pituitary hormone called FSH—short for follicle-stimulating hormone—makes a follicle start growing. The follicle is a fluid-filled structure which looks like a blister on the surface of the ovary. The egg is inside it—kind of like the seed inside the fruit. When the follicle has grown to a certain size, another hormone from the pituitary, called LH, or luteinizing hormone, causes it to rupture, releasing its egg—this is ovulation. Did you ever use one of those over-the-counter ovulation kits? You were measuring your own LH if you did."

Sarah nodded. "Yeah, I remember that. I ovulated on my own the first month, and then the next month they gave me a shot to make me ovulate."

"Right. When we give fertility drugs to a patient who is already ovulating, that's called superovulation. When the follicles get big—you can see that in an ultrasound—the body may ovulate on its own, and you get a positive ovulation kit. Most of the time, we control the timing and give the patient a shot of hCG, or human chorionic gonadotropin, and that triggers ovulation. This hormone works just like LH, but it's longer acting. After you've had the hCG shot, you wait thirty-six hours—that's how long it will take for the eggs to be released from their follicles—and then you do the IUI procedure.

"So," he looked at the chart again. "You had three of these cycles with superovulation and IUI."

"Still no go," Joe recalled.

"And your physician at this point decided not to waste any more time and went onto IVF."

"Yes," Joe nodded. "We were told there were a couple of other assisted technologies we could try, but Sarah was past forty..."

"Real old," she interjected.

"Well, 'old' is relative," Leverton shrugged. "It's just that your physician knew that time was really of the essence, and undoubtedly, she weighed the pros and cons of the various treatments with you. You might have been told about GIFT, or gamete intrafallopian transfer, where the eggs are combined with sperm and placed directly into the fallopian tubes. Yes?"

"She mentioned it, I think, but said it wasn't for us. What is it?"

"With GIFT, fertilization takes place in the body, and it's more natural. But—and this is a big 'but'—you don't get to see fertilization take place in the lab prior to the transfer as you do with IVF. And you need a laparoscopy—an invasive surgical procedure in an operating room with anesthesia. We usually only do GIFT on patients who have some problem we want to look at through the laparoscope—someone with endometriosis or a lot of scar tissue. Or someone whose insurance covers GIFT and not IVF."

"That wasn't us," Joe said ruefully. "Our plan at work covered nothing."

"Which is very common and which is also why most physicians choose the simplest and least expensive procedure when they can. That means IVF with ultrasound-guided egg retrieval in the office and transcervical embryo transfer three days later."

"That's what we had," Sarah nodded. "Our doctor said there was another one of those acronyms she might consider—was it ZIFT? But it turned out I didn't need it."

The doctor looked at the chart again and nodded. "Some women have a scarred cervical canal or some other problem in the uterus which makes transfer of the embryos through the uterus difficult. So we do ZIFT, which stands for zygote intrafallopian transfer, or TET, and that's tubal embryo transfer. In both of these procedures, you put the embryos in the fallopian tube—again, using a laparoscopy. ZIFT is done 24 hours after egg retrieval and TET is done 48 hours afterward. But it take it your transfer was easy?"

"Oh, everything was perfect," Sarah told him. "They had lots of eggs—well, lots for somebody my age—and the fertilization was great, they said."

"Well, that's good news, because it means Joe's sperm was working hard and fertilized well. We won't have to do ICSI, or intracytoplasmic sperm injection, when we get the donor eggs. If the sperm isn't up to par, we can isolate one sperm and inject it directly into the egg. But in your case, we don't need that. We'll just add the sperm to the eggs in the petri dish and let them do their thing, then replace them inside you."

"We did two of those IVF cycles, and the embryos didn't stick," Sarah sighed. "Not one of them, and they put in five embryos each time. We were so bummed," she said softly.

"That is a large number of embryos to transfer, but it's pretty standard in a woman of what we call advanced reproductive age. Since there's very little likelihood that any one embryo will implant, we put back several at a time. The risk of multiple gestation is low in IVF with your own eggs, so we can be bold and put back five at once."

Joe sighed. "All that time and money, and for what?" he muttered. Sarah looked over at him, seeing the same look on his face that he'd worn four–and–a–half years ago, the day they decided to stop knocking their heads against a wall.

"Well, that's the question you have undoubtedly asked yourself again, after waiting a long time for the answers to make sense to you. Otherwise you wouldn't be here, right?" Leverton looked from one to the other.

"I ... we were hoping that bypassing my old eggs will make a difference."

"It will make all the difference in the world," Leverton assured her. "The younger eggs from the donor will fertilize just like yours did, but will have a much higher chance of implanting. The chances are so good, in fact, that we never put back more than three embryos at a time with egg donation, just in case they *all* implant."

"Really!" Joe grinned.

"Now, with egg donation we're adding an extra person to the equation. The donor does the IVF cycle for you, and you do the embryo transfer."

"This is more complicated, then," Sarah said. She felt the beginnings of a headache, and she practically *never* got headaches.

"Complicated in that the more people, the more feelings, the more ramifications on the child. Have you talked to your families about this?" the doctor asked. "Some people are strongly opposed to what we'll be attempting, you know."

Sarah's head was throbbing. "We know that. It's us that counts. Us and the child we have."

The doctor nodded. "Even so. It brings up a lot of feelings you may not realize are there. Which is one reason why I send all my patients to a counselor. She's a psychologist who specializes in the ins and outs of being a couple trying to have a baby in this way. You'll go to see her?"

They readily agreed. Sarah was sure she needed all the shrinking she could get.

"All right. Then let me tell you a little about how this process differs from the one you went through years ago. The donor will be stimulated with medication in much the same way that you were, Sarah, when you were doing IVF with your own eggs. Her ovaries will then produce several mature follicles from which we can harvest eggs, and these eggs will be mixed in the lab with your sperm, Joe, to produce embryos."

"Do these drugs hurt the donor in any way?" Joe asked.

"Not as far as we can tell. There are some side effects associated with ovarian stimulation, but there's no evidence that fertility drugs have any serious long-term effects. Of course, they've only been on the market for 30 years, and IVF has only been around for 20, so we can't rule out the fact that something bad will turn up in another ten years. So far, though, it seems like there aren't any long-term problems."

"Joe, these are the same drugs I was taking when we were doing IVF," Sarah cut in. "And I guess these donors wouldn't be repeat customers if it were dangerous."

"I agree," Dr. Leverton said. "So, as the donor undergoes ovarian stimulation, Sarah, your participation will involve getting the lining of the uterus ready for implantation. That means you'll be taking estrogen and then progesterone on a fairly precise schedule that is matched to the donor's response. What we're doing, of course, is creating exactly the same cycle in you and her.

"We'll be measuring her blood levels and checking her follicles by ultrasound until several of them grow large enough and are ready to go. When we're happy with the size of the follicles and her estrogen level, the donor will give herself an injection of hCG to trigger ovulation. And 36 hours later, we go in and aspirate—or suck out—her follicles with a thin, hollow needle, exactly the way it was done when you had IVF yourself."

"I can guess what comes next. I go give you a sample," Joe said wearily, "and then it gets washed and diluted and mixed with her eggs this time, instead of Sarah's, and in 48 hours, they're ready to go."

"We *hope* they're ready to go. And we're leaving them in the lab for 72 hours now." The doctor shuffled around on his desk and took out a photograph with a purple tint. It was a picture of three embryos, magnified so many times that you could see the cell divisions—there were probably 8 or 12 that Sarah could detect. "This is what we're looking for—round, regular in size, and not too granulated on the inside. We take up to three of them, if we get that many, and we draw them up into a catheter, which is then inserted through Sarah's cervix into her uterus. And then we wait and see if they implant. Maybe one, maybe two—maybe all three, although that's rare."

"A young donor should give us great eggs that will fertilize nicely and produce great embryos. Most of the time we actually end up with extra embryos to freeze for future attempts. But I have to tell you that sometimes, even given all the right ingredients, you don't get the result you want."

Sarah sighed. "We know that. We've always known that."

"And when you're close to 50, it's not so easy in terms of your health. We have to think about problems like high blood pressure or gestational diabetes as the pregnancy proceeds. You may know that diabetic moms are more at risk for pre-eclampsia, preterm delivery, placental problems—even stillbirths."

"We've read about that," Sarah said. "We understand."

The doctor looked at them again, and did that trick with his finger in his eye again. He probably did that when he was thinking hard,

Sarah figured. Kind of a symbolic gesture for probing his brain for answers. "What do you say?" he asked softly.

Sarah felt Joe's hand again. She interlaced her fingers with his. "Yes," she said.

"Yes," Joe echoed. "We'd like to try."

Dr. Leverton stood up and went to open the door. The sound of a woman laughing came filtering down the hall. "Why don't you go meet with Michelle and with Lani, and they'll explain all the details to you. It's been a pleasure, and I assume we'll be seeing a lot of each other pretty soon."

Michelle was a tall black woman wearing a white coat over a long skirt and t-shirt. She handed them a list of the necessary tests they'd have to take, and explained that they could have records sent of tests done within the last year from their previous physician. But since it had been years since they'd been in infertility treatments, they would have to start from scratch. Sarah would need all kinds of blood tests and an EKG and treadmill test, to be certain her not-so-young body could withstand the rigors of pregnancy.

Michelle also handed them eight typewritten pages, each of which began, "Consent for..." There was consent for embryo transfer (which discussed the fact that they risked winding up with twins or triplets), another for embryo freezing where they had to state what they wanted done with their extra embryos in case they both died, and several others that covered every scenario of egg donation and its possible problems.

Michelle asked them to take the sheets home, read them carefully, and sign at the bottom of each page. Then she talked a little about picking a donor, and explained that they could ask for any characteristics they wanted that would match Sarah's, but the more requests they had, the longer it would be before she came up with a match. "If you just want to try and get Sarah's small build and dark eyes, that's easy. But if you're looking for a certain IQ and a great dancer who also happens to be Jewish, well, you may be waiting a while."

After 15 minutes of specifics, including the phone number of the counselor Dr. Leverton wanted them to see, Michelle handed them over to Lani, who gave them another sheaf of forms, all of these having to do with payments for various tests and services. At the end, they wrote her a check for $250, which was the price of their initial consultation with Dr. Leverton and his staff.

"I feel so tired," Sarah said as they walked out into the cloudy afternoon. It was starting to get dark, and you could smell fall coming on. They wandered down Riverside Drive for a while, cutting over at 80th onto Broadway. Joe bought them two eclairs at Zabar's, and they munched them as they walked down the avenue.

"What do you think of him?" Joe asked, licking chocolate off his fingers.

"I like him, I guess. It's too soon to say. I have a feeling I'll like him if we get pregnant and I'll say he's an asshole if we don't. But he seems pretty down-to-earth about this." She shook her head. "I didn't realize there were so few of us—only a hundred women in the world over 50, I read in the literature Michelle gave me. I don't imagine there are a whole lot between 48 and 50 either. Do I really want to be a groundbreaker?"

"Darling, you've always been a groundbreaker. The question is, do you want to be pregnant at 48?"

"Oh, no. I'm just knocking myself out for fun," she snapped. "What do you mean, do I want to? Look, I'm the one who has to live with not being genetically represented in our child. I'm the one who has to take the drugs and get the ultrasounds and sit with my goddamn legs in the stirrups."

"Hey, cut it out!" he barked back. "Don't take this out on me, Sarah. We went through enough fights over the IVF and the lousy sex."

She was silent, not really able to tell him what it was that was eating her inside. He was her husband; he had been on this path with her before, but it was still her soul she wrestled with.

Late that night, after he'd been in bed for two hours, she got up and went to the phone. She didn't know the number by heart any more, and that pained her. She sat at the window with her address book, listening to the howl of the wind. It was raining heavily, just as it had on the night of her accident. But probably, in California, it was balmy and clear. She imagined Alison, hearing the phone ring, walking over to it and looking out over the palm trees as she heard her mother's voice. A voice from her past.

The phone rang. Rang again. And then a third time.

"Hello?" The sound of her child was unmistakable. The little girl with the incredibly deep voice. She'd inherited that from her grandmother—and probably the cigarettes and coffee had encouraged her vocal chords to stretch some more.

"Hi, Alison," she said as though she said it every day.

There was a long pause. Then, "hi."

"How's it going?" Sarah had no idea how to handle this conversation.

"Good."

"I'm not disturbing you?"

"No."

"Listen," Sarah pulled on the phone cord impatiently. "We can talk in one word segments, or we can help each other out with whole sentences. How about it?"

"What do you want?" Alison sounded bored, as though she couldn't care less. How could Sarah begin to discuss this topic?

"Well," she began. "I've been thinking about you a lot lately. Wondering what you're doing, how you're doing. Because whatever misunderstandings we've had in the past, we're still blood relatives. And somewhere, there's usually a glimmer of light in between the arguments. So I figured I'd be a big girl and call you up and ..." Her voice trailed off.

She heard a sigh three thousand miles away.

"Still listening?"

"Yeah. I just can't fathom why you picked tonight to call and make a speech."

"Something's going on in my life. I wanted to include you."

"Well, good for you," Alison said sarcastically.

"I want to tell you that you'll always be my daughter, even if you never want to see me again. It doesn't go away, you know. When you give birth, that's it for eternity."

"Okay, fine, but that was your choice. If I had had a developed consciousness at that point, I might have seen it differently. If I'd been able to analyze the relationship that you and I would have, I might have opted out."

Alison often reminded her of Marilyn, that intellectual, standoffish, stuck-up double-talk.

"Alison, you didn't come when I told you I was marrying Joe, and I understand that—my marriage really had nothing to do with you.

But I'm about to do something now that really could make a difference in your life, so I'm calling to ask for ..." What was she asking for? Not an egg. Not at this point. There was too much between them.

"I just want your support."

"Okay. Shoot."

Sarah heard a rustling on the other end, as though she finally had decided to continue this conversation, and she was sitting down. She told her daughter the news, but not the way she had with Marilyn. She told it as though it were the legend of her life, the culmination of all the motherly and nurturing feelings she'd been missing out on since Alison had moved away. She told it so that it was clearly a new beginning, rather than a desperate attempt to recapture the past and bind up the wounds between them. It took her a long time, and finally, she said, "I know all this is hard for you, and that you probably think I still blame you for the accident, which I don't. But I thought of all people, you would understand. You and Jason don't want children—don't even want to get married, and that's okay. But our life choices don't have to be similar for us to back each other up. I guess that's what I want. I just need you to hear me out."

Alison muttered something, she wasn't sure what. Then she said, "I don't see why my opinion is so important to you, Mom."

It was the "Mom" that did it. Sarah was suddenly breathing easier. "I'm not replacing you. I could never find anyone who smoked and rode horses and jumped out of planes into fires like you do."

The peal of laughter on the other end broke the tension. "You make me sound like a real cowboy."

"Yeah, well it's amazing my hair never turned white over all your adventures. I suppose it's good we don't live too close."

"So what do you want me to do?" Alison asked.

"Just ... be there. Call me when you get a chance. No, I'm not leaving it to chance. I'll call you. This a good time?"

"Sure. Mom, how's Marilyn? And Lillian?"

"The same. Marilyn's not too thrilled with our decision. Lill doesn't know yet, so don't go calling up and gossiping with her about this."

"Me? Gossip? Hardly likely."

Sarah realized the conversation was over, that at least she'd made the first step. It was on the tip of her tongue to discuss the egg with Alison, but she decided to leave well enough alone. Actually, she felt a little creeped out about the idea of combining her daughter's egg with her husband's sperm. They weren't related, and it wasn't incest, but it was just too avant-garde for her.

"I think I have to go to sleep now. I'm glad I called, Ali," she said softly.

"Yeah."

The single word was as much affection as Sarah could get right now. But it was a start.

CHAPTER FOUR

The Marriage of Egg and Sperm

S arah and Joe want to have a baby. That might have been a simple thing for them years ago, but Sarah's biological clock has wound down. Her tiring ovaries cannot bring her elderly eggs to maturity, nor can these eggs be fertilized, become part of an embryo, or implant in her uterus.

The good news, however, is that the rest of her reproductive tract, with a little coaxing, can still provide a hospitable environment for an embryo. A uterus that's been given a hormonal boost can be persuaded to allow implantation, growth, and development of a fetus, and normal delivery of a baby. Just as exercise and training got Sarah through her marathon, so will diligent hormonal preparation ease the way for her pregnancy. The arbitrary timing of her natural biological clock doesn't matter anymore—she can *rewind* it, and enjoy the benefits of several more decades of reproductive life.

She will go through exactly the same process that occurs in nature with this one exception: The egg she uses won't be hers. Everything else follows just as it would have when she was 20 years younger: The sperm that fertilizes the egg will come from *her* husband, the egg will implant in *her* uterus, and she will gestate, bring to term, labor and deliver, and nurse and nurture *her* child throughout life.

A fundamental quality of all living things is their ability to reproduce, to make approximate copies of themselves, in order to perpetuate the species. Birds do it, bees do it, and most people, no matter their age, are driven to do it.

But just what is reproduction? What conditions must be present to make that big blind date between egg and sperm occur?

Before we get to the exciting story of how male and female unite, it's essential to understand how the whole system works. We'll begin with the stuff of life—the gametes, egg and sperm—housed in their gonads, the ovary and testicle.

OF GAMETES AND GONADS

Reproduction is the very essence of life, the one quality that separates a living cell from a nonliving, inorganic piece of matter. It can be divided into two broad categories: asexual and sexual. Asexual reproduction is akin to photocopying—in a process called *mitosis*, the lifeform makes a copy of itself and splits in half. Sexual reproduction, however, occurs by a process called *meiosis*. Two parent cells, or *gametes*, supply half the genetic information needed for a new individual. During an elaborate pattern of genetic multiplication and division, a new individual results with half the input coming from each parent. Mitosis is replication; meiosis is reproduction.

All cells above the level of bacteria undergo mitosis. They will grow, then split and divide into two new entities. This type of replication, for example, a skin cell within a human being—is asexual. The cell replicates all of its important components and then separates the new copy from the old copy by cell division.

Complex cells, no matter what their specialized function, contain within them a complete blueprint for the entire individual—that is, they have within them information applicable to all cells. This blueprint is stored in the form of wrapped-up bundles of a molecule called *deoxyribonucleic acid (DNA)* and is housed within the nucleus of the cell. When cell division occurs in mitosis, the new cells must each have their own copy of the DNA. The genetic material is carefully duplicated, then partitioned off into the two new cells along a plane of division and then carefully separated to ensure that each cell has the same amount and the same copies of all of the DNA.

But the problem here is that one skin cell looks exactly like another skin cell—there's no variety. With asexual reproduction, all the new individuals look just like the old ones, with the exception of some minor random mutations, which may take place during duplication of the genetic material. From an evolutionary point of view, this results in a tremendous disadvantage for the species. After all, if you can't change and adapt genetically to your environment, you're stuck. And for this reason, nature in her wisdom has allowed virtually all species of life above bacteria to reproduce sexually.

Sexual reproduction means that two individuals must come together to form a single new individual. A man and woman partner up, their genes combine and—presto!—a new baby is born. The new individual has the characteristics of both the mother and the father, and these characteristics are somehow programmed in the DNA, which is the genetic code of the new individual. When this baby grows up and wants to reproduce, he or she will get together with a member of the opposite gender, they will intermix their genes, make a new individual, and so on.

The gift we give to our children is half of the new genetic blueprint. Since the half that is chosen may be different each time, a single set of parents has the ability to make a very large number of very different new individuals. And none of the offspring will be exactly like its parents. Think of it musically. Each person is a chord, represented by four notes. As a mother, you will give two of your four notes; as a father you'll give two of yours. And the resulting child will sound those four notes in order to make a totally new chord (hopefully a harmonic one) that blends elements of mother and father.

As a species, we're crazy about genetic variety—we're constantly showing off how little Mary has one quality but her younger sister Abby is completely the opposite. We abhor the idea of intrafamilial marriage and incest, and although we may countenance cloning in sheep, we are extremely leery of extending this technology to our own kind.

Now how does all this dizzying genetic juggling go on? In order to achieve sexual reproduction and make sure that the new offspring has equal parts from both parents, the cells that will initially start the process cannot come about as a result of mitosis. That would be tantamount to making photocopies of the two parents and then gluing the pictures together. The coupling of two mitotic cells would give us too much genetic information for just one individual.

The logical way to solve this problem is to have each parent form a special new cell—this time, by meiosis—with only half the genetic information needed for a complete individual. Then two such cells could join forces and the new complement would make up the new individual. This, of course, is why *gametes*—eggs from the female and sperm from the male—have exactly one half of the genetic information needed for each human being. These cells are formed in specialized organs called *gonads*—ovaries in the female, testes in the male.

All gonads, whether male or female, start out the same. These organs are formed in the latter part of the first trimester of pregnancy within the developing fetus. A gonad is made up of a supporting structure (*stroma*) and of gamete precursors, called *germ cells*, which migrate to the area. If the fetus is male, then under the influence of the Y chromosome, the gonad differentiates into a testis. But without this influence, in the presence of only X chromosomes, the gonad differentiates into an ovary.

Where does all this occur? Before the story of gametes meeting and dividing will make sense, we need a few landmarks. First, let's travel inside the female body and take a look at the particular anatomy that makes reproduction possible.

The Female Reproductive System

To peer inside the female pelvic cavity is to view everything nature intended to create a baby. Starting from the exterior of the body, we have the external genitalia, consisting of two sets of *labia*, external and internal. These are the skin flaps around the vaginal opening that also enclose the hooded *clitoris* and the *urethra.*

The vaginal barrel is an elastic corridor about 4 to 5 inches long, lined with accordionlike *rugae*, folds that trap mucous and make the interior of the *vagina* lubricated and comfortable enough to admit anything from a tampon to a penis. The vagina ends at the *cervix*, a tight entryway to the *uterus*, which is a pear-shaped hollow organ about 3 inches long and 2 inches in diameter. Its flat, triangular cavity is lined with specialized cells that possess a unique characteristic: They allow embryo implantation to occur. The uterus is also endowed with a terrific potential for growth. During the course of a pregnancy, it increases in size from a pear to a watermelon so that it can accommodate several full-term babies. The *fallopian tubes*, terminating in

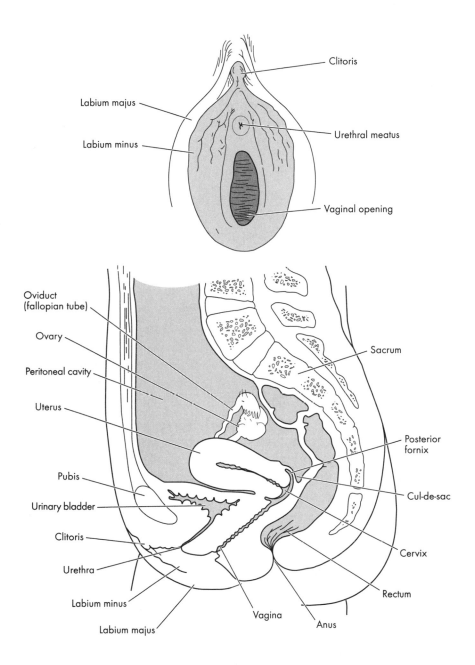

Female reproductive system and external genitalia.

floating fingerlike *fimbriae*, are 4- to 5-inch long passageways, connected to the uterus by two microscopic canals. One *ovary* sits beneath each tube, hanging back and down in the abdomen. Behind the uterus and between the two ovaries lies the **Pouch of Douglas**, the bowl-shaped ending of the abdominal cavity.

The precursors of eggs, the *oogonia*, (pronounced "o-o-gonia"), are stocked within the ovaries from the earliest months of fetal life when the as-yet-unborn female child is less than 3 inches long. They undergo rapid division by mitosis, so that about midway through gestation, there may be between 2 million and 10 million oogonia within the two ovaries. After that, they stop multiplying and begin meiosis, transforming into eggs or *oocytes* ("o-o-sites") within the fetal ovary. The eggs, encased in sacs called **primordial follicles**, remain suspended in this stage until about 36 hours prior to their eventual ovulation, whether that ovulation takes place when the woman is 14 or when she's 40.

Even before birth, when no ovulation is taking place, the irrevocable loss of oocytes begins. But nature never intended females to use all those millions of eggs they had originally. So it doesn't much matter that some 80 percent of them are absorbed back into the tissue of the ovary before birth. From that point until puberty, another 80 to 90 percent of the remaining eggs are also reabsorbed, so that a girl begins her menstrual cycle with only about 200,000 eggs. By the time she reaches menopause 40 or so years after she first begins menstruating, she'll have somewhere between zero and a few hundred eggs, and those that remain will not be capable of doing the job they were destined for. During the years right before menopause (the *perimenopause*), most women don't ovulate regularly. When they do, the eggs are almost always of poor quality, which means that they rarely result in a pregnancy.

One problem with old eggs, like Sarah's, is that by the time they've ovulated, nearly 90 percent have chromosomal abnormalities—one too many genes, or one too few at various places on the strand of DNA. When they are fertilized, the genetic abnormality persists in the embryo. The mixed-up blueprint is then copied throughout embryonic cell division. And the survival of the fittest rules with embryos as it does with most other creatures—nature rejects them, either not allowing them to implant or getting rid of them through miscarriage. (The miscarriage rate for women in their forties is higher than 50 percent.)

A young egg from a young donor, however, has far less trouble keeping the right number of chromosomes in the right place, hooking up with a sperm, becoming an embryo, and implanting successfully.

If a woman ovulates 12 times per year on average, and she ovulates from the time when she is 12 to the time when she is 52, or over a timespan of 40 years, only 480 eggs will be ovulated during that entire reproductive lifetime. Even after puberty, hundreds of eggs are discarded by the ovary for every one that is normally ovulated. That's why egg donors can supply lots of eggs and yet not alter their own ovarian function or fertility potential.

How Eggs Grow and Change

Let's go back to the early days of the ovaries' life and the functional eggs inside. The ovary is like a fruit-bearing tree with the follicles representing the fruit and the egg as the seed inside the fruit. Of course, all the fruits don't ripen at the same time. On our ovary tree, you'll always find small fruits at various stages of development.

The seeds would never spill from the fruit if they had no signal calling them to action. In order to ovulate, the follicle needs to grow to a size that will facilitate the release of the egg. Its growth is dependent on a chemical messenger called *follicle-stimulating hormone (FSH)* which is secreted by the *pituitary gland* after puberty. Without FSH, follicles simply shrivel up and die. The enclosed egg and the helper cells are then reabsorbed and incorporated into the supporting structure of the ovary. This of course is what happens to all follicles before puberty when no FSH is present, and why so many eggs are lost before a teenager has even experienced her first menstrual period. Only the eggs that remain comfortably housed in their primordial follicles will be available to ovulate later in life when they're needed.

But a small number of eggs are destined to go on to mature and ovulate. The initial part of the egg's departure from the ovary begins in what appears to be a random occurrence. At any one point in time, one or more eggs may start to take the first small steps toward eventual maturation and ovulation. The single layer of helper cells surrounding the oocyte in the primordial follicle begins to divide and to thicken.

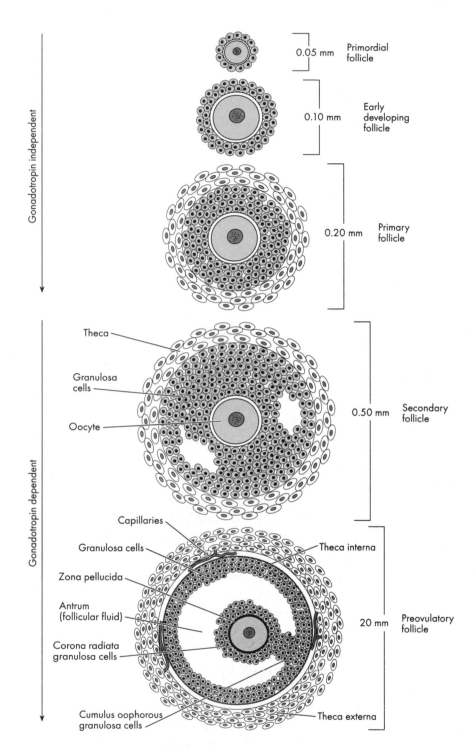

Follicle development.

At this point, the egg still has a *nucleus*, or *germinal vesicle*, which contains all the genetic material. Since it hasn't yet undergone even its first meiotic division, there are now 46 chromosomes in this immature egg. A layer of *cortical granules* lines the membrane of the cell. The egg is covered by the *zona pellucida*, the human eggshell, a protein coating that will harden to keep out intruders as soon as one sperm drills its way inside the egg. Like the prince who was the only one able to penetrate Sleeping Beauty's hundred-year forest with his sword, the zona pellucida ensures species specificity—only human sperm can penetrate this coating.

The egg is surrounded by several layers of helper cells, the so-called *granulosa* and *theca* cells. And the granulosa cells have produced a small amount of fluid, which has formed a tiny lake of follicular fluid that surrounds and protects the egg.

The Process of Meiosis

Inside each egg's nucleus sit the chromosomes that contain the DNA. Our genetic inheritance is carried on the DNA's sequence of component nucleotides, which, if laid out flat, would look like a long strand of ticker tape. It might be said that the transfer of DNA from one generation to the next is the *ne plus ultra* of reproduction. Sarah comes by her thick, wavy hair, her large feet, and her wide smile from her parents, who got their chromosomes from their parents and so on back through the ancestral line of her family. But the very elements that make her look so much like her mother and a little like her grandfather on her father's side are the ones that will prevent her from handing on her unique traits to a son or daughter of her own.

The key lies in the sorting bin of chromosomes. The process of meiosis, which means "lessening" in Greek, is something that happens to every egg, or oocyte, twice during its developmental process. In utero, the egg only reaches the most preliminary stage of meiosis, and it stays in suspended animation for years like this until ovulation, when first meiosis is completed and the first meiotic division occurs. The second division happens at *fertilization*.

In this twofold process, the egg reduces its DNA , cutting the original number of *chromosomes* in half. Although all the other cells in the body have 46 chromosomes, eggs and sperm have only 23, because they must end up with their complete complement of 46 when they come together.

When the egg and its surrounding helper cells reach the *primary follicle* stage, a moment of truth occurs. At this crucial point, the follicle, just two weeks from ovulation, must be exposed to adequate levels of FSH or it will simply be reabsorbed back into the tissue of the ovary. The egg is full-sized now, and even though it hasn't shed its excess genetic load, it probably contains all the building blocks and tools it needs after fertilization, during its difficult seven-day trek to implantation. These building blocks—energy factories and enzymes that direct fertilization and cell division as well as DNA replication—are contained within the gelatinous substance of the egg, called *cytoplasm*. Although it's usually the aging nucleus (which contains the genetic blueprint) that takes the blame for falling down on the pregnancy job once a woman is over 40, it may well be her poor-quality cytoplasm that's preventing the extension of her reproductive life. It's certainly possible that even chromosomal abnormalities may be caused by errors in DNA sorting and replication that is no longer accurately accomplished by aged cytoplasm.

Reproduction the Natural Way, Inside the Human Body

It's just like life—in order for an egg to meet a sperm, it has to get out of the house. In this case, the house is the follicle. In order to leave home, the egg must go through the process of *ovulation*. The fully mature follicle that develops from the primordial follicle (and which now contains the mature egg) is a multilayered structure: On the outside are the theca cells, which produce testosterone and other hormonal precursors of estrogen; next come the granulosa cells, which take the testosterone, convert it to estradiol, and also secrete follicular fluid. A lake of this fluid, lined by granulosa cells, pools in the center of the follicle. In one corner, the granulosa cells form a clump called the *cumulus*. The cumulus surrounds and is attached to the zona pellucida, the eggshell that protects the egg itself.

Ovulation is the linchpin: Without it, human reproduction as we know it would never occur. Once every 21 to 35 days or so, from puberty to menopause, one egg bursts out of its follicle as it leaves the ovary and has the chance to get out into the silent, inner world of the peritoneal cavity to get picked up by the fallopian tube and, there, possibly to meet up with a sperm. Ovulation is easily interfered with—pregnancy and nursing stop the process, not to mention birth control pills and any unduly physically taxing situation like studying for finals, training for a marathon, or going through a bout of anorexia. But during normal times, as we shall see next, the crescendos and surges of various hormones direct the female body to release one or more mature eggs, which, if fertilized in a timely fashion, may become a baby.

The Female Cycle

It's easiest to think of each female cycle as beginning at the time of *menstruation*. Although most women tend to think of bleeding as the grand finale of the hormone show, physiologically, it's also the commencement. The menses signify that the ovarian hormones, *estrogen* and *progesterone*, are at their lowest levels, the ovarian follicles are at their smallest size, and, the uterine lining, the *endometrium*, is the thinnest.

There are two phases to the female menstrual cycle. The first, which takes from 12 to 16 days in most women (although it can be a lot more variable that that) is the *follicular phase*.

The opening foray of the follicular phase begins with the secretion of FSH from the pituitary, which prods the primary follicles in the ovary to begin growing, starting on the path to follicle maturation and eventual ovulation. Several follicles may respond to the FSH stimulation.

As the follicles grow, the granulosa cells in the follicle walls start to produce *estradiol*, or *E2* as it's commonly called. The body actually makes several types of estrogen, but E2 is the most potent. It's responsible for thickening the lining of the uterus and preparing it for eventual embryo implantation, and it's also necessary for *feedback inhibition*, a mechanism that lets the pituitary know that FSH is working and the ovary is responding with follicle development.

Now a competition begins among the follicles—which will be the one to mature enough to ovulate? The strongest follicle makes the most E2, which makes it more sensitive to FSH, and in the meantime, the circulating E2 turns off FSH production by the pituitary, reducing stimulation to all the other follicles, which then break down, dissolving back into the tissue of the ovary.

Under most circumstances, only a single follicle per month gets its FSH tonic so that it can mature. This follicle (known as the *Graafian follicle*) then ovulates the one egg enclosed within it, which is why most human births produce only one offspring at a time. Fertility drugs, however, increase FSH levels, causing multiple follicles to develop. This, of course, is how multiple eggs are retrieved during IVF treatments and how *multiple births* occur if fertility drugs are used, even without IVF (such as the case of the Iowa septuplets).

As years pass, the FSH just doesn't do as much, even when it's given artificially in high doses. Older women's ovaries contain relatively fewer eggs than younger women's, and therefore relatively smaller numbers of primary follicles at any one time are available to respond to the FSH stimulation. This also explains why egg donors who undergo stimulation with FSH and then egg donation are not losing their eggs any faster than they would ordinarily, since the primary follicles, if unexposed to FSH, would simply die of natural causes. (This also explains why women who are on birth control pills for a long period of time without ovulating still lose eggs at the same rate and undergo menopause at the same time as they would if they had not used oral contraceptives.)

As the dominant follicle approaches ovulation, it grows like crazy, adding 50 percent or more to its volume every 24 hours until it's about an inch across. The granulosa cells in its walls are pumping out E2, which is helping to thicken the uterine lining and prepare it for implantation. The estrogen also changes the nature of *cervical mucus*, which becomes copious, slippery, and receptive to sperm just before ovulation. (One of the natural techniques women use to judge when they are most fertile is feeling the consistency of this mucus, which can be stretched out between two fingers right before ovulation.)

As the pituitary receives the message from E2 that the FSH has done its work, it switches gears and gradually prepares for the midcycle surge of *gonadotropins*. Although the levels of both hormones increase, the dominant player here is *luteinizing hormone (LH)*. This hormone, humming along in the blood at a very low level in the early half of the cycle, jumps to 10 or 20 times its former rate prior to ovulation.

After about 38 or 40 hours of LH stimulation, the dominant follicle is ready to ovulate, and the cells around the egg let it know that it's about to be released. This is the cue for the egg to complete the process of meiosis that began so many years ago but has been in suspended animation ever since.

At this point, the membrane of the nucleus surrounding the chromosomes disappears, and the chromosomes line up, kept in place by a delicate spindle of cell structures called *microtubules*. Now, the 46 chromosomes divide. Fifty percent stay in the main oocyte, and 50 percent move to a little satellite known as the *first polar body*, which rides along the top of the main cell. This process is similar to cell division in that each of the two daughter cells has the same number of chromosomes. However, the polar body, separate from the main egg but still surrounded by the zona pellucida, has very little of the cytoplasm.

There is now a half-set of double-stranded chromosomes present in the egg and in the polar body—23 in each—and they both have a double amount of DNA because the strands have not yet separated.

The 23 chromosomes remaining in the egg are aligned again by a new spindle, one that will eventually turn them into 23 single strands of DNA. If fertilization occurs, these 23 strands will align with the 23 strands coming from the sperm. But if no sperm come to call, the egg will die with meiosis half-completed.

The new gamete has only half of the genetic information that it needs. And it's perfectly happy to stay that way until the individual reproduces. Then the half from the female gamete will join with the

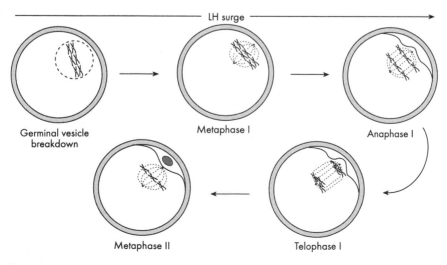

First meiosis.

half from the male gamete, resulting in one whole set. But the picture is not complete until the second meiosis, which occurs in the mature egg right at fertilization. We'll continue that part of the story in a few moments, after the two gametes have come together.

The egg is now prepared for ovulation. LH induces a cascade of hormonal changes in the wall of the *dominant follicle*. It allows a small hole to open in the wall so that the follicular fluid can drain out, carrying with it the mature egg. The egg still needs a lot of protection for its journey to meet the sperm, and so it leaves the follicle still surrounded by the cumulus, that sticky cloud of granulosa cells that enveloped it when it was inside the follicle. The cumulus is insurance that the egg will reach its destination at the mouth of the fallopian tube and will adhere to the fimbriae, or fingerlike projections of the tube. In addition, this protective barricade will shield the egg from the hostile environment of the abdominal cavity where immune cells, blood, and toxic substances lurk.

The old follicle, minus its egg, is now called a *corpus luteum* (Latin for "yellow body") and this structure begins producing another gonadal hormone, progesterone, (or P4), one of a class of hormones called progestins.

It is progesterone that will enhance the readiness of the endometrium to receive an egg. If the egg is successfully fertilized and the embryo implants, the hormone of pregnancy, hCG, will be produced by the precursor of the placenta, which is known as *trophoblast*. This hormone is closely related to LH, which means that it can stimulate the ovary. During early pregnancy, hCG stimulates the corpus luteum to remain alive and produce E2 and P4. These hormones, in turn, help keep the pregnancy going by maintaining the stability of the endometrium.

Each event in this chain must happen in sequence like one domino falling on the next. So if the embryo doesn't implant, we get no hCG and there's nothing to keep E2 and P4 going. Two weeks after ovulation, the corpus luteum dies. Consequently, E2 and P4 levels plummet, and the uterine lining, no longer receiving any hormonal stimulation, sloughs off in the process of menstruation. And the cycle begins all over again, continuing until natural or surgical menopause, or a trauma to the hormonal system such as chemotherapy or radiation.

Follicle maturation and the degradation of unselected follicles continues throughout a woman's reproductive years until the aging

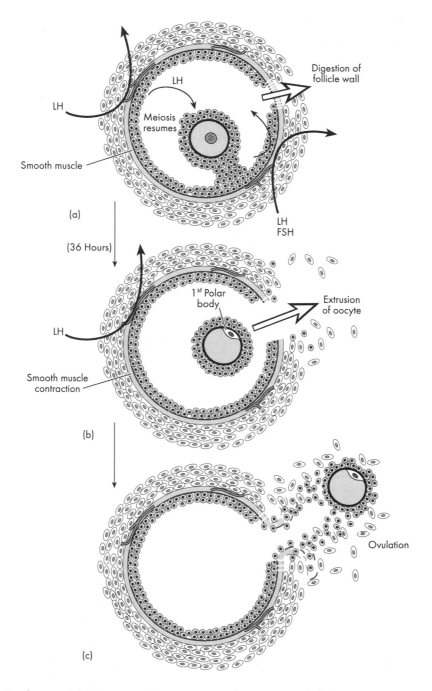

Ovulation: (a) LH surge; (b) extrusion of oocyte; (c) follicle-secreting egg.

process accelerates the rate of egg depletion and eventually all the functional oocytes in the two ovaries are gone.

The Male Reproductive System

Before we can get to the adventure of the ovulated egg, we need to examine the male side of things to get a little background on the sperm that will travel to meet this egg. The sperm either must be waiting at the entrance to the fallopian tube or arrive a short time after the egg for the great blind date to take place.

The various organs that are necessary for the development and transportation of sperm are the *testes* encased in the baglike *scrotum*, the *epididymis*, the *seminal vesicles*, the *penis*, the *cavernous bodies* or *corpora* within the penis which become engorged with blood to create an erection, and the *vas deferens* (the tube that carries the sperm from the scrotum up to the corpora). The *urethra* (which carries both urine and semen) traverses the penis.

During puberty, the same system begins revving up in boys as in girls. The hypothalamus in the brain speaks to the pituitary, which in turn, speaks to the testes, telling them to begin producing the male gonadal hormone *testosterone*. (Men also produce estrogen, by the way, but in far smaller amounts than women; and women also produce testosterone, but in far smaller amounts than men.)

Under the influence of this hormone and FSH from the pituitary, the testes manufacture new spermatozoa throughout the male life-span—trillions of the little swimmers are created and discarded over the years. It takes 48 days for a sperm cell to develop in the testis, and during this growth period, the sperm precursors in the *testicle* have their requisite component of 46 chromosomes. But as they mature, they, like the eggs, also undergo meiosis.

The difference between sperm and eggs, of course, is volume. In order for a mature egg to maintain its large volume of cytoplasm, meiosis sheds chromosomes into small, inactive polar bodies. In this way, one mature egg results from two meiotic divisions of an immature egg. But in the male, two meiotic divisions give way to four active and functional spermatozoa. By the time they leave the testis and move to the epididymis for another 14 days to mature, they too are reduced by half the number of chromosomes. Each spermatozoon is long and

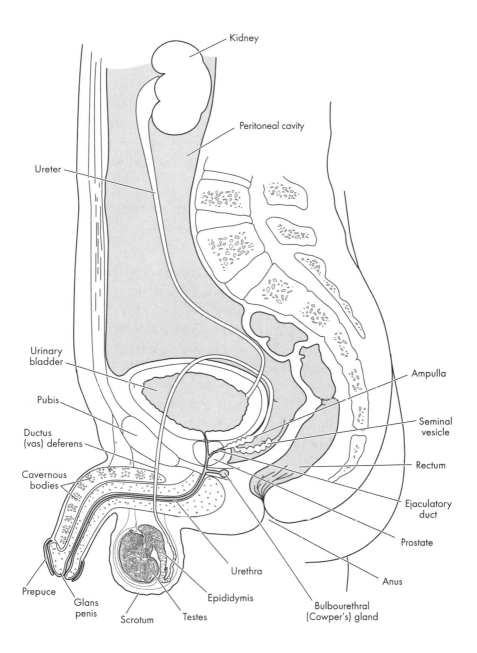

Male reproductive system.

slender, with chromosomes jammed inside the sperm head, and a long tail to propel the cell along.

The mature sperm in the epididymis are actively transported out of this waystation by strong muscular contractions in the vas deferens. They are propelled up out of the scrotum and around the bend to the *ejaculatory duct* within the *prostate gland*. There they are combined with *seminal fluid*, the sticky, gluey liquid that will help to take them along the last part of their journey. They will finally come out of the ejaculatory duct, into the urethra and from there, down the length of the penis and out into the vaginal canal, hopefully not too far from the cervix.

The Sperm's Journey

The seminal fluid rapidly forms a clotlike coagulum around the sperm, giving it enough substance so that it won't drain out of the vagina. Its high pH and buffering qualities also protect it from the acidic (and potentially lethal) vaginal environment. Once inside the female reproductive tract, the sperm swim randomly, moved along by the mechanical pull of gravity. The most hardy are rewarded at the top of the vaginal barrel with a wave of slippery cervical mucus that protects the opening of the cervix. At ovulation, this mucus is receptive to sperm because of its alkaline nature, which protects the sperm from the naturally acidic environment of the vagina, and also because of its longitudinal structure, which helps the sperm to pass up into the uterus.

Mucus is a very interesting substance, made of water held together by a loose protein network, something like Jello. But the protein in Jello isn't well-organized, so it's easily cut into blocks. Mucus, on the other hand, contains well-organized, longitudinal protein fibers that stretch easily but can't be cut. Imagine, if you will, the long, sticky bands of cervical mucus like many thousands of rope ladders, suspended from the upper genital tract for the sperm to climb up. Within minutes of ejaculation, the hardiest sperm are out of the perilous vaginal melieu and up and away into the safety of the mucus.

The sperm can survive for two to four days in the cervical mucus, but of course, they have a better shot at reaching their goal if they get through immediately. A normal ejaculate contains between 50 and 500 million sperm. But almost all of them die off as they struggle to reach their goal. Only a few will reach the rendezvous to attempt to fertilize the egg, and only one will be successful.

The Main Event: Fertilization

After ovulation, the egg, released from its home in the ovary, floating in a mixture of follicular fluid and peritoneal secretions, starts tumbling down toward the depths of the peritoneal cavity. But the fimbriae of the fallopian tubes puff up, and opening their "fingers," filter through this fluid in the Pouch of Douglas as a sea anemone might filter seawater. The cumulus and its egg stick to the fimbriae and are carried by ciliary action into the interior of one of the fallopian tubes, or *oviducts*. These tubes are much more than just conduits to the uterus. Their function is so specialized that no substitute, biological or synthetic, has ever been devised.

The cumulus mass with the egg inside it travels through the wide terminal portion of the tube called the *ampulla*, where it calmly waits, somehow secure in the understanding that it has reached the meeting place. The ampulla, only 2 to 3 inches from the uterine cavity, is lover's lane. It is here that the sperm must meet the egg. It may either be waiting there when the egg arrives or get to the rendezvous shortly thereafter.

The sperm are determined to keep their date, but it's not easy. Only a few thousand of the original horde have passed through the cervix, and they proceed, a dozen or two at a time, up through the upper genital tract, searching the mecca of fertilization, the fallopian tube, for an egg. Conception will only occur if the sperm are present in the ampulla before ovulation or, at the very latest, on the day of the event. As with warriors storming the enemy castle to find the kidnapped princess, time is always of the essence. If the sperm get to the site more than 24 hours after ovulation, the egg will die and all they will find is the cumulus. After swimming the perilous moat of the vaginal canal, scaling the castle wall on mucus rope ladders, and finding the meeting place at the ampulla, the sperm will find their quest to have been futile if they are late.

These hardy troupers are given a boost during their ascent in a process called *capacitation*. The cervical mucus of the female reproductive tract—as well as the culture media in the laboratory during an in vitro procedure—induce biochemical changes in the outer membranes of the sperm, so that they become capable of fertilization. On their own stomping ground, in their own male fluids, they remain under the influence of the potent *semen* that keeps them subdued and appears to inhibit fertilization.

But as the seminal fluid comes off the sperm inside the female or inside a test tube during *sperm washing,* the sperm become revitalized, stronger than ever. (Think how much faster Olympic swimmers go when they shave their bodies!) Several boisterous sperm, like Lilliputians swarming over Gulliver, finally make contact with the cumulus. This is a huge place, a veritable cloudbank with no land-marks. It is thought that the sperm react to electricity—if you put them in a drop of culture medium, they tend to go right to the surface, reacting to the electrolytes and the orientation of the charge at the edge of the fluid. So similarly, the sperm go for the surface of the clump sur-rounding the egg.

The commandos of the reproductive tract are now few in number. Hundreds of thousands have perished, and only the fittest hover around the outer layer of the egg, fighting to get inside. The suitors struggle, battering along the edge of the egg. It may take up to an hour for the winner to break through one spot on the zona pellucida and at last achieve fertilization. The others may keep battering against the now-locked gate for several more days, even as the successfully fertil-ized egg undergoes its repeated cell divisions.

The Hard Battle for Fertilization

Even when the triumphant sperm reaches the egg, its battle is not over. At the edge of the egg, it still has to make its way through the human eggshell, the zona pellucida. The sperm recognizes a particular protein site on the zona, confirming that it's a member of the correct species, and it binds to the site. This is the way inside. The sperm head goes to work now, its long dartlike top, the *acrosome,* releasing enzymes that will allow the sperm to digest its way through the zona. The enzymes from the acrosome melt a narrow slit in the boundary that keeps the sperm from its goal, but they do no damage to the egg itself. Now the movement of the sperm becomes hyperactivated, its tail thrashing in an exaggerated mating dance that helps to propel it through the zona and toward the inner membrane of the egg.

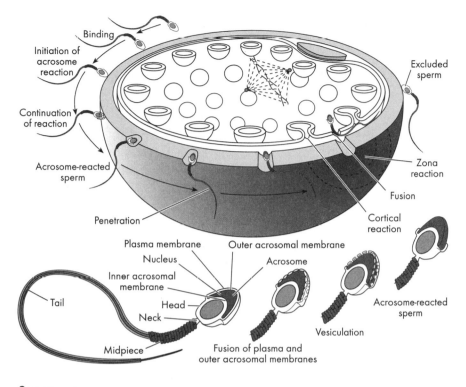

Binding

Initiation of
acrosome
reaction

Excluded
sperm

Continuation
of reaction

Acrosome-reacted
sperm

Zona
reaction

Fusion

Penetration

Cortical
reaction

Plasma membrane

Outer acrosomal membrane

Nucleus

Acrosome

Inner acrosomal
membrane

Tail

Head

Acrosome-reacted
sperm

Neck

Vesiculation

Midpiece

Fusion of plasma and
outer acrosomal membranes

Sperm enters egg.

As soon as the egg becomes aware that a sperm has bound to its cell membrane (the *oolemma*), it releases small packets of chemicals from the cortical granules beneath its surface into the space just under the zona pellucida. These substances harden the zona so that it acts as a barricade to keep all other sperm out.

Sometimes, however, more than one sperm does manage to get inside. In this event, called "polyspermy," both sperm try to combine their genes with those of the egg in a cellular ménage à trois. The resulting zygote has 69 instead of the usual 46 chromosomes and can neither implant nor form a normal baby. But nature makes sure that this doesn't occur very often—it takes place in about only 8 percent of eggs fertilized in vitro.

How is it that one side of the egg knows that the other side has been penetrated? After all, the sperm is so tiny, and there's plenty of room in the cumulus for many more. The answer is that the information probably travels through the membrane that surrounds the egg—and the word goes out not to let anyone else in.

The entry of the sperm head into the interior of the egg is the magical moment of fertilization, and many theologians and philosophers deem it the beginning of life. Technically however, this is not the case. Fertilization is not one isolated event, but rather an unfolding series of happenings that lead inexorably to the development of a new genetic individual. At this point, the story is still not halfway told.

Now the egg becomes the active partner. The soft, pliable oolemma, with the consistency of a Jello-filled plastic bag, folds inward and encases the sperm head in its cytoplasm, the inside filling of the egg. It sheds its excess DNA into a second polar body in order to permit the intermingling of genes with the sperm. This new polar body now rides along adjacent to the first polar body right under the zona pellucida. At this point, the DNA remaining inside the egg coalesces into a small spherical structure called the female *pronucleus*. This will be the maternal contribution to the baby's genes.

The sperm, meanwhile, knows that it has come home to rest. The sperm head "decondenses," releasing its chromosomes into a spherical structure called the male *pronucleus*. And out of the male pronucleus emerges a *sperm aster*, a collection of microtubules that reach out like the points of a star, pushing the male pronucleus away from the

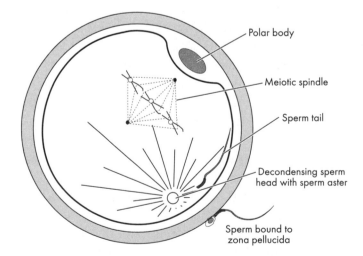

Polar body

Meiotic spindle

Sperm tail

Decondensing sperm head with sperm aster

Sperm bound to zona pellucida

Fertilization: decondensing sperm head with sperm aster.

oolemma and toward the center of the egg. These microtubules reach to all points within the egg, finding the female pronucleus and pulling it in toward the center of the egg, in close proximity to its male counterpart. The couple is irrevocably drawn together.

At this point, the fertilized egg is called a *zygote* or *embryo*. Sixteen to eighteen hours have passed since the sperm head melded with the egg membrane. It is at this stage that embryo cryopreservation is usually done in an assisted reproduction cycle where more eggs have been fertilized than will be transferred back. But the interesting thing is that male and female haven't yet become one. Their genes are still separate.

The search of the egg and sperm to find each other represents an almost desperate biological yearning. Yet even when they meet and combine, the two gametes continue the dance. The *two-pronuclear stage* is the most crucial, since it is here that the randomly produced halves of the DNA of two individuals will make a third, completely different set of DNA.

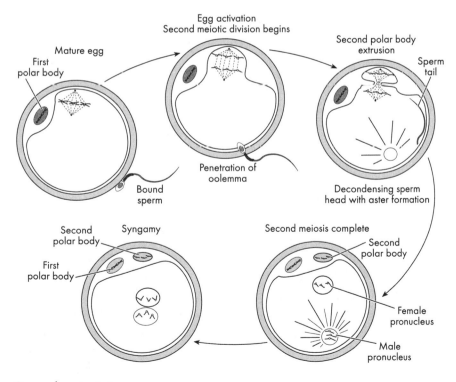

Second meiosis to syngamy.

The pair of pronuclei approach each other, and within a few hours, their outer membranes fuse in a process called *syngamy*. The zygote now has a full complement of 46 chromosomes—23 from the female and 23 from the male. And of those millions of possible combinations of genetic inheritance in each gamete that we began with, only these strands of DNA are left.

There is so much room for error here. If you get one extra chromosome (a *trisomy*), the fetus won't form properly—the most common of these is *trisomy 21*, or Down's syndrome. But if chromosome 21 is missing (*monosomy 21*), the fetus won't survive at all. Other chromosomal abnormalities will result in heart problems, gastrointestinal difficulties, mental retardation, and other, multiple handicaps. This is why the embryo, the blueprint for implantation, is so crucial. It must divide, make more copies of the cell's DNA in exactly the right order, and have enough energy left for the long journey to the endometrium.

Development of the Embryo: From Fragile Zygote to Powerful Blastocyst

About 30 or 40 hours after insemination, the zygote cleaves in two, beginning its pattern of mitosis, the type of division used by every other cell in the body. Every 12 hours or so, the cells split in half, so that 2 becomes 4, 4 becomes 8, and 8 becomes 16 embryonic cells called *blastomeres*. (Since human cells don't necessarily divide at the same time, there may be temporarily uneven numbers.) Each blastomere has the same number of chromosomes and same intracellular structures as its mates, and up to about the eight-celled stage, each one, if housed within its own zona pellucida, could conceivably become a person all by itself.

Of course, no matter how many divisions take place within the protective environment of the zona, the total volume of cells can't exceed that of the original egg. So each time the cells of the embryo split, the two daughter cells are one-half the size of the mother. During this division process, there may be some fragmentation of individual cells of the embryo, and the two polar bodies undoubtedly start coming apart as well. No longer needed, these satellites and the DNA captured inside them simply become part of the cellular debris.

This dividing ball of cells is now propelled either by peristalsis (a wavelike contraction and relaxation of the muscles in the fallopian tube) or by ciliary action of the fallopian tube toward its final home in the uterus. This is a crucial time. Before this ball of cells actually settles in the endometrium, it is in no-man's land, a fragile voyager with no roots, no home.

Approximately five days after ovulation, the embryo is a ball of 100 to 200 cells known as a *blastocyst*, with a fluid-filled center known as a *blastocele*. Since it is still approximately the same size as it was after only one cell division, it is now packed solid. So the blastocyst expands, pumping additional fluid into its blastocele, and inflates like a water balloon as the zona pellucida stretches to the breaking point. Finally, it cracks, and in a process remarkably similar to that of a chicken egg, it allows the embryo to slip out, so that its cells come into direct contact with the endometrium. This process is called *hatching*. (During in vitro procedures, we occasionally have to help nature along. In *assisted hatching*, we actually create a small opening in the zona in order to make things easier for the embryo.)

If the lining of the uterus has been properly primed with estrogen and progesterone, it is in a favorable state to receive the young embryo. At this point, seven to eight days after it began its whirlwind tour of ovulation, fertilization, migration, alteration, growth, and hatching, the embryo burrows into the endometrium, where if all goes well, it will settle in for an eight-month stay.

If implantation is successful, the next developments can unravel seamlessly. The embryonic cells, now called *trophoblast*, send out fingerlike projections that invade the maternal endometrium, holding on for dear life. Cells of the child-to-be interpenetrate cells of the mother-to-be. And trophoblast produces the vital pregnancy-specific hormone, hCG, which we can detect in the maternal circulation about eight or nine days after ovulation, or about five days prior to a missed period.

As trophoblast continues to grow, a group of cells differentiate into the *placenta*, which passes blood supply and nutrients to the growing embryo. The midsection, a tiny handful of cells in comparison to the thousands that now exist, becomes the *fetal plate*, the beginnings of the growing fetus. Blood vessels now start to develop on both sides of the division between the endometrium and trophoblast, leaving only

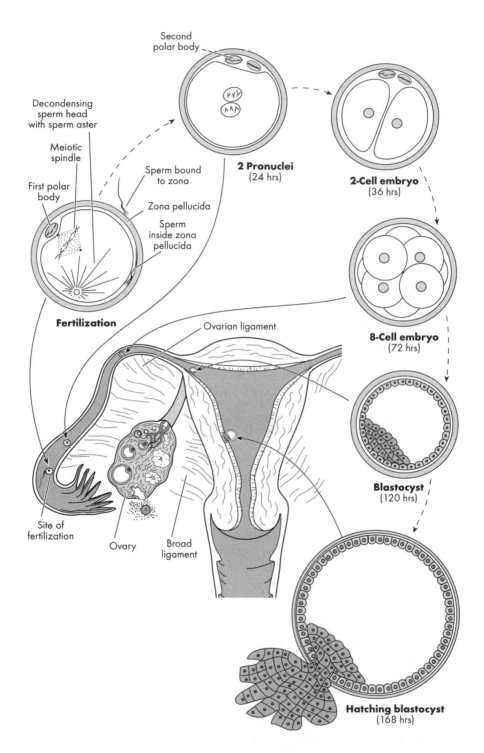

Second polar body

Decondensing sperm head with sperm aster

Meiotic spindle

First polar body

Sperm bound to zona

Zona pellucida

Sperm inside zona pellucida

2 Pronuclei
(24 hrs)

2-Cell embryo
(36 hrs)

Fertilization

Ovarian ligament

8-Cell embryo
(72 hrs)

Site of fertilization

Ovary

Broad ligament

Blastocyst
(120 hrs)

Hatching blastocyst
(168 hrs)

Female reproductive system with egg, from fertilization to hatching blastocyst.

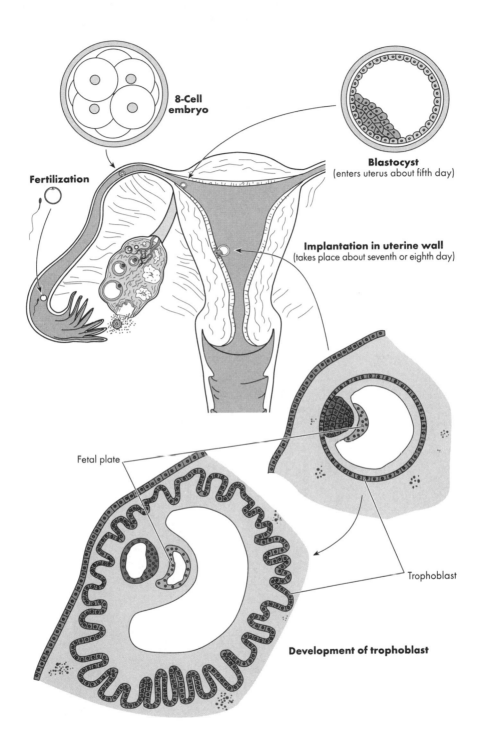

8-Cell embryo

Blastocyst
(enters uterus about fifth day)

Fertilization

Implantation in uterine wall
(takes place about seventh or eighth day)

Fetal plate

Trophoblast

Development of trophoblast

Trophoblast implants in endometrium.

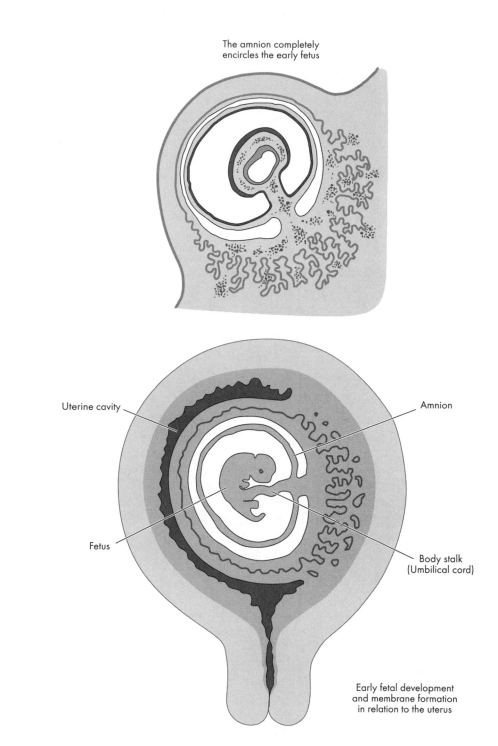

The amnion completely encircles the early fetus

Uterine cavity

Amnion

Fetus

Body stalk (Umbilical cord)

Early fetal development and membrane formation in relation to the uterus

Development of placenta and fetal membranes.

three layers of cells separating the maternal and fetal circulations. Only two weeks after implantation, a new life has begun.

The Window of Implantation

There are several reasons why implantation might *not* occur. The first is poor egg quality. The second reason is that the endometrium may not be receptive to the embryo at the exact time that we want it to be. In humans, the uterine lining is only receptive to embryo implantation during a one- to three-day period of time each cycle—during the vital window of implantation. If the embryo tries to hatch out of its zona pellucida at any other time, the uterine lining simply won't accept it.

Obviously, the lining has to be prepared in some way to be receptive to the implanting embryo, and it might be difficult to sustain this degree of preparedness for very long. But that's not the whole explanation of why implantation is so tough.

Certainly, in natural reproduction, there could be no implantation without ovulation. So ovulation might have to precede the preparation of the uterine lining. But assuming we could get a nicely primed endometrium when we want it, why wouldn't it stay that way?

What actually happens is that the window opens about five days after ovulation, then slams shut about three days later. This is probably a tactic on the part of the reproductive system to prevent the implantation of embryos which are developing too slowly. It eliminates abnormal ones before they can latch on to the endometrium. (Actually, most abnormally developing embryos don't get that far—they tend not to reach the blastocyst stage or, if they do, they may not hatch from the zona pellucida.)

In order to get a receptive endometrium, you first have to stimulate or "prime" it with estrogen for a sufficient period of time. In a natural cycle, the developing follicle starts producing E2 right after the menstrual period. As the dominant follicle grows, it increases its output of E2, especially during the last few days prior to ovulation, so that the uterine lining thickens and prepares itself for the progesterone stimulation that's about to follow. After the follicle releases its egg, it turns into a corpus luteum, a busy factory of progesterone production.

You have to have estrogen to prime the endometrium and make it susceptible to progesterone. And you have to have progesterone in order to cause the changes within the endometrium that will make it susceptible to implantation. Without E2, you'd never get P4 receptors, and that would mean you'd never get a response to P4 even if you gave it externally. Consequently, you'd never get an embryo that would latch on to the uterine lining. Both E2 and P4 are critical.

Once progesterone secretion begins, the endometrium goes through a series of very predictable changes. So if you take a piece of endometrial tissue (a *biopsy*) at any time during the *luteal phase* of the female cycle, it can be "dated" by observing specific criteria on specific dates of the cycle.

These changes actually correspond to critical stages within the endometrium as regards embryo implantation. During the first half, or preovulatory phase, of the cycle, the endometrium thickens in response to the estrogen stimulation. During the second half, or post-ovulatory phase, progesterone induces tissue changes which pinpoint the number of days that have elapsed since ovulation.

The egg, too, is running against the clock since it can only be fertilized during the first 24 hours after ovulation, after which time it has to make its way toward the endometrium to implant and must reach its destination exactly when the lining is primed and receptive. How does the body coordinate all this? It can't rely on the timing of the female cycle, because for some women, the typical pattern is every 21 days and for others, it may stretch to 35 days or more. So the coordination signal

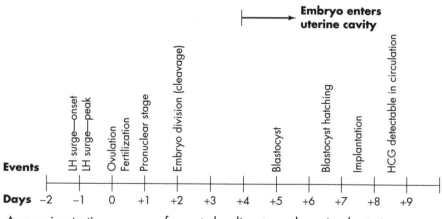

Approximate time course of events leading to embryo implantation.

between embryo and endometrium must be ovulation. For the egg, this means extrusion of the polar body and fertilization. For the endometrium, this means the beginning of progesterone secretion and the changes in the lining that will lead inexorably to the opening of the window of implantation seven days later.

When we examine tissue samples of the endometrium throughout a cycle with a scanning electron microscope (SEM), which gives us a three-dimensional image, we can observe specific changes in the surface appearance of the cells that make physical contact with the embryo. In contrast to the microscopic appearance of the cross sections of endometrial tissue that changes throughout the menstrual cycle, the surface cells appear to be the same whether any progesterone is present or not. But in biopsies taken during the postovulatory phase, right around the time that the window of implantation opens, we find small bumpy structures called *pinopods* protruding from the surface of the endometrium.

Just prior to implantation, the pinopods suck out fluid from the uterine cavity, squishing the embryo up against the endometrium like an orange against a wall. Forcing the embryo up against the surface of the endometrial cells may help the hatching embryo to make cell-to-cell contact and to implant.

When we're preparing a recipient for egg donation at the USC ART program, we have her go through a practice cycle, a stimulation identical to the one that she will undergo when she's actually synchronized to a donor. At the end of this cycle, we take a sampling of her endometrial tissue to be sure that she's getting the appropriate estrogen and progesterone response.

We check the biopsy under the microscope to identify the exact changes that progesterone has caused in the uterine lining. That way, we know whether or not the estrogen priming was adequate and whether or not the progesterone response was appropriate. The following month, when we need the recipient to be perfectly in sync with a donor, we'll have a precise timetable.

When we need to align two cycles of two different women, the window of implantation becomes even more crucial. We have to be sure that the embryos produced in vitro from the donor eggs are in synchrony with the endometrium in the recipient, which must be properly primed with E2. While the eggs are obtained from the donor and mixed with the male partner's sperm in the laboratory, the recipient needs to receive both E2 and P4 so that her endometrium will accept the embryos when they are transferred back.

The more particular we can be about the window of implantation, the more success we'll have in the future coordinating IVF and egg donation cycles, as we'll see in the next chapter.

CHAPTER FIVE

A CYCLE BUILT FOR TWO—OR THREE: ASSISTED REPRODUCTION

Pregnancy is simple for some, impossible for others. There are many cases where this joyous, amazing event can't happen naturally, and this is where we look to medical science to override some of nature's limitations. Assisted reproduction has changed the way we view and remedy reproductive failures. And as technology moves forward, we'll have an increasing number of tools at our disposal.

Assisted reproductive technology (ART) has moved some of the early steps in fertilization and embryonic development from the human body to the laboratory. So far, however, we can do nothing to manipulate the steps that come prior to the development of the primary follicle or after embryo implantation. You must have a primary follicle in the first place to get an egg out of it. Only a primary follicle that responds to FSH can grow into a preovulatory follicle capable of ovulation. Before that, what goes on is independent of hormonal stimulation and outside environmental stimuli.

Nor can you do anything in a laboratory to alter embryonic life after implantation. Once it occurs, it has to remain where it is—you can't transplant an implanted embryo like a tree. If it should accidentally put down roots in the fallopian tube—an ectopic pregnancy—it can't be picked up and moved to the uterus. And implantation has to happen in a uterus—there are not, as yet, any plans for an artificial womb (although a few radicals in the field have been musing about transferring human embryos into cows and apes). For now, if you've had a hysterectomy and you want a baby, you need to find a gestational carrier.

While technology can't do everything—at least not yet—it can enhance the reproductive process from follicle maturation to embryo implantation. Assisted reproduction may be necessary because of male factor infertility, female factor infertility, or both. To help with male blocks to fertility, we combine eggs and sperm in a petri dish, which saves the sperm a lot of work. These laboratory techniques up the odds on fertilization by concentrating sperm in high numbers and keeping them close to the egg for a longer period of time than they'd have in the body. To help with female blocks to fertility, we can move eggs out of the ovary. This allows them to bypass scarred or absent fallopian tubes and to arrive in the uterus at the right time in the right stage of development.

But before we step into the laboratory, let's briefly examine the more "natural" types of assisted technology that can help the processes happening inside the body. By manipulating the menstrual cycle and the deposition of sperm, we can still give nature a leg up.

In the simplest of assisted technologies, *intrauterine insemination (IUI)*, we monitor the woman's cycle using ultrasound and blood tests with or without the use of fertility medications. At the time of ovulation, we ask the male partner to produce a sperm sample, which we separate from the seminal plasma and then insert through the cervix into the uterine cavity. We do this in order to get the sperm as close as possible to the fallopian tube where fertilization occurs naturally.

In another relatively "natural" type of ART, *gamete-intrafallopian transfer (GIFT)*, the eggs are removed from the ovary and then placed together with sperm at the entrance to the fallopian tube. (This is a preference of religious couples who may feel that this type of ART is closer to the way God intended conception to occur.) Simple, yes, but quite traumatic for the woman, since the gametes must be put back inside by means of a laparoscopy, an invasive surgical procedure. But GIFT is only an option for women with normal fallopian tubes. If the tubes are damaged, blocked, or absent, the egg and sperm would have to be deposited inside the uterus. Unfortunately, unless fertilization has already occurred in the laboratory, implantation rarely occurs this way.

So the safest bet for virtually all causes of infertility, and especially for women with damaged or absent tubes, is to take the guesswork out of that big blind date between egg and sperm by having it take place in a petri dish in a laboratory: This means *IVF*, *in vitro fertilization.*

In this type of ART, the follicular fluid containing the eggs is sucked out, in a process known as *aspiration*, from the preovulatory follicles in the ovary, the eggs are identified and separated from the follicular fluid, the sperm is collected in a cup and separated from the seminal plasma, and the gametes are then mixed together in a petri dish. After 72 hours, the resulting embryo is transferred back into the woman's uterus.

If you let the female body do its thing naturally, you'll get one follicle per cycle, and hope it will yield one egg. But to increase our chances of a pregnancy during IVF, we artificially stimulate the ovary to produce many large follicles, from which many eggs can be extracted. The most efficient way to achieve this end is to shut down the normal reproductive cycle and create a new one from whole cloth.

A STIMULATED CYCLE

In order to stop the natural female cycle, we administer a medication called Lupron. Lupron is a GnRH-agonist, which blocks the action of natural *gonadotropin-releasing hormone (GnRH)*, the hormone put out by the hypothalamus that drives the pituitary gland to start up a woman's natural cycle. For the first few days of administration, Lupron actually stimulates the pituitary, but then, after about 7 to 10 days, it achieves *down-regulation*, shutting off the pituitary so that it can't put out its requisite hormones, FSH and LH. It's like putting a hormonal clamp on the ovary. Each day, the woman undergoing a stimulated cycle gives herself a subcutaneous injection with a tiny syringe, similar to those used by some diabetics to self-inject insulin.

When the Lupron has done its work, estrogen levels drop, ovulation stops, and the uterine lining thins out—the body is in a temporary, artificially induced state which resembles menopause. The lack of stimulation ensures that the follicles won't compete among themselves for dominance, which works out nicely when the stimulation regimen begins, since we want to encourage as many follicles as possible to develop at the same time. When the endometrium finally sloughs off (since it's receiving no estrogen or progesterone to keep it thick and juicy), a period results. This is the sign that the down-regulation is complete.

At any time after this, the ovaries can be artificially stimulated so that the woman will produce multiple follicles, all maturing at the same time, a process known as *superovulation*, or "controlled ovarian hyperstimulation." The beauty of this is control and timing—if a woman is using her own eggs, she can begin superovulation when it's convenient for her and her doctor, and with third-party assisted reproduction, the donor's superovulation can be synchronized with the preparation of the recipient's endometrium. Most fertility programs start stimulations on a particular day of the week, knowing that follicle aspiration usually takes place 11 to 15 days later, which facilitates the timing of all other procedures.

It's FSH that causes follicles to grow, naturally or artificially. So we can get multiple follicular development with daily injections of FSH; various brands, such as Humegon, Pergonal, Repronex, Fertinex, Follistim, and Gonal-F are used. A woman has to have enough primary follicles present in the ovary to respond to the FSH. If she's nearing menopause, there will probably be only one of these waiting to grow, and no amount of stimulation from the outside will alter the single follicle process that normally occurs in the body. But if she's of normal reproductive age, she can easily grow from 10 to 20 good-sized follicles.

The injections of FSH continue for 7 to 12 days until the follicles reach a healthy preovulatory size, and as we monitor their growth, we can raise or lower the dosage if we need to get them to go faster or slower. At our clinic, patients take their injections in the evening, and we see them the next day so that we can measure their follicles by ultrasound, take blood to get an E2 level, and then decide whether to change dosage.

When a woman—either an IVF candidate or an egg donor—is going through a stimulated cycle, she begins with a course of Lupron. When she has a period, we know that she has down-regulated successfully. The ultrasound taken at this time will show that her uterine lining is nice and thin and that the only follicles in her ovaries are small, apparently ready to respond to stimulation. At any time after that, she starts her FSH injections. (In the bad old days, with the cheaper, older formulations, she would have had to give herself a big intramuscular shot daily, but today with the new recombinant FSH formulations, she'll only have a small injection, like those she gave herself when she was taking the Lupron.) When she starts the final phase of the stimulation, it's time for her to come into the doctor's office for regular monitoring.

The patient's first visit to our office comes after her first four days of injections, and we check her every other day until ovulation is imminent, when we see her daily. When the follicles reach a good size (about 20 millimeters or four-fifths of an inch in diameter) and the E2 level indicates that the granulosa cells within the follicles are working at the correct level (about 200 picograms per milliliter per large follicle), the decision is made to stop the Lupron, stop the FSH, and trigger ovulation with 10,000 IUs (international units) of *human chorionic gonadotropin (hCG)*. The patient is given careful instructions to inject herself exactly 36 hours before follicle aspiration is scheduled.

This hormone, hCG, you may recall from the last chapter, is the marker of pregnancy, the same one that is produced by the implanting trophoblast. (Depending on the dose of hCG administered, a urine *pregnancy test* may be positive for as long as a week after the injection. A blood test may be positive for as long as two weeks afterward.) When pregnancy occurs, the rising hCG levels in the body stimulate the corpus luteum in the ovary to provide continuing progesterone support for the growing trophoblast. In assisted reproduction, we use hCG instead of LH to trigger ovulation because they're so much alike. (The half-life of LH is so short that it would disappear from the circulation within an hour or so, and we'd have to give many injections in order to simulate the LH surge. But hCG is long-lasting, so it can be given just once.)

Ovulation occurs between 38 and 40 hours after hCG is administered, so we have to schedule the follicle aspiration for no later than 36 to 37 hours after the hCG is given. If we wait just an hour longer, the follicles will begin to release the eggs into the peritoneal cavity. If we jump the gun and do it too soon, the eggs may be immature or may still be firmly attached to the inside of follicle and won't come out when the follicular fluid is aspirated.

ENTER THE CLEAN, WASHED SPERM

Whether we're talking about two- or three-party reproduction, the recipient's husband must be ready with a sperm sample right after the follicle aspiration procedure. Sperm can be added immediately after the eggs have been brought to the laboratory, but most programs inseminate about two to four hours later to more closely approximate the actual time of ovulation.

In addition to the vital sperm in an ejaculate, there is a great deal of seminal plasma, white blood cells, dead sperm, and other debris. So we have to separate the sperm from the sticky seminal plasma before we can add them to the dish holding the egg.

When sperm rush into the vagina, the cervical mucus acts as a filter to get rid of the unwanted semen. The filtering is what gives the sperm their get-up-and-go, and it's what you need for capacitation to occur, which prepares the sperm to go through the acrosome reaction, the necessary step before fertilization. As anyone who has ever tried to wash off the remains of love making with plain old water knows, semen holds on for dear life. Similarly, in the laboratory, where there's no natural fluid environment in which the sperm can divest themselves of their gluey covering, it must be artificially substituted.

You can separate sperm from seminal plasma in several different ways, all of which are based on two principles:

- Sperm is heavier than the rest of the fluid and, when put into a centrifuge, will automatically go to the bottom of the centrifuge tube
- Good swimmers ("motile" sperm) will swim into whatever solution is placed around them.

The procedure that most facilities favor these days uses a *density gradient*, which is a solution of microscopic particles that are heavier than water. The semen is placed at the top of a test tube filled with the density gradient, and it's then centrifuged at high speeds. The centrifugal force pulls the sperm to the bottom of the tube, and in so doing, filters out the lighter debris, which gets stuck in the density gradient. At the end of this "spin cycle," the sperm are rinsed in fresh media, then centrifuged again. We now have "washed" sperm.

The sperm are deposited into the petri dish with the mature eggs which have been retrieved a couple of hours earlier, and then nature is permitted to take its course. Sixteen to eighteen hours after the sperm are introduced to the eggs, fertilization can be affirmed by microscopic examination. When you can see the female and male pronuclei lining up in the dish, you know the sperm's job is done.

An Embryo in a Petri Dish

Now egg and sperm have come together, by one means or another, and an embryo has been formed. We now have about four or five days before the blastocyst stage, when the embryo must go back into the reproductive tract in order to implant.

So what do we do now? If the woman's fallopian tubes are open, we could put the embryos right inside the tube. After all, in nature, embryos live in the tube for five days after ovulation. About 10 years ago, two procedures were devised that did just this. *Zygote intrafallopian transfer (ZIFT)* and *tubal embryo transfer (TET)* both replaced the embryo into the fallopian tubes at different stages of development. But getting the embryo into the tube requires a laparoscopy—which means general anesthesia, an operating room, extra risk, and extra cost. Consequently, these procedures are only used today in unusual circumstances.

A better alternative is *embryo transfer*, where the embryo is placed through the cervix directly into the uterine cavity, where it will eventually implant. This simple office procedure is very much like an IUI and takes minutes to complete. The only question with this treatment is *when* to put the embryo back in the body.

After some trial and error, we have come to the conclusion that the best results are achieved when the embryos are transferred to the uterus after being cultured for about 72 hours. As the zygote divides during its first three days of existence, the laboratory is actually a better home, physiologically speaking, than the uterine cavity. But at some point after that, the embryo's metabolism changes and the secretions in the uterine cavity are adequate to meet its metabolic requirements. As culture media get better and better, it's very likely that all embryos will be grown to the blastocyst stage prior to embryo transfer. The best embryos will then be selected and just one or two embryos will be transferred simultaneously by the transcervical route.

Once the embryo is back in the uterus, there's nothing more we can do but wait and hope. If all systems are go, the embryo hatches from its zona pellucida and implants into the uterine cavity between six and eight days after follicle aspiration. And we know we've achieved our goal if hCG, that all-important pregnancy hormone, shows up in the patient's bloodstream a few days later.

The newly pregnant mother generally continues taking progesterone as a precautionary measure for the entire first trimester in order to ensure that P4 levels are adequate to stabilize the endometrium and keep the pregnancy going. The rising hCG levels in the blood stimulate the ovaries to produce progesterone naturally, and at the end of the first trimester, the placenta takes over, doing everything it would have, had the pregnancy been generated naturally. The new mother will now make all the hormones she needs—including prolactin—so that at the end of the nine months, she'll be able to nurse her baby.

EGG DONATION: A CYCLE BUILT FOR THREE

If a woman has undergone chemotherapy or radiation, or if she has gone through menopause, either natural or surgical, premature or timely, then two-party assisted reproduction won't help. You can add all the FSH you want, but if there are no follicles to respond, you still won't have an egg to call your own. Third-party reproduction allows us to use another woman's eggs to obtain embryos (by fertilization in vitro) for transfer and implantation. The process goes on exactly as it would have if the recipient were using her own eggs.

Of course it's not only the eggs we're concerned with, but the endometrium as well. In an older woman like Sarah, who isn't making estrogen and progesterone the way she did in her reproductive years, the endometrium is a thin strip, not at all receptive to implantation. So we must artificially prepare the "nest" in which that hatching embryo can grow. That means that we must also control the timing of follicle stimulation in the donor and, simultaneously, the proliferation of the endometrium in the recipient.

The donor and recipient must be hormonally in sync. The first woman has to be stimulated with FSH-like drugs to ripen the follicles, and at the same time, the second must receive estrogen and progesterone to prepare the endometrium to receive the embryos. The donor undergoes a standard IVF cycle (usually stimulated, although it's possible to do a natural cycle without medication as we'll discuss in a minute), while the recipient gets estrogen during the first part of her cycle and then adds progesterone on the day that the donor undergoes follicle aspiration. It's as simple as that.

But in the early days of egg donation, we struggled to get all the elements right. Initially, we were worried about how much estrogen to give the recipient. We knew a minimum amount would be necessary to get things started. But how much was too much? And how long should we continue giving her the estrogen? It turned out that the length of estrogen stimulation wasn't important—what counted was having enough of the hormone in the system to prime the endometrium.

On the other hand, the timing of progesterone administration had to be carefully chosen. We needed enough of it to make those crucial changes in the uterine lining so that it would acquire receptivity to an implanting embryo. What's more, we needed the changes to happen exactly when we wanted them to.

So the crunch always comes down to that window of implantation, to making the right guess as to when the embryos will be sufficiently developed so that the endometrium is ready and waiting.

NATURAL CYCLE IVF

A stimulated cycle is not the only option in IVF treatments. If a woman has been ovulating, and she's not getting pregnant because of damaged or absent fallopian tubes, it may be possible and even preferable to use natural-cycle IVF. We occasionally use it in donor-egg cycles as well. Remember that the world's first IVF baby, Louise Brown, was the product of a natural cycle. If you can capture one egg from one dominant follicle and avoid hyperstimulating the ovary with medication, you may be better off in several important ways.

When we first tried monitoring natural cycles at the USC ART program in the late 1980s, our early results were disappointing because we kept missing the magic moment of ovulation. Urinary measurements of the LH surge just weren't accurate enough. We had much more luck when we substituted the hCG injection midcycle. Now we knew that the follicle would get LH-like stimulation and would be ready to aspirate 36 hours later. Our pregnancy rates jumped from zero to about half what we were getting with stimulated cycles, which was pretty good. These cycles were easier on patients and less traumatic to the ovaries and endometrium, and they could be repeated on a monthly basis. Of course the drawback was that we had only one shot—there were no extra eggs to freeze for future cycles.

In the future, when we can manipulate immature eggs, this won't be as much of a problem. Once again, we look to new laboratory techniques to make the difference. We can see a time when in addition to using that one dominant follicle, we could also aspirate those that are not yet ready to ovulate and grow them out in the laboratory, providing several more chances at pregnancy. As our culture media improve, natural-cycle IVF may become much more popular. The more elements we can play with, the more creativity we develop, and the more hope we have to increase IVF pregnancy rates.

ART: SUCCESSES AND FAILURES, JUST AS IN LIFE

There are so many factors to consider when you're assisting nature in the laboratory—the quality of the eggs and sperm, the synchronization of the two womens' cycles in egg donation, the aspiration, the ability of the gametes to go through meiosis and mitosis in vitro so that they can end up as properly cleaving zygotes. Having seen how astoundingly difficult conception can be in nature, we take all necessary precautions in a laboratory to smooth the way. The air is filtered, quality-control procedures are impeccable, anyone who goes in and out wears sterile scrub suits, masks, hairnets, and booties. But even with the various culture media, the centrifuges, the incubators, and pristine laboratory conditions, the process is still fraught with failure.

We generally retrieve about 14 eggs in a typical egg-donor aspiration, and usually about 10 of them fertilize. Since we occasionally get 100 percent implantation rates, we never transfer more than three embryos at a time in a donor situation. The other six or seven will be frozen for future transfers—in case this one doesn't work, or in case the recipient wants more children in the future.

It's a risk, but so is everything in life. You've got embryos coaxed into being from two gametes, the right chemicals, temperature, and timing. You've got an older uterus well prepared to act *as if* it were the young, pliant organ of its former days. You've got a dedicated staff of professionals who have checked and rechecked all the ingredients and steps that must be taken. And you have a couple who have invested blood, sweat, tears, and considerable dollars in order to make this last chance at conception work.

The chances for success or failure in getting pregnant the natural way are very much based on the vagaries of two people and their random decisions about when and how to mate. But with third-party reproduction, you have to factor in the donor's and recipient's compliance with their schedule of medications and office visits, the synchronization of both women's cycles, the physician's careful titrating of medication dosages according to changing ultrasounds and blood tests, an extraordinary laboratory staff, and finally, some great eggs and one good sperm.

With so much orchestration necessary, it is astounding that this one new chord, a unique mixture of male and female, actually comes into being. But it does, again and again, and the vibration lingers in the air for a lifetime.

CHAPTER SIX

JOE COUNTS HIS BLESSINGS

If you have the right tools, you can do any job. Joe had always been convinced of this. He wasn't particularly handy, but if he had a good instruction book and a great set of screwdrivers, he could probably build anything simple—a bookcase, a crib, a flight of stairs.

So on a misty October Saturday, when Sarah was at her tai chi class, he decided to hang the Colombian hammock that his friend Paul had given him. He turned on the Elvis CD that Sarah had just bought him, and "Jailhouse Rock" blasted from the speakers.

The hammock spilled out of the bag in the closet, its pink, green, blue, and yellow mesh a riot of color on the floor. This gift had arrived after Paul and his wife split up and Paul moved into an efficiency on the Lower East Side and had no room to turn around, let alone swing in a hammock. Joe and Sarah didn't have trees, but they had a great loft on Greenwich Street with high ceilings, and there was hanging room aplenty.

The hammock didn't go with anything much in their place, but it had pizzazz. It also had the flavor of Tahitian idyll about it—Joe and Sarah and the baby could lie around in it, snuggling close and being a family. And until the baby came, he and Sarah could practice making love in it while trying not to fall on the floor.

Joe smoothed the hammock flat and stared at it. It was such a basic thing—just some colored strings woven together. But it provided comfort and decoration. Neat to think about living in a culture where that was all the bed you needed. The beds he'd known had been like minefields. It would be good to start fresh, maybe get a new mattress, or new sheets. Or just use the hammock. Simpler.

He measured, then put tester marks with a pencil on two of the columns that lined the center of the living room. He could run it from column to column, and when it wasn't in use, he could hook it up to the ladder on the far wall that led to the roof. The hammock would overlook the Hudson so they could get all the benefit of the brilliant sunsets—whenever the view wasn't smogged over, of course.

He whistled along tunelessly with "Blue Suede Shoes," drilling a hole—not too big—then tapping in the anchor and placing the hook. He did the same on the other side, then stretched out the hammock and it was installed. Beautiful. Tropical. Not bad for a city kid who hadn't known a hammer from a wrench when he was growing up. Joe grinned.

Slowly, he lowered his lanky frame into the mesh. He sat down gingerly at first, then put all his weight on it, and the hooks held. He sighed with pleasure. Everything in life should be that easy—like making a baby. He swung his feet up and put his hands behind his head, closing his eyes, imagining a palm tree above him and a soft ocean breeze caressing his face. All those years of trying, all those stomachaches and fights. But that was over now. He had really high hopes for this donor business.

He would never tell Sarah, but secretly, he thought this lousy situation was worse for him. The man is supposed to be the One—he's supposed to please his wife in bed, he's supposed to be able to get it up any and every time, and he's supposed to be virile, potent, all those good things. And the clincher was that the doctor promised he had such an astronomical sperm count. After years of failure, Joe wasn't sure about that. Maybe Sarah and the doc were in cahoots, and he really didn't have one good sperm to call his own. He felt like he wasn't making the grade as a man.

He remembered nights when he just wanted to leave rather than walk into that bedroom again, that performance arena where he felt like a gladiator facing the world's toughest lion. The opponent wasn't

Sarah or him or the baby they couldn't produce, it was something that they couldn't see or feel or smell. It was like there was a hungry predator in their bed, feeding on them, laughing at them. *Hey, you want to get your wife pregnant, buddy? Let's see you try. And try. What a loser.*

So he got mad, and wanted to stop trying. He'd been an only child, and it hadn't been that bad. His parents were plain, working-class types, not terribly emotional or brilliant, but regular guys. Their worlds didn't revolve around having a child, and sometimes—especially during his rebellious teen years—he thought they would have been perfectly happy without him. When he got married, he hadn't had any expectations that his life would be that different from his parents'. But it was. And he and Sarah were terrific together, except for this one thing.

It was more her than him, actually. Maybe if her relationship with Alison hadn't been so crappy, she wouldn't have been so desperate for another child. Except Sarah was crazy about kids. She probably should have had a tribe of them when she was young, but she had such a disastrous first marriage, it never happened. And now she had a really good marriage, so she wanted it to bear fruit.

Elvis jumped into "Hound Dog," and Joe played air guitar for a few seconds along with the King. Then he sighed, and got up to get something to eat. He rummaged through containers of cooked spinach and eggplant dip, then finally settled for a peanut butter sandwich and a banana on the side. (He kind of liked junk food, but he would never go overboard like his idol. Frying and mashing the thing together, ugh, it gave him the creeps.) He dropped a piece of bread on the floor as he tore into the loaf, and he sighed, nostalgic for their dog, Quin, who had finally died of old age last spring. Quin, a stray from the streets of Jersey City where Joe's parents lived, was a canine vacuum cleaner. You could drop anything, from cookies to onions, and she'd scarf it down.

The point was, did *he* want a child as much as she did? Yes, he thought so, but the idea was so abstract. You could see other people's kids, and enjoy playing with them, and you could remember your own childhood and think about how you and your folks got along, but none of that was real. What he'd come down to, through all these years of heartache and blood tests and injections and bad sex, was that it was worth it if he could eventually pass on something of his own to the next generation. He wasn't sure what it was of himself that he wanted to preserve for posterity, whether it was an attitude toward life or a vision of the future, or a way of taking risks. And the way he saw clear to doing that was having a child of his own ... flesh and blood. Yes, that was why the idea of adoption left him cold. If he had the right tools, he could cut off a piece of himself and tamp it down here and hook it in there and watch it grow into someone quite different from himself or Sarah.

A child. *His child.* Some days he saw himself hugging an incredible little girl, with soft brown curls (like his) and a quick mind and great sense of humor (also his). Other days, it was a boy, the two of them having heart-to-heart talks in the park, going to games, eating ice cream cones. And on a few days, not many, he had one of each, looking almost the same, but not quite. Twins who fought over toys, made up, ran around making messes. Two kids who were unique and special.

When he was seven, his mother got pregnant. He remembered how excited he'd been about having a baby brother—he was positive it was a boy!—and how he'd started making these paper mobiles of stars and ships and trucks and sticking paper clips in each piece so he could hang them up with strings. He couldn't believe how lucky he was going to be, to have a pal on the premises, a little brother to show the ropes to. And then, one day, his mother got really sick and was taken to the hospital and when she came back, there wasn't any baby. And she and his father told him she would never have any more babies, ever.

He didn't cry, but he was very quiet, and the next day, he threw out all his mobiles. He went inside himself, and though he had plenty of friends, and did all the normal boy stuff, he somehow felt he'd lost something he could never recover.

Elvis was crooning, "Love Me Tender" when Sarah walked in, looking a little dazed, as she usually did after her tai chi breathing. Joe personally could never get into that meditation-type hocus-pocus, but Sarah said it did wonders for her and anyway, it would help her with the labor and delivery, so she intended to keep it up.

"Did you get around to hanging the ...? Oh, Joe, that looks so fine!" She ran up to the hammock, throwing her jacket and bag on the floor. "Can I sit in it, or will it fall down?"

He gave her a hurt look. "Are you implying I can't make things work?"

She bopped him on the head. Then she made a face and he knew she was thinking of something else that wasn't working between them.

"Let's both sit down. That'll show you." He shoved her backward and she fell into the hammock, giggling, grabbing his head, and pulling him toward her. They kissed lightly, but then she wrapped her legs around him and drew him in. The kiss held, welding them together.

He'd had plenty of girlfriends in his life by the time he ran into Sarah, and had had a near-miss with marriage to a woman he would have been really miserable with. He and Wendy had lived together for a year before deciding that a wedding would be a horrible mistake. They really had nothing much in common and had come together because of an attraction that wore off long before the year was out.

After Wendy left, Joe was all prepared to be a dedicated bachelor. But Sarah changed his mind. He'd never met anyone like her—mature but silly, thoughtful but impulsive. She had seen beyond his self-assured, sometimes smug manner. She'd listened to him—not just to the things he said but also to the things he meant. She was funny and quick, determined and extremely dependable. Even when they fought over some stupid thing, like what time they were supposed to be at someone's house for dinner, he knew he could count on her starting the apology on the way to the event. And when she woke him up in the middle of the night one night to tell him she loved him, he felt this wave of delirious happiness. This was right. It didn't matter that there were 12 years between them   who cared? That sense of coming home at last was something not that many people had in their lives.

He put his hand under her jacket and felt the slight swell of her breast. She was so warm.

"Joe, not now." She squirmed away from his hand.

"What?"

"I need to do something now."

"Do what? I was just snuggling. For God's sake, why do you think I'm always trying to get in your pants when I just want to get close?"

"I do not!"

It was one of their oldest fights. She constantly assumed that he wanted intercourse when he touched her. Ever since the planned encounters they needed to coincide with her cycle, she'd interpreted any foray into the private sector of her body as a request for sex. But he was a touchy guy—he just enjoyed the feel of her. He loved sex too, but with Sarah, there was so much more to intimacy. Why couldn't she understand that?

He pulled away abruptly. "This is not an invasion, okay?"

"Joe!" Her voice sounded harshly above the drone of Elvis. "We made a date to go over the finances. That's all."

"That date was for 11:42, exactly? It can't wait?" Actually, he wasn't feeling like sex. He had thought *she* was when she grabbed him. Was he ever wrong.

"Look, we're scheduled to see the counselor next week, and that means they'll start the matching process with a donor. I think we should have all our homework done."

"Yeah, sure. Whatever."

He shrugged off his disappointment and walked across the room toward the desk, thinking of other times in other years when they hadn't had sex on purpose. Nowadays sex was always related to pregnancy, and they were always nervous about "wasting" good sperm on a rollicking good time. He was always nervous about those appointments in the doctor's office when he had to put on a smarmy sex video or leaf through the old magazines to get himself aroused enough to come in a cup.

Now that he was 36, it might be even harder. He hadn't had a sperm count done since they gave up on the IVF treatments six years ago. Maybe he wasn't as studly as he had been then.

As he grabbed the files from the desk, he wondered if he thought about sex too much. But supposedly all men did. He just wondered if they thought about when and why they were supposed to have sex, as opposed to just wanting to have it.

"'For a woman over 45,' he read, 'the following tests are required.' Okay, this is just the standard stuff you had before—mammogram, electrocardiogram, and treadmill because they worry about heart disease in an older mother (that should be a breeze for you), chest X-ray, endometrial biopsy—isn't that where they take a sample of the lining of the uterus to check for abnormal cells?"

"Yeah, whew, that one was really uncomfortable," Sarah muttered. "What else is there?"

"You'll need a new Pap smear, a urinalysis, and a hysterosalpingogram. Oh, that's the one where they shoot dye through your fallopian tubes to be sure they're open."

"I really loved that one, too." Sarah got out of the hammock and walked over to her husband, slipping an arm around his waist. He sensed it was an apology, a way to tell him that she hadn't meant to turn him off.

She read over his shoulder: "'The blood tests: A fasting cholesterol and fasting glucose (because they're worried about an older mom getting diabetes), triglycerides,' other general-type blood tests,' to make sure I'm not secretly dying. They also need an FSH to see what my pituitary is putting out, a thyroid test, and a CBC—I think that's a complete blood count."

Sarah and Joe would both need an HIV test, tests for all strains of hepatitis as well as for syphilis. And Joe would have to have his semen checked yet again—the volume, motility, and morphology, as well as a culture to make sure that no extraneous bacteria could hitchhike their way into the culture dish and overgrow the embryos.

The list went on and on until Joe's head began to ache. Her, him, and the donor too would be poked and prodded, and tested for every known condition in *Tabor's Medical Dictionary* that might prevent conception or implantation or result in a deformed, sickly child. In the old days, people just went to bed, rolled over on each other, and a couple of weeks later, the rabbit died. This was a whole other ballgame.

And of course, it was costly. Their insurance would pay for most of the preliminary testing, but after that, they were on their own. They'd been told by Lani, the woman in Dr. Leverton's office who took care of insurance, that on the West Coast, there were several programs where some of the assisted procedures were also covered. And when the primary insurer didn't take care of all the expenses, it was possible to get a supplementary indemnity plan. In that case, even if the lab work wasn't taken care of, the doctors' fees would be covered. In Massachusetts and Arkansas, coverage was mandated for most assisted reproductive procedures. And in some plans in other states, the patients paid half and the insurance took care of the other half. Eventually, Lani had assured them, most insurers would work out an itemized rate with providers.

But Joe had scoured their policy and discovered that that wasn't going to be the case with him and Sarah. They had good benefits at Bemer & Truscott, but infertility was not one of those necessities of life, according to the ad agency. There was a fringe benefit tacked on so that you could get a great executive physical anywhere in the country—they'd spend up to $1000 on you to go to the Mayo Clinic and have every diagnostic test in the book for wellness care—but for some reason they thought that it would be too expensive for them as a company to cover fertility. This was even after Lani told them that fertility treatments represented less than 2 percent of medical costs in the United States. Joe knew of other friends of theirs with HMOs and PPOs where it worked differently—with the HMO, they'd see group doctors and would copay $5 or $10 for each visit, and with the PPOs, they'd choose their specialist from the list of participating doctors. After their deductible was taken care of, they'd get copaid visits. Of course, egg donation was still considered "investigational" by most of them and therefore not a "covered benefit." But with Joe and Sarah's insurance plan through their company, it would be really costly. They would be reimbursed for the initial visit with Leverton, where he diagnosed Sarah as "infertile," but after that they were on their own.

He held up the list from Leverton's office:

OOCYTE DONATION

- Follicle stimulation and cycle monitoring: approximately $2000
- Follicle aspiration of donor: $1500
- Embryo transfer to patient: $500
- Embryology laboratory charges: basic cost $2500. [This may be higher with ICSI procedure ($500 extra) or embryo freezing and storage charge ($500 extra)].
- Serum hormone determination: basic cost $600. These cover FSH, LH, and E2 tests during stimulation and the first two pregnancy tests after embryo transfer. Any additional tests are charged individually (usually $40 to $60 per test) by the lab.
- Cycle coordination fee: $2000. This includes donor screening and matching, coordination with recipient, donor's nonhormonal blood tests (including tests for HIV, hepatitis, and syphilis), and donor support, including any postcycle testing necessary. Not included are any special tests requested by the recipient such as Tay-Sachs, thallassemia, or sickle-cell disease.
- Donor compensation fee: $2500

- Facility fee: $1500 (includes facility charge for both follicle aspiration and embryo transfer).
- Cost of donor's medication: approximately $2000. This includes 2 two-week kits of Lupron, about 30 ampoules of FSH, and 1 vial of hCG as well as the recipient's estrogen pills and progesterone suppositories. Costs of hCG and the FSH are about $50 for each ampoule when obtained through the doctor's office. Some insurance companies may cover some of the medication costs even if IVF is not a covered benefit.

Joe let the figures hang in the air for a second before picking up his calculator. He punched in the numbers and whistled.

"Yes, tell me," Sarah insisted.

"It's $15,100 *if* we have no extra added tests."

"And if we don't need double doses of medication, which you have to have if the follicles aren't growing large enough."

"Face it, sweetie, FSH is like buying Beluga caviar—this is the high-priced spread."

"Actually, I know a way to get it cheaper." Sarah took off her shoes and plopped down on the floor to rub her insteps.

Her extra-large feet got sore quickly—Joe could just imagine how she'd be nine months' pregnant. "How do you mean?"

"I was eavesdropping on this other patient at the office when she was talking to her husband about getting 'leftovers' from cycles of couples who got pregnant sooner than they expected. They'll sometimes sell the medication privately for $20 or $30 an ampoule. It's not completely legal, because the FDA says you're never supposed to resell a prescription, but she told me no one's ever been slapped in jail for doing it."

"Hmm. We'd be the first. I know our dear boss would love that."

"Well, we don't have to stay with Leverton. I've heard about programs in California where there's a three-for-one deal."

He eased back in his chair and stuck his hands in his pockets. "Oh, come on. This I gotta hear."

"No, it makes perfect sense. I know there are a couple of programs where they do it like a game of chance—you get three tries for one flat fee. That's more than just the cost of a single cycle, of course. If you hit it the first time, the doctor wins; if it takes you three times, you win. But you have to sign on for the whole deal."

"Sarah, I am getting a little dizzy here. This is our baby we're talking about, not the boardwalk at Atlantic City."

"But we have to pinch pennies, Joe. There's a chance we won't get pregnant on the first cycle."

"Don't be ridiculous—of course we will." If they hit it on the first shot, that was 15 grand, about the price of one year for their child in private school. Wait a second—Joe swallowed hard. That was at today's prices. By the time their little one was ready for high school, $15,000 would be cheap. If it took two cycles, $30,000, or a new car. Three cycles ... oh God, he didn't want to think about it. Of course, they'd been through three IVF cycles years ago, when they only cost $7000 apiece.

Something else they couldn't count on was having a perfectly healthy child. What if something went wrong during Sarah's pregnancy? They might require high-tech after-birth as well as before-birth care. They would have to redo their wills, and they'd need to set up trust funds for their child, just in case they both died before she was through with college. They owned the Tribeca loft and also a small condo in central Jersey that they used for rental income; there were reasonable-sized mortgages left on both of them. In the worst-case scenario, if for some horrible reason their child had special physical or psychological needs, they could sell all their real estate and use the cash for medical bills.

And then there was the question of who could be a legal guardian. It had to be someone much younger than either of them, and from the way Marilyn had reacted to Sarah's announcement about the baby, it wasn't going to be her. There was Alison—he knew Sarah had mixed feelings about her daughter, but he would certainly consider her. If she would consider accepting.

"Oh, why didn't we meet years ago?" Sarah sighed, reading his mind the way she always did. "Why couldn't we be a normal couple right out of college with young eggs and juicy genitalia?"

"Your genitalia are wonderful, thank you. I don't want any changes. Sweetheart, human reproduction is flukey. We could just as easily have had problems if we'd started trying decades ago."

"I suppose. But when I was 20, even 30, I had good eggs and I was almost always ovulating. After 45, even when you're still bleeding every month or two, you may or may not be ovulating. Precious few eggs left, and those that are left aren't any good. The good ones are all gone, thrown away with the Kotex pads."

"No use crying over spilled eggs, Sarah. So we pay the money and do it the new-fangled way. We're lucky, we both make good bucks and have nice bonuses every year. Money goes in; money goes out. At least we have something important to spend it on." Joe had always thought, growing up with not much at all in Jersey City, that socking your income away for your retirement never made any sense. Money was to be earned, enjoyed, used for something really crucial. Naturally, they were going to be spending more as their kid started to grow—the baby stuff, the clothes, the lessons, the schools—but so what? If they had a child of their own, nothing else would matter.

"Listen," Sarah said, turning the CD player off and the radio on to a soft, classical hum. "At the tai chi studio, you know they have this bulletin board, and there was an ad posted this week about adopting baby girls from China, so I called the number. Maryanne—this woman in my class who'd been going through infertility treatments for the last five years—she and her husband just got back from the mainland with this wonderful eight-month old girl. Joe, I was thinking—I know you're suspicious of these agencies, but this one is different. The whole process takes approximately a year, from first application to adoption. The agency fee here in America is $6700, and the expenses in China— the orphanage donation, the court fees, the child's medical exam—are about $6500. Everything else is just airfare and travel in China, a home study to approve where we live, application translation fees, all that kind of thing. So it ends up costing just a little more than one cycle— maybe $18,000 or $19,000. Would you consider it?"

He didn't have to think. "No," he said bluntly. "I know we talked about adopting, but I've given it a lot more thought than when we first considered it years ago. Now I'm sure. Maybe this isn't fair to you, because we've already signed off on your genes, but I know that you're going to be taking care of her when she's inside you—eating all that good stuff and exercising and sleeping right and playing all the great symphonies, and Elvis, to your lovely big belly. You'll be participating in her life, even before she's here.

"If we had to have a sperm donor, maybe I would consider it. But we don't—and that gives us at least one connection to this child, which is better than none. Plus I want to see you pregnant. I want to go get you oysters and asparagus at all hours of the night because you have a craving, I want to go to Lamaze classes, be with you in labor doing all your tai chi breathing, and hold your hand when you deliver our child. I want to be there from the start—from conception. I want to feel that I can relate to her in every way."

Sarah smiled. "Wow. Okay. No trips to China. I see you've already decided on a girl."

"No, not really."

Sarah came over and put her arms around him. "What happens, happens."

"It's going to happen," Joe said. It was a statement, not a wish.

CHAPTER SEVEN

Counselors and Therapists

Having a baby when you're pushing 50 can cause more emotional upheaval than a death, a marriage, and a birth all rolled into one. You are grieving over the loss of your own genetic input; you are bonding with your partner and a donor in a scientific ménage à trois, and you are bringing new life into the world. It's hard on you, your spouse, your family, and the child to be. So many feelings crowd in together—frustration, anxiety, stress, and depression play around the edges of your consciousness. You have no other topics to discuss but reproduction, sex, identity, and money. You have to get over the old hurts of your years of infertility, you have to make choices about the type of donor you want to be represented in your child-to-be, and you have to be open-minded enough to accept the child— or children—that come from this high-tech adventure. You have to deal with your neighbors' upraised eyebrows when they see you, slightly lined and gray-haired, with your belly out to here. You have to decide whether to tell anyone, even your own parents, that you are using someone else's egg, and you have to think seriously about how you'll deal with this matter when your child is old enough to understand. Most important, you have to stay connected to the people in your life whom you love and who love you, whether you are partnered or single, because it is crucial to have a great support system when you're having a baby at an advanced age.

Since most reproductive endocrinologists have neither the expertise nor the time to deal with these complicated issues, they commonly request their patients to be screened by a professional psychotherapist or counselor. The psychologist may be part of the program and have an office in the doctor's facility, or, as in our practice, she may be "off-campus," and see patients on a referral basis. All the therapists connected with ART programs are experts in the emotional ramifications of egg donation.

People often ask me how I decide whether particular couples are good candidates for this procedure, and frankly, it's not easy. I am very reluctant to make these decisions alone. Any time there's a question about a particular couple or single woman, I share the situation with the nursing and laboratory staff. After all, this is a project that takes many hands, hearts, and minds. If we make the decision to go ahead, we'll all be working together to achieve success.

The first step is to sit down with the prospective parents and talk to them seriously about the ramifications of parenthood, and the job of raising children (or multiple children). Usually, this type of discussion is enough to dissuade those who truly had not given the process enough thought and those who had come in for a consultation just to learn about the egg-donation process. Since it's a tough road to travel, many need just a little guidance so that they can eventually make their own decision.

It's not uncommon for women to come in alone asking if I would keep the egg donation secret from their partner. They may be so desperate to cover up the fact that they're aging, they can't even share it with their husbands! I remember one 42-year-old woman who came in and told me that she didn't want her fiancé to know that she intended to use both donor egg and sperm. The couple had been unsuccessful up to this point trying to conceive, and he'd been sniping at her about being too old to have a baby. Her plan was to come in for treatment and then simply turn up pregnant and tell her fiancé that she had conceived in the natural way. I told her this deception might ruin her relationship and would certainly argue against the blossoming of a healthy family. She said thanks and never came back.

When I was first confronted with these types of requests many years ago, it set my teeth on edge. I'd get indignant and preachy, trying to point out the error of starting life with a lie. A child born of such deception might very well find itself in a broken home. But over the years, I've come to the realization that many people who might be perfectly rational about most other things in their lives lose all sense of perspective when dealing with reproduction. I still won't be party to a lie, but I am more empathic to those who are desperate to cover up the truth.

And then there are even harder cases, where a couple walk in who just don't seem to have the potential to be good parents. Their motivations seem questionable, and their relationship appears weak. My first reaction, and that of my staff, is to turn them away. But how could I possibly assume that within an hour, I can figure out two other human beings? The most "together" people can turn out to be manipulators; and the most bonded relationships can be on the verge of crumbling. On the one hand, the arrival of a baby could help this struggling couple put down roots, but just as easily, it could deliver the coup de grace to their marriage. How are we to judge?

The answer is, we try to get as many opinions as possible. Since I'm not an expert in evaluating the psychodynamics of relationships, I want an opinion from someone who spends her time peering into the depths of the human mind and spirit. Ideally, this person should be a professional, independent of our office, so that he or she can maintain a clear vision. I get very close to all my patients and their families, so it's harder for me to stay uninvolved.

And when it doesn't work out, when years of treatments have led down a disappointing road of "maybe next time?" What do I do then? Many individuals who have been through years of infertility treatments are "addicted" to the office visits, the care and nurturing they get from the staff, and their sympathy and eagerness for the process to work. It can be hard to *stop* trying to have a baby. For this reason, I want someone working alongside me who can be objective. I also want to make sure that couples contemplating an ART procedure know all the facts and know themselves. A little introspection and a lot of information go a long way when you're considering egg donation.

Although we recommend that everyone go through a counseling session, it is specifically required when the woman is older than 50, when the couple shows ambivalence about their decisions, or when there is something unusual about their situation—for example, when the husband is much older than the wife. The cost of counseling is not included in the general menu of fees. The counselor's service is paid directly by the couple unless the counselor is affiliated with the doctor's practice. A typical one-time consultation with a referral from the doctor costs about $250 to $300; if the couple returns for additional appointments, it generally costs about $150 per hour.

After the recipient and her partner have met with the psychologist, she and I, and my office staff who have also had contact with the couple, can make a more reasonable assessment of their case.

THE MANY HATS OF A THERAPIST

A therapist or counselor serves multiple purposes in the egg donation process. She is an expert in all the psychosocial issues that may arise for a couple and the impact those concerns may have for the two individuals contemplating this procedure, their families, and their futures. She acts as the go-between for physician and recipient and physician and donor. She finds out what the couples' expectations are and helps them to question their needs and wants. She interviews donors and tries to assess what they feel about their contribution even as she tells them honestly about the difficulties of the medical process—from the shots to the time constraints to the side effects of the medications and the discomfort of the aspiration. She is obviously interested in the way donors view their own future fertility, whether or not they've already had children of their own. The therapist or counselor also needs to find out how donors will deal with never knowing a child that comes of their gamete. If the donor is related to the recipient, she probes the family dynamic for sibling rivalry, trying to head off any competition or jealousy that might arise from this unusual situation. Clearly, she would want to find out whether the sibling donor might wish to impose her own parenting ideas on her sister's child and whether this would lead to conflict in the family. She gives and evaluates psychological and personality tests in order to make the best match between donor and recipient. Hopefully, she will be the inspiration for more thoughtful use of ART procedures.

The psychologist is there to raise all the questions that the couple may have wondered about but not voiced. For example, it's important for her to find out how the couple feels about dying before their child reaches maturity. Have they selected a guardian in the eventuality of their deaths? Is there any residual jealousy or anger on the wife's part about her husband but not herself being represented genetically in their child? Does the husband feel guilty about the same issues? Have they discussed together what they imagine about their ideal anonymous donor? What about a related donor? Is the couple aware that the likelihood of multiple births is high with egg donation? Can they handle the stress and financial burden of such a drastic change in lifestyle? And what about the leftover embryos? Suppose they have frozen several in the eventuality that they won't hit it on their first cycle, but they get pregnant with twins? Will they want to have more children in future? Will they consider donating them to another couple? Or can they deal with the idea of destroying embryos that they don't use?

When reproduction was something that a man and a woman just *did*, no one else had to be involved. You could tell the world or keep it quiet (at least until the fourth or fifth month when a protruding belly would blow the secret for you). You certainly didn't have to spill your guts to a stranger who might express concerns about whether or not you would make a suitable parent.

That was then; this is now. People who are having children after the traditional age for childbearing has passed may be very confused about their motives and actions, and this confusion can have a deleterious effect on the baby and on their parenting efforts. Then too, there's a third person involved. The donor is an integral part of this "family," even if she wishes to remain anonymous. If she chooses to be present at the sessions—or if she is related to the couple—her feelings must also be taken into account.

Another factor that must be considered is the affiliation of doctor, patient, and the patient's partner, and also, of doctor and donor. The psychological component of the doctor-patient relationship is something that has often been discussed in relation to other types of treatment. A physician who cures your cancer or helps you walk again or restores your vision becomes a miracle-worker—and the most exciting part of it is that he has worked this miracle just for you.

The trust and vulnerability inherent in the egg donation process is a striking example of this phenomenon. After all, when a physician offers an infertile couple the ultimate prize—a child they were unable to have on their own—he can easily take on superhuman qualities in their eyes. The psychologist acts as the voice of reason here—she's supposed to remind all the parties involved that they are only human,

and their humanity is exactly what makes them simultaneously powerful and fallible. Although science can give a little oomph to the natural process of making babies, it cannot make that new life—or the
lives of the parents—perfect. People have to be realistic about their
hopes and dreams, because sometimes, achieving a lifelong goal doesn't
resolve the stress, depression, or anxiety that was there to begin with. I
often tell couples to be careful what they wish for, because they're quite
likely to get it.

THE STRESSES OF THE PROCESS: EXPECTATIONS, HOPES, FEARS, AND DREAMS

By the time a couple has decided to accept an egg from another
woman, they have usually been through years of unsuccessful IUIs and
IVFs. Many were charter members of their local chapters of RESOLVE
(a nonprofit education and advocacy infertility organization) and have
been going to meetings for years, trying all the medications, all the
doctors, all the protocols they've ever heard about. Although there are
those who are just trying to have their first child at this stage, or their
first child in a new marriage, most have been trying for a long time and
are burned out by the infertility grind. They often make peace with
their second choice (using a donor egg) by denying that they ever had
a first choice (having their own genetic child). The weight of their
repressed anger about not getting what they expected out of life can be
extremely heavy.

Elaine Gordon, Ph.D., the counselor who sees most of the recipients and donors in our program at USC, says that she tries to find out
what couples really want when they say they want a child. She usually
asks first if they would consider adoption. (Years ago, after unsuccessfully trying egg donation herself, she adopted a daughter.) Some
would, and have. It's quite common for a couple to start up an adoption process while they are in the midst of IVF or egg donation cycles.
And sometimes, when both work out, they get an instant family. But
the options for adoption to older parents are extremely limited—either
they must accept a child who's not of their race, or deal with the
vagaries of private adoption through advertising or word of mouth, or
they must take on a special-needs child. Not everyone is willing or able
to do this.

After the adoption question is cleared up, Elaine Gordon tries to get couples to own up to their grief and disappointment. "It's important to mourn what you couldn't have so that you can move on," she says, "otherwise you may contaminate your new family with old hurts and regrets. Hopefully, when you have this child, you'll be able to respect and welcome the differences you see in him or her into your family."

Gordon tries to prepare a woman for the possible comments about her child's looks, which may bring up feelings of not being connected to her offspring all over again. The practice you get fielding questions in a session can serve you well when you're in the park with your stroller. Probably the best response to "You and little Susie look nothing alike!" is "You're absolutely right." Getting defensive and anxious is useless. (There are a surprising number of egg-donation moms who swear that there's an incredible resemblance even though they have no common genes with their child. Whether this is wishful thinking or a strange accident of fate, or the environment of the uterus has more of an influence on fetal development than we think, it makes many women feel better.)

Gordon also helps couples with their guilt about waiting so long. Many couples never thought about having a child when they were younger because they were involved with too many other things, or they just weren't ready. Now that they're past the age for natural reproduction, they blame themselves—maybe it's too late now and will never happen. If they'd started on the donor route when they were just 45 or even 40, they would have had more time to spend with their child-to-be. It's important for the counselor to assuage these fears and suggest that they trust that there was a good reason they didn't start this process earlier.

Gordon says, "I ask them if it's going to do any good to beat themselves up about this for the rest of their lives, or if they're just going to get on with it. This way they see that the healthy choice is putting the past to rest, in whatever way they can."

She points out that by the time couples have decided to go the egg-donation route, they may have a lot of work to do to repair their relationship. "Infertility has been a hook for you to hang junk on," she says. "It doesn't cause your problems, but it's a great excuse for why your marriage is rotten or your self-esteem is low." A couple's intimate life may be in shreds thanks to years of planned sex. Despite the fact that most therapists encourage couples doing IVF cycles to have "sex for baby making and love making just for you," there's a great deal of frustration and anger left in the bedroom.

A therapist has to determine if only one party has voted for the donation process. Perhaps the man is completely fed up with monitored sex and wants his life back and throws down the gauntlet: No more IVF for me! If you want a baby, we'll do it some other way. Or it can be the woman who fears the man will leave her if the sex doesn't get better and a baby doesn't come soon. The coercion inherent in this lack of cooperation has to be addressed by the therapist and the couple.

Many counselors say that often the woman is very protective of her husband. "I'm so glad it's me going through all this—he could never make it," one woman was quoted as saying. She was concerned about her husband feeling "less manly" after all their years of in vitro, as though there were a sign tattooed on his forehead saying that he couldn't produce. He had also had difficulty getting an erection whenever she was ovulating because he was so tense, which totally turned her off the rest of the month, when he had no trouble getting it up.

Several women confessed that they no longer found their husbands sexually attractive, although they would never have hurt their spouse's feelings by saying no when he wanted to be intimate. There were other women who felt less feminine the longer this process took. "I always looked down on women who churned out kids year after year," one woman said. "I couldn't stand it when they'd boast that all their husband had to do was look at them and they got pregnant. Then when I couldn't conceive, I started to feel lacking, like I wasn't really a woman. A long time ago," she went on, "I dreamed of a baby that would be the perfect amalgam of the two of us, because we were so much in love and this would be the culmination of it. But now I can't be part of it genetically, so I have to be more practical. I just want a baby, period."

Although choosing to go the egg-donation route was a hard one for many women because they would be losing their genetic stake in their child, at least it took the burden off by-the-numbers sex for more "natural" infertility treatments. Now they could try again, but this time, without all that pressure in the bedroom.

Gordon is concerned about doctors who feed the hope that an older woman will be able to succeed with her own eggs—maybe not in this cycle, maybe not the next, but sometime soon. "If the doctor isn't direct with the patient, she's not going to stop, even if she's 48 and it's clearly hopeless. Remember that the doctor sees 20 patients a day; the woman sees only one doctor. So for that time, she's all his and he's all hers, helping her through this extremely difficult life crisis. It's hard to separate, for him as well as her. Though this is unfair to the patient, many doctors shrug and say, well, she'll go to another practice and try again—why not keep her here if she wants to be here?" There are, of course, miracle stories about women over 50 conceiving without medical assistance, but they're rare. This lack of medical intervention means that we have no measurement scale—we'll never know how many women at this age had unprotected sex in order for this one conception to occur. Natural conceptions in women over 45 are not common enough to justify years of unsuccessful cycles. Many fertility centers stop offering IVF to women over 43, and virtually all stop at 45, since the success rates for this age group are extremely low.

But the statistics on successful pregnancies are excellent with egg donation, no matter what the age of the mother. So it's a logical step for someone who's been through the trauma of IVF to start thinking about actually having the baby as opposed to struggling with getting pregnant. You don't have to take your temperature or play junior chemist with your urine and an ovulation predictor; you don't have to have sex at certain times in certain positions; you don't need to be filled with anxiety about that telltale drop of red appearing monthly on your pants.

"There are couples who see this child as the golden apple," says Margot Weinshel, Ph.D., consultant to various ART programs through the Ackerman Institute for the Family in New York. "Each time, the task becomes a little more difficult, a little more costly. It's terribly expensive—you've spent down all your savings on IVF, then you sell the co-op as you start in with egg donation. But isn't it worth it if you get a baby? So you've already spent $50,000 on this—what's another $10,000 if you have a reasonable chance? It's very seductive, and you want to keep going."

A counselor has to be realistic with the couple on all these issues, but she also has to allow them to make their own way through the minefields of reproductive medicine and the various feelings it stirs up. She can't do it for them.

WHO'S A FIT PARENT?

What a terrible question, and yet, if doctors and psychologists want to practice responsible medicine, they have to ask it, and try their best to answer it. An egg and a sperm are just bits of tissue, but an embryo becomes a fetus, which is a human being. When a couple or woman comes to a physician and asks him to help them have a baby, he is, of course, concerned first, that he should do no harm. This means he wants some reassurance that this life will be appropriately nurtured, guided, and protected.

Some programs have personality parameters for inclusion; most do not. Most programs will allow in any single woman or couples who have no obvious psychiatric disorder, such as schizophrenia, that impairs their thinking, or one that has required lifelong medication. With bipolar disorder, it's a hard call, since Lithium, the major treatment drug for this condition, has been shown to cause developmental problems to the fetus such as cleft palate and cardiac disorders. Off drugs, the mother might be unstable. So most programs request a trial period, with the permission of the mother's prescribing doctor. If she is able to be drug-free and fully functional for several months, she can return to the program where she applied and begin the egg donation process again.

Antidepressant drugs like Prozac are so commonly used that it's hard to be judgmental about a patient who tells you she's taking them. Usually we do ask the mother-to-be to stop for a few months, with her psychiatrist's approval, to see how things go. But what about the father? If he's taking any psychotropic medication, should we ask him to stop? We probably should, to be certain that he can be functional without being medicated. However, the mother is the one carrying the child, and whatever nutrients or medications she's taking will have a biochemical influence on the baby; his won't. That may be an uneven division of responsibility, but that's how nature stacked the deck. And this is one aspect of the parents' health that we aren't tampering with right now.

Then there is the question of the relationship. Marriage is rarely a snap, even when you don't have a major crisis like infertility to gum up the works. Many couples are evidently trying to shore up a bad marriage by having a child; others are obsessed with raising the "perfect" child because all their grown children turned out "rotten." Still others want to replace a child who has died.

At Columbia-Presbyterian Hospital in New York, a female psychologist interviews the mother-to-be; a male psychologist interviews the father-to-be, and then they have a general session together.

"It's amazing how much people hide from each other," says Jane Rosenthal, Ph.D., a psychoanalyst and consulting psychologist to Columbia-Presbyterian's infertility and egg donation program. "There are so many secret compartments in a marriage, you don't know which one to open up first. In one case, we had an older couple—she was fifty and he was in his mid-seventies. Her grown child had just left home, and she was eager to be a mother again. When we asked each one separately how much they'd discussed illness and mortality, the woman went into detail about how they'd selected a guardian and done a lot of financial reconfiguring. The man confessed that they hadn't touched the subject. And that was just the tip of their iceberg. It was clear that they weren't communicating about some really essential issues, and we turned them down."

The programs routinely ask about family problems—drugs and alcohol, violence, or emotional abuse—but it's virtually impossible to know when people are lying. "People see us as gatekeepers," says Rosenthal. "They want to put their best foot forward. You have to listen very attentively when people talk to you to pick up on something they're omitting in a story, or a time lapse that's not accounted for, or a kind of defensiveness. And still, you may be in the dark. You need to listen with a couple of sets of ears, one for the actual information, and one for the implied."

There are much more rigorous standards for adoption than for egg donation. The agencies require home studies because they want to see how the prospective parents live and what kind of environment their child will grow up in. Then again, agencies are dealing with a child that already exists; reproductive programs are interviewing potential parents with potential children.

With egg donation, all you have is a screening, and very few program counselors see the mothers- and fathers-to-be more than once. "This isn't therapy," says Andrea Braverman, Ph.D., of Pennsylvania Reproductive Associates in Philadelphia. "We want to give them all the facts and find out what their expectations are. We have to try to ascertain that they will love and respect their baby, whether they're having IVF or egg or sperm donation. We can't do much more than that."

Most counselors agree that good candidates for egg donation are people who are solidly grounded in their lives and want a child to enrich and enhance it, rather than to fix something that's broken. They should be people who trust themselves to be able to manage in difficult situations—they won't be devastated if their child gets up five times a night or if the sitter cancels at the last minute. The parents-to-be should be mature, caring, and loving and concerned about one another rather than just themselves. They shouldn't be afraid of setting limits or disciplining a child; they should evidence a real interest in "kid" things; they should be willing to be tied down to mundane child-care chores after years of freedom, and should seem like people who could deal with a wild hooligan even when tired or incapacitated by age or disease.

Linda Applegarth, Ph.D., therapist for the egg donor program at The Cornell Medical Center, says that her goal is to make parents-to-be as comfortable with the process as possible and to prepare them for future issues. "Right now they're dealing with getting over infertility or making a choice between a known and anonymous donor, but later on they'll need to think about fears they might have that their child might not love them as much because she won't be completely genetically related. Or how other family members will or won't accept that child. Or what it will be like having a teenager storming around the house when you're ready for Social Security." Applegarth feels that many older couples never consider the fact that they're beyond the age where most people contemplate pregnancy. "All of us have the sense that we'll live forever and we don't want to miss out on any life experiences. I don't think this is significantly different whether you want a baby at 35 or at 50."

Is this screening process enough? We never question the mental health or motives of healthy young people, who can have babies without science poking its nose in a couple's private business. Why should these individuals be so scrutinized just because they're older? Jane Rosenthal feels there is good reason to be cautious. "I think we're letting too many people slip through the net because we don't yet know what filters we should have," she says. "It's not that many years since we've known how to do donor babies, so the children who've been born in this way aren't old enough yet for us to be able to pick up on our mistakes."

IDENTITY, FEMININITY, AND OLDER MOTHERS

Counselors who see postmenopausal women desperate to have children have to ask themselves what this phenomenon means in terms of the bigger picture. People don't jump from one developmental stage to the next; rather, they evolve into it—for example, a girl is a child one day, and then, adolescence worms its way in as she starts looking through *Seventeen* magazine and comparing new hairstyles with her friends. One day, she's a teen grappling with budding sexual feelings and bad acne, and then she gets her first job and she's supposed to be a responsible adult. There's always a little left from the previous stage as we move into the current one; for some, stages hang on and on.

Menopause creeps up out of the reproductive stage, tiptoeing around in the early forties as menses become irregular, and then moving in with full force in the late forties or early fifties when hormone levels drop drastically. Menopause is a major milestone for women because it signals a time when they don't have to answer to everyone else's needs. They can be free and do what they choose—if they choose to. They can sell the house and get a great apartment in the city; they can go back to school; they can travel the world; they can stay with a mate, live alone, or forge a new relationship. In our culture, the advent of menopause is also a frightening prediction of the future for many women who feel less attractive and less womanly. Of course losing the ability to procreate does not imply a loss of femininity, but many women, and men, for that matter, read it this way. (This is even truer in other cultures than it is in ours—certain groups in Africa and the Middle East permit a man to take a new wife when the old one can no longer bear him children.)

So for a woman past menopause to choose the childbearing role consciously can be looked upon as a psychological glitch. Though it's not an aberration, it certainly is unconventional and defies society's prescribed expectations—this is the time in her life when a woman is *supposed* to bake cookies, go to the golf course and the shopping mall, and enjoy her grandchildren. Why would she opt to push a stroller to the playground or become a Girl Scout troop leader? Why would she delight in becoming a caregiver to a child at a time when she might possibly have to become a caregiver to her parents?

And if she tinkers with the stuff of her menopausal years, what will she do to her old age, and her extreme old age? Is she having a child at

50 to ensure that she will have a strong young adult in 20 years who can push her in a wheelchair or take her to her dialysis appointments? Or is she having this child at this time because she is committed to taking the very best care of herself so that she can be a vital 80-year-old who goes on Elderhostel retreats and volunteers for the local literacy program? Will childbearing at menopause stretch her or limit her?

Most therapists feel that this depends entirely on the woman. There are "old" fifties and "young" fifties, just as there are senescent 80-year-olds and vibrant 80-year-olds, according to Sandra Leiblum, Ph.D., who interviews donors for the infertility program at Robert Wood Johnson Medical School in Piscataway, New Jersey. It's difficult to tell in one or two sessions what will happen to any particular individual over the next few decades. Pregnancy and childbirth, as we know, are the ultimate tests of a woman's body to perform. But you don't know if you'll meet that test when you swallow your first estrogen tablet and get matched with a donor. You don't know whether your fantasy of being an older mother will match up with reality. And neither does your doctor.

Before an irrevocable choice is made, it's important to sort out all the issues you may have had as a woman throughout your lifespan.

- Are you enjoying your life? Do you have many activities, projects, and friends to share experiences with? Or are you a hermit, sticking close to home and perhaps just those few loved ones who make you feel comfortable?
- Did you have children before, with this partner or another? Did you feel you did a complete job of parenting, or is there a nagging feeling that you left something out that you have to do over?
- Did you never have children, possibly because you were in a marriage where it was hard enough dealing with each other, let alone negotiating childcare? Or did you never have children because you couldn't, and you have gone through life feeling less than adequate as a woman?
- Do you like your body or do you always expect more of it than it will give?
- Do you feel that your worth as a woman has a lot to do with being a mother?
- Do you think your husband thinks less of you now that you're older?

- Do you think you could go to your grave *without* a child, or will you grow into a bitter old lady if this process doesn't work?
- How do you see yourself as an old, old woman? Can you imagine yourself sick but still functional? If you do contract a life-threatening disease, do you think you are you the type of person who will fight it or succumb to it?
- Do you roll with the punches, or are you flummoxed by change? Can you picture yourself doing whatever you have to to raise this child, even if your partner should die prematurely?
- Can you imagine your partner raising your child alone if you should die prematurely?

Answering these questions—and there aren't any *right* answers, by the way—won't necessarily tell you whether you're a perfect candidate to have a baby at an advanced age. What you will discover is that you probably have some big issues that go beyond the question of motherhood. Having the technology means that it's possible to have a baby at an advanced age. But society hasn't yet caught up with science, and we may not be ready for all the unknowns that surround collaborative reproduction.

With the guidance of the counselor, it's crucial that both parents-to-be examine their deepest hopes and expectations. If you don't do it at the outset your child will pay for it later.

MATCHING DONOR AND COUPLE

Once you've decided to go ahead with the process, you have to find a compatible donor. Most programs around the country have a group of young women under the age of 35 who are willing and able to donate eggs. (We talk more about the donor's side of the story in Chapter 9.)

You can choose an anonymous donor, as Sarah and Joe did, you can use a family member and salvage a portion of your genetic background, or you can sit down with a donor selected by the physician and psychologist and get to know her. You can learn how long her parents lived, that her mother was a great pianist, and that her Uncle Ed, just like your Uncle Larry, was a terrific comedian with an infectious laugh.

Andrea Braverman explains that the women she sees in her program in Pennsylvania have generally been with her since they were IVF patients. After a number of unsuccessful cycles with their own eggs, they have the option of switching over to egg donation as long as they are under the age of 47, the cut-off age for this program. Couples are eligible to be matched with a donor in the order in which they've entered the program. If they reject her, the next couple on the list is called. Most couples request a basic physical similarity, and if they can, the programs attempt to match the two women's builds, coloring, and hair texture.

In our program at USC, we match recipients to donors both anonymously and nonanonymously, depending on a couple's preference. Even in anonymous donations, we show the recipients a donor's application form so that they get a detailed account of that person's personal characteristics; her family, school, and work history; her personal and family medical history; and her fertility history. In Braverman's program and many others, the donor is asked to write an essay about herself, why she wants to participate in the program, what type of couple she would like to donate to, and how *she* feels about disclosure. Then the couple can see a broad range of mental and emotional parameters that may help them to decide which donor to choose.

In several clinics, the couples play an ever-larger role in making the decision. Many of these clinics have a photo album of the donors for the recipients to scan. To many psychologists this seems a little too much like a dating service. "I wonder about the advisability of giving the couple this chance to make their fantasies real," says Margot Weinshel of the Ackerman Institute. "I know of some instances where a couple didn't like the woman's appearance—she was too fat or they didn't like her smile. There were others where the man was really enthusiastic and the woman rejected the picture— because the donor was *too* attractive and she was jealous of her husband's interest in her."

But not having a picture allows the fantasies to run rampant, and people often conjure up an ideal that they would never have dreamed of insisting on for a mate in real life. What is slightly disconcerting is the deep-seated sexism that comes up time and again in the matching process. Sperm banks are rarely asked whether the donor is a hunk, but recipient couples constantly ask if their donor is attractive. There have been husbands who shamelessly ask whether the donor has large breasts!

Matching certainly isn't all about looks; to a great extent, it depends on the size of the potential donor pool. We have a considerably larger one in Los Angeles than in most other cities. In some communities, there aren't that many young women willing to give up their eggs, even for a price, so the selection process is more straightforward. Usually, the older the recipient, the less picky she is—she wants to cut to the chase and have her baby.

Elaine Gordon often finds that couples would like to meet the donor in person, and if it's all right with the donor, she'll arrange a meeting for the three of them in her office. "Of course everyone is on his or her best behavior, but you do get a lot out on the table," says Gordon. The general feeling in the psychological community is that the more issues you can handle early on, the better.

But not everyone feels comfortable with a stranger in their midst—especially in the midst of their baby. And for that reason, they prefer to keep it all in the family.

THE EMOTIONAL UPS AND DOWNS OF RELATED DONORS

How close is close enough? How close is too close? You can use your grown daughter as your egg donor, or your sister, your cousin, or your niece. Some of the best donations happen between sisters and cousins who have had close relationships in the past and want to join in this ultimate bond together.

As a physician who strongly believes in the power of kinship, I always ask my patients at the initial interview if they have a family member who might be willing and able to donate. This is one reason why many women go to their families first. You inherit 50 percent of your chromosomes from each of your parents, you share 50 percent with a sibling, 25 percent apiece with an aunt or niece, and 12 percent with a cousin. This is an enormous advantage over having no genetic linkage with your baby, both physically and emotionally.

Family donations can be wonderful, but they can also create havoc. If you have a terrible relationship with your sister, if you've always been in competition for one thing or another, this may not be the best course of action. You may also be nervous about what this intermingling of genes might mean in terms of having certain relatives breathing down your neck while you parent your child. And therefore, many couples request anonymous donors.

What goes on between sisters can be both good and bad, and it's vital that the counselor try to fathom what they really feel. Does it bother the wife to think about her sister's egg mixing with her husband's sperm? Have they talked about the possibility of the child's donor-aunt one day protesting about their parenting decisions? All the anxiety has got to come out into the open, or it can fester and grow into a destructive family situation. One of the more bizarre tales in the reproductive literature is the one about the husband of the recipient who fell in love with her donor sister. After his wife got pregnant with her sister's egg, the husband and sister ran off together. Now, we have to assume that something was going on between the husband and sister long before egg donation came into the picture. But the end of the story is particularly horrifying: A woman left to fend for herself with the pregnancy created by the two who abandoned her.

Perhaps no counselor could have caught the nuances of these interlocking relationships, but we must make a concerted effort each time, with each family. And counseling against certain relatives donating for one another is often necessary. There can be a lot of strained feelings, and coercion is something we always worry about.

Suppose you had an aunt who brought you up when your father left home and your mother died of breast cancer. You would be indebted to this woman for taking you in and raising you as though you were her own child. And then, perhaps, when she was 51, she decided to marry the man she'd been going with for seven years, and they were eager to have a child of their own. Although you're now just 20, you can relate. If you were with someone you cared about passionately, and if you were financially able to swing it, you'd probably want to get pregnant, too.

But your aunt is too old to conceive on her own, and she asks you if you'd help out. How can you refuse? You would feel overwhelmed with guilt if you didn't do it. The procedure sounds a little strange, and you don't know if you can give yourself shots, but you'd risk anything for your aunt.

In the situation just described, this is a reasonable request, although the niece is quite young and slightly apprehensive. It's the job of the therapist and the physician to figure out how well or poorly she will tolerate the donor experience. If she is a virgin, for example, this is not a good way to be introduced to the poking and prodding of her genitals. The same would be true if she had been raped or had serious fears about sex. It's also important to see how envious she feels about her aunt's new marriage. She may not acknowledge that she's upset, and yet, hidden feelings about this may surface later, after she's donated her eggs and her aunt is pregnant.

What about a mother–daughter donation? Many therapists are dismayed by transgenerational situations because of the broader implications. All of us have conscious and unconscious fantasies about our parents. When you have a *real* situation—say, a mother carrying a child that developed from her daughter's egg and her new husband's sperm—it seems a little like incest, even though the two have no genetic ties. What will it mean to the family and their offspring in the future? The role confusion inherent in this situation can be extremely troublesome, to say the least.

One of the most disturbing mother-in-law stories to come out of this complex interfamilial matching happened when the older woman's newly married and pregnant daughter was killed in a car crash. The bride and her husband had been going through IVF and had frozen several other embryos. The mother offered to carry a child for her dead daughter. But the widowed husband wasn't so sure that he wanted to be a single father with a mother-in-law who was clearly going to be around *all* the time. Within the year that followed his wife's death, he met another woman and wanted to have a child with her. His former mother-in-law threatened to sue for custody of the embryos, insisting that she wanted to preserve her daughter's memory through her child. Eventually, the husband gave her what she wanted; she got pregnant and raised the baby by herself. Many in the family felt that she was desperately trying to replace the child who had died. The situation was far from ideal for all concerned.

There are certain connections that are better not made among family members, and staff at ART clinics can choose not to become a party to some procedures when they feel that those actions may result in significant harm to the people involved. Counselors can help ART staff and clients sort out the extremely volatile issues that could be damaging, and can help persuade the parents to think of the child first, their egos second.

GETTING OVER THE LOSS OF INFERTILITY

At Beth Israel–Deaconness Hospital in Boston, Alice Domar, Ph.D., sees very stressed-out women. If the hopeful mom is 42, and has been trying with no luck to use her own eggs for years, she is undoubtedly more depressed than if she just joined the program at 52 and has no option but egg donation.

"One of the things I remind women who are 'settling' for an egg is that the whole thing is not as unequal as they think. Yes, their husband is the one whose DNA will appear in their child, but on the other hand, they're the one who gets to carry the baby, and nurse the baby, which usually produces the strongest parent-child bond."

"Sometimes women tell me that they're worried they won't love their child, that they'll feel they're carrying an alien inside them. The interesting thing is that many moms feel that way anyhow—there's some person in there who's invaded your inner space. So you have to overcome your initial aversion. Most women get over it by the fifth or sixth month; others may need therapy to deal with it."

Domar uses stress management techniques, including meditation, mindfulness, cognitive restructuring, guided imagery, and group meetings to deal with the more difficult aspects of IVF and egg dona-tion. She has conducted several interesting studies that indicate that high levels of stress hormones in the blood can disrupt the natural reproductive process. In repeated programs with women who had no physical barriers to pregnancy such as tubal blockage but who spent years unsuccessfully undergoing IVF procedures, she has experienced astounding success. Between 36 and 42 percent of the women in each group became pregnant after learning to calm the savage beast within. As they worked through their mind–body treatments, their levels of anxiety, depression, and hostility plummeted.

Domar has also found that it's extremely helpful for women to visu-alize the child they're hoping for. "Most picture themselves pregnant or holding an infant in their arms. Only one imagined a six-year-old in Oshkosh overalls. I think it's important to get across that a little baby when you're 50 is one thing; but that child's going to grow up, and you'll be a lot older." A whole different ball game. And one day, when that child is verbal, he or she is bound to ask, "Mommy, where did I come from?"

So what will you say?

DO WE TELL? THE ISSUE OF DISCLOSURE

Years ago, adoption was something done under cover of darkness. Once a young woman had relinquished her baby to the system, she was dead and buried as far as her child was concerned. The adopting parents become the baby's parents, and that was that. It was not until grown adopted children began often futile searches to locate their birth parents that the question of disclosure came up. Suppose you had a rare bone disease and only a blood relative could donate marrow that might save your life? Suppose you were an alcoholic and wanted to know if the condition went back a generation or two? Suppose you were of a different ethnic background from the people you lived with and wanted to find your roots? What if you just wanted to *know*, because you'd never felt that you belonged to the people you grew up with?

The reasons were so good, the former prohibition was lifted. And there are many blended families today where both the birth and adoptive sets of parents work together to raise a child.

With egg donation, however, the verdict is still out. Some psychologists counsel the recipient and her partner to tell no one, particularly the child. Learning that his DNA owes nothing to his mother cannot help, but only hurt an impressionable youngster—or so this line of reasoning goes. Other professionals believe just as strongly that it is the child's right to know everything about his or her parentage, and if you're going to be honest with your child, you will also have to disclose the truth to your parents and siblings. Since secrets of any sort can destroy a family, you should come out in the open.

What is the nature of this argument? The school of silence, represented by many East Coast therapists, takes its lesson from studies done on children of sperm donors. It was found that many kids learned the truth at particularly inopportune times, like right after the death of their fathers or during a difficult divorce. In one such family, the father who was walking out on the unhappy teen's mother fired one last parting shot at him: "You're not my kid anyway!" At this particularly impressionable age, it can be devastating to be told that you're not who you think you are, and that the person you believed to be your father is not related to you.

Several of the parents interviewed for this book confessed that it was partly an ego choice not to tell. One new mother of 51 said that she had always looked younger than her years and no one—not even her parents—questioned her when she began wearing maternity clothes. They were thrilled that after all these years, she had finally become pregnant and never asked how it happened. Many of the couples who want to keep quiet about this procedure insist on anonymous donors who match as precisely as possible with the mother-to-be. They may be uncomfortable discussing what they considered their "failure" at IVF. When the decision is finally made to accept an egg from someone else, it's more comfortable not to think about all the ways in which you've compensated for your loss. Sometimes, couples who are conflicted about this choice never arrive at their scheduled appointments with the therapist. They would rather pretend that nothing out of the ordinary is happening, and choose not to examine their extreme anxiety about the truth coming out.

The physicians themselves tend to feel this is not a matter that need be discussed. In a 1992 study done by Leiblum and Hamkins, it was reported that 56 percent of physicians surveyed thought that the child need not be told; 21 percent were neutral, and only 22 percent thought it was a good idea to tell.

Then, there's religious and cultural pressure against disclosing. The Catholic church and the conservative right speak out as loudly against using artificial means of beginning life as they do about terminating life. The belief is that God should be the only instrument of procreation—to bring forth life in any other way is an aberration. (This is why IVF is also frowned on, even when the mother's eggs are the ones in the petri dish. Some liberal church authorities will permit GIFT, since the egg and sperm are not joined outside the body.) So for any observant couple who decides to flaunt doctrine and do it anyway, they're going to keep quiet about it or risk the censure of their priest or minister, as well as the congregation in general. The policy here is usually "don't ask, don't tell."

Orthodox and Hasidic Jewish feeling is that there is nothing wrong with egg donation, although sperm donation is frowned upon (having another man's sperm in your wife's body seems perilously close to adultery). Since the child must be born of a Jewish mother to claim his or her heritage, both the egg and the uterus in which the embryo grows must be Jewish. This has become a problem in the last few years, since there is a high proportion of Jewish women who are unable to conceive, but few Jewish donors. One way that some more liberal rabbis have skirted this issue is to interpret the law so that the mother is the one giving birth, no matter who the donor may be. This group is not in favor of disclosing the truth, however. It's generally easier to tell your friends that this late-life baby was a *mitzvah,* or blessing, from God.

Certainly, there are benefits to not disclosing. Never telling eliminates a good deal of stress in your life because you'll avoid confrontations with friends, relatives, and eventually, your child. Society will just accept what you've done as yet another miracle of high-tech medicine. If you are not troubled by "sins of omission," you can live conscience-free.

It is true that a couple's private business, particularly in the realm of sex and baby making, is their own. But having a child isn't so private when there are so many people involved—the couple and their family, the donor and her family (if they are related, these are the same), the child-to-be, any godparents or guardians who may be considered in the eventuality of the parents' death, the physician, and the therapist.

And think about the future. I have to remind couples that technology leaps forward at a dizzying pace. Only 10 years ago, egg donation to menopausal women was pure fiction, but today, Louise Brown, the first test-tube baby, is already 20. And though ART is widely available, it's nowhere near as common as it will be when soon-to-be conceived child is 10 years old and the world is a great deal more technologically advanced than it is today. In that still-hazy future, gene splicing may be practiced in the high school biology laboratory. Or you may have your entire genetic code saved at home on a CD-ROM, just in case someone needs the information to transplant a new organ or find out the details of your genetic susceptibility to particular medical treatments. Consequently, when any teenager can find his or her genetic parents by browsing the Internet, the notion of keeping genetic paternity a secret may be laughably irrelevant.

So as the playing field expands, there are wider ramifications of keeping silent. There are also many good reasons for telling.

Carole LieberWilkins, M.A., a California psychotherapist who counsels adoptive and pre-adoptive groups, suggests that keeping egg donation a secret can damage the entire family. Secrets are generally kept to cover up nasty habits that we are ashamed of. Most people are silent about extramarital affairs and drug habits because they fear censure. The truth of the matter is, even if you're not a blabbermouth, it gets harder and harder over the years to keep privileged information hidden. Few secrets stay in the closet for a lifetime.

If you never really resolved your infertility issues, you may have more difficulty coming clean about how you achieved pregnancy, and therefore you may balk at telling your children the complete truth. But the fact that you couldn't conceive on your own is certainly nothing to be ashamed of, and keeping a secret about your child's heritage can conceivably be detrimental to all parties concerned. "The knowledge of where we came from, that's information that belongs to each of us," says LieberWilkins, who is herself the mother of one adopted son and one donor-egg son. "Our genetic makeup is highly significant to forming an identity. It is *not* true, in the case of third-party reproduction, that what the kid doesn't know won't hurt him."

My own bias is in favor of telling the truth. As a civilization, we've spent the last 200 years evolving away from demystification and toward more information gathering, understanding, and acceptance. Are we better off knowing that the earth is not the center of the universe? It probably doesn't matter one way or another. It doesn't take anything away from our development as loving, caring individuals. Would it really make a difference if we knew that we had spent the first three days of embryonic life in a petri dish in an incubator instead of in our mother's fallopian tube? Would it matter if our father's sperm had to be injected into our mother's egg? So why would it matter if the egg or sperm that had carried our DNA had come from someone other than the parent with whom we grew up? You might as well get all the facts out on the table. And remember the DNA-on-the-Internet argument.

Even though we always discuss disclosure, I don't ask couples to come to a decision before we go ahead with treatment. It's simply unrealistic to predict how people will feel in the future when they've got a real, palpable four-year-old running around. But I do feel that it's vital to raise the issue at the outset and at least start thinking about it.

Consider this: If you don't tell, you are first, perpetrating a family secret that can easily backfire; second, you are allowing your child to grow up living a lie; and third, you are asking your child to assume a burden that was yours to begin with. People will comment on your physical dissimilarities, and you'll have to cover the truth about the reason; pediatricians, school nurses, and athletic coaches will ask whether allergies or predisposition to disease run in your family, and you'll have to fudge those answers, too. One lie leads to another, and any one of them can have severe consequences. So disclosing is an ethical as well as a psychological decision.

Jane Rosenthal, with the Columbia-Presbyterian program, suggests that we all dream at one point or another that we are not the child of our parents anyway. Especially during times of turmoil, when we are struggling for our independence and want nothing more than to get our lousy parents off our backs, we fantasize that we come from someone else, someone nobler, finer, kinder. Didn't you ever imagine that you were the daughter of an heiress, a wonderful, loving, smart, funny mother who would always be there for you? So it's not damaging for a child to learn that, in fact, something like this is true, that part of her came from another woman that she may never meet, but who has certain characteristics that she can relate to.

Rosenthal also points out that we haven't been doing third-party reproduction long enough to realize what the larger ramifications of disclosure are. If you tell a child about sex too soon, or about the fact that his parents were never legally married but simply live together, this type of information can be overwhelming and terrifying. Also, different kids take big news in different ways. Some want to know why the sky is blue, and others couldn't care less. For the laid-back child, who accepts everything in stride, it may not cause a wave to know that his "mother" is really two women; for the sensitive, fragile flower, it could trigger an identity crisis. And you must also consider how you will educate the world once you have educated your child, so that he or she will be treated fairly and decently despite being different.

If you do decide to tell, how do you manage it successfully? Elaine Gordon says that, as with any other piece of vital information, you mete it out in appropriate bites, giving the child what she wants when she's ready for it. When your child wants to know, "Mommy, did I grow in your tummy?" you can easily answer, "Yes, and even though Mommy's eggs weren't working, we got Sally's to help us out." That's all you need at the beginning unless the child wants to know who Sally is. A little later, as you fill in the blanks about the reproductive process, you can tell your child that making a baby requires one egg from the Mommy and one sperm from the Daddy, and if either parent can't supply the needed parts, you can borrow from other people. Keep it simple, and let your child's curiosity trigger your response.

LieberWilkins suggests that if you start telling the story early on, even before your child is verbal, there will never be a time when he didn't know he was the product of three people rather than two. She suggests that children who know from the beginning are fine about it—they don't feel like outsiders; they don't feel different; instead they feel they are special because they have more heritages than most people do. One mother of twin boys explained that from their very first days, they would all say a prayer before bedtime. As they knelt by their cribs, this mother would thank God for their good health, for their comfortable home, and the good food they ate. And then she'd add, "and thanks to the doctors who helped us to get you, and the generous lady who gave Mom and Dad what they needed so that you could be born."

The introduction to the "generous lady" is stage one in allowing your child to see that there was someone else involved in his procreation. Then, as he gets older, you can progress to stage two, where you make the connection between this lady and your child. He will eventually learn that the lady was generous because she gave a portion of herself—an egg—that became part of him.

This brings up the fact that if you're going to be honest about your child's parentage, you also have to be honest about how babies are born, both naturally and with the new technology. Many savvy donor-egg children know their birds and bees long before any of their classmates, and they are eager to share their information. If you have given your child a good, rudimentary home course in sex education, don't be surprised if your child's teacher calls in a panic because other parents are dismayed about what their kids learned from your kid in the playground.

DEALING WITH THE FAMILY AND SOCIETY

What will your parents say? What will society say? Do you really want all that hassle?

A lot of people are horrified by the idea of women having babies after 45. (Most program cutoff dates range from 43 to 47, ages that are variously seen as premenopausal, although some programs, such as ours, will accept women into their mid-fifties.) This means that the woman or couple who picks up the gauntlet must be prepared for a battle, whether implicit or explicit. It's not nice to fool Mother Nature, but we're doing just that, and some people object strongly to it.

What's wrong with her that she can't let go of the Mommy role? That's what the neighbors will say, perhaps even what her own mother will say. Isn't she selfish to want to bring a child into the world who is obviously going to have to care for her in just a few years? And what if the child is damaged or handicapped in any way? It will be hard enough to take care of her own health at this stage of life if she has a healthy child, but with a sick one, watch out! That's a burden no one would willingly shoulder at any age.

If she has already been through years of infertility, the assumption will be that repeated failure got to her, and now she's lost it. If she never had a child, it will be assumed that she is an overachiever, or is desperate to bring back the youth that she squandered. Think about the ridiculous premise of the movie *Father of the Bride, Part II.* Think how we all laughed at the mother and daughter in adjoining delivery rooms, giving birth at the same time. It's the stuff of modern comedies, not real life.

How can an older mother answer these criticisms? More importantly, how can she square her decision with herself and her spouse? In my experience, the women or couples who are committed to having children in their later years are not flakes by any means but people who have reached nearly every other goal they have set for themselves in life. They are comfortable in themselves and their marriages, and they have overcome a lot of obstacles—physical, mental, emotional, and social—to get where they are today.

We know from numerous studies of different groups that the best families tend to have the following six characteristics:

- They spend time together.
- When they're together, they communicate; they don't just sit in the same room watching TV or reading the paper.
- They have a commitment to one another; each is concerned about the well-being of everyone in the family.
- They have a communal as well as a personal ability to handle stress.
- When one family member succeeds in any endeavor, the others give their sincere appreciation for what they did.

- They tend to have strong religious or spiritual feelings; they count their blessings for being alive and having one another.

How can you see the potential for those qualities in a woman when she comes in for an initial interview? You can ask about her birth family or about her genetic children from her earlier years, but you can never be sure that what you see is what you get. And that's the problem society has with assisted reproduction for older women—we just don't know enough about these new families. Despite the sincere attempt at a mental health overview, some will work out; others won't.

But that's been true of every family since humans started clustering in groups. The more tolerance we have for social change, the more chances we have to do it a little differently and maybe a little better next time.

CHAPTER EIGHT

SARAH'S SECOND—
AND THIRD THOUGHTS

Everywhere she went, she saw young women. Any one of them might be her donor, the genetic parent of her child. Their faces, bodies, hairstyles haunted her. One was too perfect, the next too sloppy, one looked emotionally detached and the next looked like a walking nervous breakdown. How would her doctor, a relative stranger, ever find a person who was qualified—no, who was just adequate?

"I want a person who's nondescript and fabulous, all at the same time," she told Joe as they walked into their bedroom after a late dinner with friends. "I don't want her personality and characteristics to override yours, but I want her to be exceptional. I know, I know, we could get the perfect donor with the perfect family history and still manage to produce a little brat. The baby might be nothing like her mother—after all, so many traits skip a generation."

"Hey, no way *we* could make a bad seed!" Joe protested. "You're so worried about the donor's input, Sar—but remember what Leverton said. It's not all nature, a lot of it's nurture. The environment we give our child, the values our kid sees in us, the experiences he or she will have in life—that's what shapes a person."

"Yes, true. But DNA is powerful. We're inviting a total stranger to ally her chromosomes with yours. Frightening." It was the Saturday night before their Monday appointment. Dr. Leverton had called in the morning to say he had a tentative donor match he wanted them to consider, and he wanted Sarah to start her medications on Monday for the practice cycle. "So for that reason alone, I want her to have motherhood in her bones, in her cells. She has to have NURTURER emblazoned on her forehead."

"You'll never meet her, never have to get used to her not picking the baby up the instant she cries, so what difference does it make?" he asked, slightly exasperated. Sarah was getting into what he called one of her "knots," where anything and everything tied her up inside, and she found it difficult to break free.

"It does. I have a feeling that if she is really tender and compassionate, even if she's a little nutsy, this mixing and matching of genes could work. Then whatever you and I give her will temper the mix." She pulled off her sweater and stood in front of the mirror in her bra and jeans. "I want you to see *me* in our child, reflected through a prism of what we get from the donor. I don't want the donor overshadowing me. Does that make sense?"

Joe put his arms around her and gathered her in, letting his chin rest on her golden curls. "You throw a long shadow, lady. Honest," he murmured, and kissed the top of her head. "Are you going to take everything off now?" he asked expectantly.

"I was getting ready for bed," she shrugged. "Why, did you have something else in mind?

"Yeah, I mean, I wouldn't mind." He nuzzled her neck and eased her bra straps down her shoulders.

"I don't even want to think about your gametes getting cosy and intimate with a stranger's in a petri dish," she grumbled, tuning into the sensation of his hands on her.

"I promise not to enjoy it, even vicariously," he swore, rubbing her nipples with the palm of his hand until they stood up at attention.

"If you knew her, met her, you'd be checking out everything," Sarah sighed, her breast brushing her husband's chest.

He leaned back, lacing his hands around the back of her waist, to appreciate her better. Her body was so lovely, nicer than it had been at 40.

"You complain about me!" Joe shook his head. "You'd be the one who'd want to meet her family, take her out to lunch, listen to her sneeze. Just to see what you might be getting a pint-sized version of."

"Hey, when you look at my DNA, you should be happy I'm not passing it on. My stiff-as-a-board sister and my looney mom. If we can erase Lillian's obsessive-compulsive nature from our family tree, that will be a blessing."

They fell into bed, wrapping their legs around each other in a practiced way, but Sarah was simply too anxious to yield her body to Joe's hands and mouth. There was something stuck in the back of her head, and it wouldn't let go.

"Sorry," she said after a few futile moments of touching and retreating. "I think I'm just too preoccupied."

"Talk to me," he urged her, lying back, lacing his fingers under his neck. He wasn't that interested in sex himself, tonight, and it puzzled and worried him. This wasn't the first time. Was it a sign of age? Or had the Baby-That-Wasn't so completely taken them over, he was losing sensation in his groin?

"Don't get me wrong. I'm really excited—maybe too excited," she confessed. "Starting Monday, even though it's only the practice cycle, we're going in with a really good chance of success—and yet I still have this sense of dread," Sarah said so low he could hardly hear her. "Suppose Leverton and the counselor let a bad one slip through, some woman who would be responsible for attention deficit disorder, or depressive tendencies? Suppose she has a tic? Could she pass those on?"

"Hey, I'm not perfect either. I will surely give our kid something you don't like—like my terrible sense of direction. Sarah, I look at it this way—this baby, wherever she comes from, is going to be a whole lot more than the sum of her parts. It's not like she'll inherit a gene for happiness from me, a gene from the donor for flower-arranging, and so on. It's such a mix. Think of Alison——"

Sarah cut him off. "Exactly! Exactly what I mean. I was thinking when Alison was born, how I lay in the hospital bed and examined her tiny fingernails and saw how much they resembled mine, and that prominent forehead and the dreamy look in her eyes. That was a wonderful feeling. I think I needed that feeling of connectedness to get a jump-start on the incredible number of chores and scutwork you have to do for an infant."

"But she didn't stay that way," Joe reminded her.

"No, you're right. By the time she was 12, we would stand in front of a mirror together and she'd say, 'Mom, we look nothing alike!' She was dark and had a peachy complexion and I was blonde and sallow, and she was tall like her father and I was short, and I had a long face and she had a round one. Then, as the years passed, we started looking a bit more like each other. But we're nothing alike as people—as women."

"Remember how the counselor said there are a disproportionate number of egg-donor babies who look just like their gestational mother, even though they share not one gene in common? Our child could turn out more like you than Alison did."

"Yeah, I guess." Sarah sighed and turned out the light. "Sorry, did you want to watch Letterman or something? I'm bushed."

"I'm tired too." Joe rolled over, spooning into his wife's back. "You smell so good. I hope she smells like you."

"Well, we'll have to douse her with cranberry juice in that case. I feel like I have cranberries coming out of my pores with this bladder infection. Ugh. Why doesn't the body behave the way you want it to? Every year it cooperates a little less."

"I don't know. I'm not the doctor. Close your eyes, would you? You'll be in a better mood tomorrow."

She *was* fine after a sound night's sleep—she didn't even hear Joe sneak out at 7 to go get bagels. But her mood blackened with the arrival of the Sunday paper. She was flipping through the sections when she reached the magazine and stopped dead. The cover story just made her day.

"Hey, lady, what's your problem?" Joe walked in with the bagels and a gallon of milk. "You look like you just ate a lemon."

She made a noise deep in her chest and thrust the paper at him. "Look at this—some 51-year-old has an egg-donation baby and they make a big stink. She's a terrible candidate—a single mother, no support system, seeing these off-the-wall doctors who talk about fertility treatment like they're prospectors in the Alaskan Gold Rush. They seem irresponsible—like they'd be willing to put a baby into anyone who paid them. It just shines such a bizarre light on the thing. Oh God," she sighed, "I want to be normal. Just ... I want to be quiet and private about this birth, but everyone's going to jump down my throat as soon as I do it."

Joe picked up her feet and placed them on his lap as he sat beside her. Sarah felt her husband's warm kiss on her upper lip, but the salty tears at the back of the throat took away all the pleasure.

"You're just extrasensitive right now," he explained gently. "This wouldn't seem so bad if you didn't feel so on edge about our donor. Sarah, you hate being out of control, and not having any way to make the final cut is eating at you." He swept the paper onto the floor.

"I want a child, I want a child, that's all I keep thinking. I wonder if all the people they write about have the same stuff going on inside. Or do some of them do it because it's another collectible—Marilyn would see it that way—or because it's the ultimate challenge? This lady in the story—she just seemed lonely, like she had nobody and at least a kid would take the edge off. Whew. Some bioethicist they quote in the article says all the progress that's been made scientifically has been done for the benefit of the parents, not the children. I worry about that. How much of this is our crazy *shtick*?"

Joe was quiet for a minute, wanting to stay out of Sarah's knot. No sense both of them getting tied up. "We're human," he said at last. "I can't say I cut myself out of the loop. But on the other hand, I'm gonna be a goddamn good father. And you'll be a great mother, if you can ever stop second-guessing yourself and your motives. Sarah, you've talked to a counselor, to the people at RESOLVE, to Lotte, to me, and to Leverton. You've filled out all the forms and thought seriously about everything connected with the subject of this child and you and society."

"Yeah, true. I could write a dissertation on this stuff," Sarah agreed, stretching out full length on the couch. "Have I discussed using donor eggs with my family? Yes, everyone but my mother who would undoubtedly laugh and say, you're out of your mind but I can't stop you. I don't know that it's worth the argument. Have I thought about what happens when I die, leaving my newborn alone with you? God forbid. I promise to haunt you both."

"But ghosts can't breast-feed."

"Yeah, that's the really sad part about being dead."

"What else has been eating at you?"

"The number of embryos. You know, until that couple had seven children at the same time, I didn't really think about multiple births. But boy I do now! Thank God, with an egg donation, they only transfer three in one shot. If we insisted on five, we could get five babies. Yikes, no! I'm not about to deal with the Sophie's choice thing."

"You mean selective termination or selective reduction?"

"Exactly. Deciding to put all those *potential* children in there, and then having your wish come true, but you get too much of a good thing. So then you have to decide if you're going to remove some of those *actual* children just so the others have a better shot at making it. What a can of worms." She shuddered and hugged herself, as though she'd had a sudden chill.

"I have a question for you, sweetheart." He thought she looked beautiful then, with her old torn gray Henley shirt and no bra and the sun shining through her gold curls.

"What, something new? Something we haven't chewed over like a stale bagel?" She took a poppyseed from the bag and ripped it in half with her teeth. "Shoot."

He looked grim, and his voice was tight. "Suppose we don't make it. Suppose we get the embryo and it doesn't implant? What will this do to the two of us? Will you still need me when I'm 64?"

She stared at him, this man she loved and knew better than anyone else in the world. "You know sometimes you're a real brat. Geez, Joe, our relationship is not just based on this imaginary child—and it never was for however many years we've been together. What is it?" Her voice had a hard edge to it. "You think I'm going overboard suddenly? You think I'm ruling you out? Bull. If we can't have a child, we'll need each other more than ever. I don't mean in desperation—I mean support, like I was saying this woman in the article didn't have." She got up and went to the window.

"Sorry. I'm sorry."

"Yeah, okay."

"There is another thing we haven't really been through."

"What's that?"

"How about a birth defect, or multiple defects? Or multiple defects with multiple children? I think if all three of them had birth defects, I'd fall apart."

She raised her eyebrows. "What are the statistical chances of that?"

Joe shook his head. "Pretty low, I would think. Leverton did say that birth defects go up with age, but it's the age of the donor, not the recipient; so we should be okay."

She sighed. "All right, just one more. What do we tell our child, or children, about their background?" She looked at Joe. "We can't lie."

"No. I think it would be good to always have it out there on the table. To start on Day One talking to our baby about Mommy, Daddy, and the Other Woman."

Sarah chuckled nastily. "Leave it to you. I can see the new bedtime stories for kids in the making. Very racy."

"Well, it would be lousy to spring it on him when he's 16 and taking the SATs or 14 and going to his first dance or something."

"Absolutely. But this Other Woman thing ... it has messy overtones."

"Yeah, let's talk about her. Who do you want? What kinds of genes are you looking for?"

"I'm not fussy," Sarah said. "Someone small and blond like me, preferably a college grad. But not too smart—I can't bear those little kids who know more than their parents."

"Yeah, I agree." Joe sighed. "Personally, I don't want to know too much about this person, except that she's healthy and has great eggs."

A shiver went through Sarah. The hopes and dreams of years all resting on some stranger's shoulders. Such a huge responsibility for all of them. And the odd thing was, not to know, not to talk to her and get under the surface of polite conversation. Never to get under this woman's skin although she would soon be under Sarah's.

They spent the day catching up on paperwork for the office, taking a walk, going to the movies. While they were shopping at the Fairway Market for dinner, they saw two men start scuffling with each other on Broadway, and then a police car screamed up beside them and people gawked as the angry duo was escorted roughly away. But neither Sarah nor Joe was particularly focussed. The movie, the unpleasant incident, the food they ate all seemed a wash of movement, inexorably bringing them to the next morning, when they would be presented with their potential match in Leverton's office.

Neither of them slept particularly well, and they were up at six, moving silently around the apartment, dressing and making coffee the way they usually did on Monday mornings. When they arrived at the doctor's office, there were already three couples ahead of them, so Sarah went out into the corridor and took off her shoes so she could practice her tai chi and breathing. Joe opened up his laptop and played solitaire. No use trying to think much.

"Mr. and Mrs. Girard?" A nurse they'd never seen before, looking preternaturally cheerful for that hour of the morning, came to escort them in. She smiled at Joe as she looked around for his partner. "Your wife?"

"Here I am." Sarah, who couldn't have been concentrating that hard on her tai chi practice, saw the nurse through the glass window and was back in a flash, struggling into her shoes. They followed the nurse down the now-familiar hallway and entered an examination room.

"I'm going to take some blood for an E2 test and then Doctor will be in to see you." Joe watched the young woman swab the inside of Sarah's arm with alcohol, then prepare the needle. She seemed to have four hands, putting on her latex gloves, pulling off the needle cover, quickly making contact and piercing the skin, pulling back the needle until blood flowed, then swabbing the arm again and covering it with a Band-Aid as she pasted a prepared label on the tube of blood. "Just a minute now," she said, briskly closing the door behind her.

"It's amazing how she got right in there, no hesitating, no halfway measures," Joe mused. "Don't you wish you could live your life like that?"

Before Sarah could answer, there was a knock at the door and Leverton, in maroon surgical scrubs, walked in with another young man who was dressed the same way.

"Hi, how are you guys today?"

Sarah decided not to tell the truth. "Fine, thanks."

"So, we begin. I'd like to introduce Dr. Sirak, who'll be in on Sarah's various procedures and will see you for appointments, if I'm unavailable."

They all shook hands and made a little small talk, and Sarah decided she liked this fresh-faced young man. Anyway, she kind of had to.

"Geoff has also worked with your donor, and will be able to tell you a little about her."

Sarah sat up straighter. "What's she like?"

The young man smiled. "I can't say she's the spitting image of you, but I think you would be quite happy with the similarities. She has your coloring and build, and dark eyes," he looked down at Sarah's chart, "which you requested. And I think I should tell you that this donor has been with us for three cycles, which have resulted in two pregnancies. That's a very good sign."

Joe had a small smile on his face. He knew Sarah would never have asked, but she would have been dying to know. "Absolutely."

"She was on the lacrosse team all through college. She makes a living doing car detailing. She's 26, unmarried, but she has a long-term boyfriend. She'll be available to donate just about the time you'll be ready. And from the time I've spent with her, I can tell you she's really neat."

"Neat?" Joe asked.

The doctor nodded. "Yeah. Genuinely nice person, thinks about others—she really wants to help women have babies when they can't. Here's a copy of the essay she wrote to be accepted into our program."

Leverton asked if they would read it after they left the office, so that they could get onto Sarah's protocol, so she folded the paper and put it in her purse, where it began burning a huge hole.

"You're going to start on estrogen today—you'll be taking it for the whole cycle. Then we'll add the progesterone halfway through. We'll take a look at your endometrium on the ultrasound to make sure it's thick enough and then if the practice cycle goes as we assume it will, and your biopsy looks good, you and your donor will get going next month. "He looked at his watch." I guess we'll start December first. How's that sound?"

"I could be pregnant by New Year's?"

"It's possible—actually, quite likely."

They glanced at each other, not daring to believe him.

"I think you know the drill, but let me mention the basic rules and regs again. Assuming you do get pregnant this cycle, you should be laying off alcohol, if you drink, and making sure your diet is nice and balanced. Lots of veggies, fruits, grains, lean meats. Of course, prenatal vitamins with enough folic acid so that your baby or babies will be able to avoid neural tube defects like spina bifida. And you should keep exercising—well I *know* you don't need instruction in that."

Joe shook his head. "Hardly."

Leverton paused and looked from one of them to the other. "Remember that this is an elective process. You can decide to back out at any time. If you get nervous or feel you don't understand something, you call us, okay?"

"We want to keep going," Sarah said, and Joe gripped her hand. "We *really* want to keep going."

"Good." The doctor scribbled on a prescription pad and ripped the page off. "So get out there, and get your meds, and let's get started."

The Girards were interrupted by the nurse, who gave them another stack of papers—a calendar with daily dosages of estrogen and progesterone that Sarah was to take, a consent for her endometrial biopsy, another consent allowing the doctors to use part of the biopsy for some sort of implantation research, another instruction sheet for how to prepare for the biopsy, and another prescription, this one for antibiotics that she was to take prior to the biopsy. Then they went into see the financial counselor before they left and wrote her a large check. Then they walked out into the bustle of the upper West Side. Joe had an early morning meeting, so he took the first cab, and Sarah went across the street to a pharmacy to get her estrogen.

She was told she could come back in 15 minutes, but she said she'd wait, and wandered over to the food-and-supplements aisle. Like many of the trendier new pharmacies, this one had a selection of herbs and herbal teas. She picked one called Women's Liberty. Then she took the donor's essay from her purse. She unfolded the paper and looked carefully at the words written in an even, round script.

"'I have always believed that women were really the first sex,'" it began. "'This is because God gave them the responsibility of keeping the human race going. This is a totally terrific and awesome thing to have to do, and men couldn't begin to accomplish it, even if they had our biological equipment. Which they don't. And besides, they don't tolerate pain well. But they're good for other things,'" she added above the line with a little carat pointing at the phrase.

Sarah sighed. The girl was naïve in her assessment of how the world of men and women worked, but she was thoughtful and kind of funny. Yes, it could work out. She was feeling a little more secure. She continued reading.

"'I would like to have children one day, if I meet someone who's right for me and when I'm ready. Right now I want to finish my education and become more secure financially with a job and a place to live that's really a home. I grew up with a mom who was a single parent and I saw how difficult that was for her. I want to finish college (she never did) and have a job that makes me feel like a person before I start a family. And in the meantime, I can help someone else.'

"'One reason I would like to donate my eggs to a woman who needs them is that I know she's going to have the resources to take care of a baby. I think the world in the future will have better families because more planning will go into making them. And even though right now you have to have money to afford an egg donor like me, I hope eventually, everyone will be entitled to this gift.'"

Sarah put the paper back in her purse, feeling teary again. She frankly didn't know whether she would have been able to do the same when she was 26 and selfish and nutsy about her first marriage falling apart and being left as a single mom. But there were some incredibly generous people in the world, and she counted herself fortunate that she had run into one of them when she needed her.

She picked up her prescription, and paid for it along with the herb tea, then caught a cab to the office. Her e-mail was blinking rapidly, and her voice mailbox was full.

"Sarah, you want to look at some pix with me?" Kimberly, one of the vice presidents, knocked on Sarah's door and walked in without an invitation. She was one of those business-first-next-and-always women, married to her job. She trusted Sarah's judgment implicitly when it came to certain ads. For some reason, she decided that she was too young at 29 to be able to accurately judge the higher-bracket accounts that appealed to her parents (that is, Sarah's) generation.

"We've got four models, and they all have something to recommend them. I'm at a loss," Kimberly put the head and product shots down on the desk on top of the project Sarah was currently working on. "What do you think? It's the Luxury of Time ad, you know, you have to be a Rockefeller to afford to tell time with a watch like this one." The product was similar to a ladies' Rolex, with a jewel-encrusted face.

Sarah examined the first woman, a perky forty-something who would be better in a homes-and-gardens ad. Her hands were smooth, with squared-off nails that were pretending to be younger than they were.

Number 2 was a thin, dark beauty who probably used to do swimsuit ads in her youth. She looked a little scrawny, like she wasn't fed enough. Her hands were positively skeletal.

She liked the third woman, a definite presence in her fifties with very done gray-blond hair. But there was something too executive about her. If she had to work for a living, even if she owned the company, she wouldn't be wearing a watch like the one they were pushing.

The fourth candidate jumped off the page. A true aristocrat, with hands that said she'd lived and traveled and known several lovers. The face had perfect cheekbones, the white hair was done neatly in a chignon, and the hands had prominent blue veins that graphically portrayed her blue blood.

Sarah waved the picture at Kimberly. "No contest—it's her."

Kimberly's face fell. "Are you kidding? This one's older than God. Look at those arthritic fingers, and the bulgy veins. Yech. Don't tell me you want to scratch Number 2—she's like Audrey Hepburn or something."

Sarah's stomach did a flip-flop. "She's too young and too thin."

"Well, there are thin, young rich women who would buy the Luxury of Time watch. Or have their husbands buy it for them," Kimberly protested.

"No!" Sarah's voice sounded shrill in the spacious office. She toned it down at once. "Sorry, I mean, I think the fourth woman is a countess or a Guggenheim or something, a person who's been around long enough to appreciate this watch. She knows her mind, and she doesn't have to have a husband buy anything for her. She knows what she wants. And that is my opinion," she said firmly, gathering up the shots and handing them back to Kimberly.

As she went about her day, she wondered how much influence her opinion would have this time. It was a clear split—old versus young. The very qualities that Sarah saw as sophisticated and mature, Kimberly saw as over-the-hill and old-hat. But what really troubled Sarah was that "yech" Kimberly had added when she spoke about the model. What would her reaction be to seeing Sarah eight months' pregnant? For the first time, she wondered what type of impact this high-tech pregnancy would have on her job. In the fast-track world of advertising, a great belly on a 48-year-old could win her a pink slip. Oh, they'd find another way of letting her go, of course, but the discrimination would be there, hovering over everything.

"Tough, I'll fight it," she murmured, reaching in her purse for the estrogen. And there in her office, she took her first pill, washing it down with her now-cold herbal tea. There was no turning back now.

CHAPTER NINE

THE DONOR'S RIGHTS AND THOUGHTS

Most of us think of our body's parts and fluids as integral to our being—the "pound of flesh" demanded by Shakespeare's Shylock is a horrifying as well as a humiliating extraction, a fate almost worse than death. It's not easy for most people even to donate blood, although it takes less than half an hour and requires only a stick in the arm with a needle. In a pinch, if a friend or relative is about to have an operation, or when there's a radio blitz at Christmas, some of us will break down and donate. There are an unusual few who have a standing appointment to give a pint every 60 days, and an even smaller segment of the population who donate platelets, bone marrow, or even a healthy organ—but these individuals seem to function on a different plane than the rest of us. They feel that they are obligated to give back to society just a little bit of what they were given at birth—good health and an open heart.

The situation is much the same with anonymous egg donors. Unlike a sperm donor, who only needs to go into the quiet ante-chamber of a doctor's office with a *Penthouse* tucked under his arm, an egg donor is in for a rocky ride. She is subject to considerable manipulation of her private parts on a regular basis, she must ingest or inject a battery of drugs which can cause unpleasant side effects, and she must be at the beck and call of the reproductive endocrinologist as he carefully adjusts the timing of her cycle to that of the recipient's. She must avoid sex with her own partner when she is particularly fertile, just in case she should get an egg fertilized the old-fashioned way. Then, when her follicles are aspirated, she must be placed under conscious sedation and have her insides poked repeatedly as the doctor passes a needle through the back wall of her vagina to get to the eggs in her ovaries.

But enhancing fertility by taking eggs from healthy volunteers has only been possible within the last decade. When egg donation started as a logical extension of in vitro fertilization, eggs were obtained by means of laparoscopy—surgery including general anesthesia. That is why most eggs were donated by women who were undergoing IVF themselves and were willing to share a part of their egg harvest. Embryo freezing was not yet a reality, so it would have been wasteful to produce more eggs than the number of potential embryos that were intended to be transferred.

The advent of the transvaginal-guided follicle aspiration process turned egg retrieval into an office procedure and made the whole experience much simpler. However, it's still no piece of cake. For all the discomfort, inconvenience, and invasive medical techniques performed, there are young women—some of whom have not even thought about starting their own families—who offer their eggs not once, but as many as 10 or 12 times to people they will never know. And though they are paid for their time and trouble, most say that they would gladly do it again for no money, just to make sure that someone who really wants a child will be able to give birth.

FINDING THE DONORS

When we started our own egg donation program at USC in 1987, the demand for this type of infertility therapy was relatively low, since the technology was brand new and its potential benefits were relatively unknown. Our patients were mostly young women in premature menopause; we asked them to track down their own donors, who turned out to be sisters or good friends.

But our program turned a corner when Dr. Mark Sauer joined us, bringing with him several women who had been recruited by Dr. John Buster for the now-defunct ovum transfer program at Harbor-UCLA.

This was the procedure in which the donor was inseminated with the recipient's husband's sperm, and the uterus was flushed five days later in a race to get that embryo out before it implanted in the wrong woman.

These women had answered ads that Buster's team had placed for fertile women who had already completed their families. They had to fall into the category of "my husband just looks at me and I get pregnant." Two hundred had originally answered the ad. The field was eventually narrowed to about twenty. And about half of that number ended up in our program.

They were a unique group—exceptionally altruistic and willing to subject themselves to a battery of unknown risks. We paid our volunteers a fee of $500, which included up to three uterine flushing procedures.

But we soon discovered that our much-hoped-for egg harvest was not to be accomplished with flushing, and though we knew we would do better with laparoscopy, we were reluctant to submit the donors to the unnecessary trauma and risk of this type of surgery in order to capture their eggs for IVF procedures. It was one thing to ask a sister or best friend to go through this trauma; quite another to request it of a volunteer in an experimental program. But luckily, ultrasound-directed egg retrieval was perfected right about this time, which moved the procedure out of the operating room and into the office and made it tolerable for many more women.

We seemed to have no shortage of donors. The process was so new and newsworthy, we got 10 phone calls each time a piece about egg donation appeared in the paper. Word of mouth was just as great a method of recruitment—donors themselves brought friends and most volunteered for several cycles.

We still had no idea how ovarian stimulation would affect future fertility, so we only took women who had completed their childbearing. An infertile woman might bring her sister who hadn't yet had children but was eager to keep her genes in the family. She would sign any disclaimer or consent form we put in front of her. So eventually we bent the rule, since we had no proof that this process would harm her in any way. Over the years, as our donors had more kids after donating we were able to confirm to a reasonable degree of certainty that women under the age of 35 had no decrease in pregnancy success after follicle aspiration, and that lack of prior fertility had no bearing on the case.

Eventually, we began to accept women into our "commercial" donor pool who hadn't had children. Other IVF programs followed suit, finding as we had that egg donation could overcome the age-related decline in fertility that we'd seen in our patients. As the demand for egg donors increased, so did the fee for their services. In our practice, we gradually increased to $2500 per cycle, although as of this writing some practices on the East Coast were offering $5000. We never advertised at the beginning, although recently, we have begun to do so in order to let potential donors know how to find us.

When the women come to see us, we want to make sure, first, that they're good medical candidates. If they qualify in all of the aspects of our screening process, they enter our donor pool. We match them with recipient couples anonymously or not, depending on their preferences. These donors are free agents—we don't "employ" them, and we don't pay them. Instead, the infertile couple takes care of their various costs by paying them a compensation fee after the donation process is completed.

The women who respond to ads or decide to make the first call to a doctor's office have different motivations, according to Andrea Braverman, Ph.D., of Pennsylvania Reproductive Associates. "Women who are already mothers understand exactly what they're donating," says Braverman. "They're usually very thoughtful about their own kids and how this impacts their family. The nonmothers often see it as similar to donating blood—they think they're doing something positive and also, they get paid. It's important to counsel them about the fact that these are potential children they're helping to make, children who will be genetically linked to them."

Each reproductive program has a responsibility to educate these women about the consequences of their donation so that they go into the process with their eyes as open as possible. And they have a responsibility to be as careful and accurate in the screening process as they can be. It's wonderful to have many donors clamoring at our door to get in, but we have to be certain that they meet every requirement, for our future well-being and also for theirs.

DONOR REQUIREMENTS

In theory, any woman who produces eggs can be an egg donor—so if she chooses to do so, she could be a candidate from the time of her first menstruation through her menopause (although a 43-year-old egg is still an old egg, whether it's coming from a donor or a recipient). Even women over 35 don't get pregnant with the same alacrity as they did before they turned 30, so most programs won't take them over this age as commercial donors. However, if an infertile woman comes in with her fertile sister who happens to be 36 or 37, we'll be glad to take her. (The oldest donor we ever had in our program was 40, donating for her 42-year-old, postmenopausal sibling. In this instance, we were concerned about possible genetic anomalies in a egg from a donor of such advanced reproductive age, but things worked out perfectly. We were all delighted when the recipient conceived during her second cycle, had a normal amniocentesis, and delivered a healthy child at term.)

In most cases, however, we set an upper age limit, and we certainly set a lower one. Theoretically, a girl of 16 could be a donor, but we feel strongly that you need some life experience to counteract the psychological trauma that might result from superovulation and follicle aspiration. Even though 18 is the generally accepted age of consent, we hold the line at 21 (although we did accept one very mature 20-year-old who was donating for a family member).

Every program has its own requirements—age limits vary widely around the country. Some IVF groups insist that donors be at least 25; others won't allow anyone to donate if she's over 30. All donors undergo a complete physical exam and routine blood tests to make sure they're in general good health. In addition, they must be free of genetic diseases that they could pass along to offspring as well as transmissible infectious diseases; naturally, the donors are routinely screened for AIDS, hepatitis, and syphilis.

The next step is the medical and personal history. Each program asks extensive questions about the donor's reproductive and sexual past, her belief system, her goals and accomplishments, and her education (including SATs, GREs, or other standard scores). Many programs also include a psychological and personality profile. Donors are asked detailed questions about the health of all members of their immediate and extended families. This information, of course, tells the program whether the donor will be suitable for them, but it's also valuable as an introduction to the recipient couple so that they can know as much about their potential donor as possible.

The most common means of matching recipient and donor is by physical characteristics—you want a donor to look a little like the woman who carries the child. So height, weight, hair color (and how it may have changed throughout her life), eye color, and skin tone are carefully recorded. There's no stipulation that the blood types of the two women match, unless the recipient couple decides to keep the donation a secret.

Before the new candidate accepted into our donor pool, she meets with the physician and IVF clinical nurse specialist. In our practice and many others, she is scheduled for a session with a psychologist as well. Her assessment should show that she never experienced a major sexual trauma; that she currently has no unusual life stressors; that if she is stressed, she has a variety of adaptive coping skills; that she has supportive and stable interpersonal and/or marital relationships; that she doesn't bounce around from one job to another; and that she is relatively stable, economically. She is asked to describe herself and her decision to become an egg donor, and whether she has any preferences for the recipient parents.

She must then give her informed consent to the various medications, scheduling constraints, and procedures that she will have to undergo as an egg donor. It's also vital that she agrees not to have sexual intercourse from the start of her menstrual period throughout the two-week period when she is taking hormones to prep her for egg harvesting. The counselor must prepare her for all the hassles of donating and be pretty certain that she won't develop physical or emotional reactions to this procedure. If she's someone who tends to obsess about things that are out of her control, she is probably not a good candidate for ovum donation. The best donors have a full and complete life of their own which gives them a lot of pleasure and satisfaction.

Not every donor gets a psychological screening—in many practices, if the young woman seems comfortable with the information she gets from the doctor and nurse, is a good match to the recipient, and passes her physical and personality assessment, then fine, she's on board. But since there are many women who disqualify themselves after going through the battery of tests and learning of the various hazards and discomforts they might experience, it's obviously useful to have a psychological assessment. We feel it's important not only at the time of making a decision about donation, but also in the future, when other elements in a woman's life may cause her to reflect seriously about her choice. The field is yet too young to know the long-term consequences of making the decision to give away these precious pieces of tissue.

LONG-TERM EFFECTS OF DONATION

It's apparent that a woman has had a positive experience as an egg donor when she asks if she can donate again. Most of the negative feedback we get has to do with not knowing whether a pregnancy occurred, not having a chance to meet the recipient couple, and the temporary impact on the donor's own sex life. These are relatively minor complaints. But how will giving away gametes affect a donor 10 or 20 years down the road? We all grow and change, and the decisions we made in our youth often seem strange or even repellent in later life. The regrets that many women have years later about abortions make us wonder what they might feel in retrospect about donating their eggs. Although most donors interviewed said that they regarded their experience as similar to giving blood, they might conceivably change their minds as they grow older and more reflective about the motherhood experience. And at that point, they would not necessarily have access to the therapy and counseling they might require.

Follow-up studies, both physical and psychological, should be a bare necessity for every woman who ever participated in such a program. Each clinic and facility should bear the obligation of tracking these women and making available to them any counseling or therapy that might become necessary. And while they're at it, it would be useful to contact sperm donors—who have been around a lot longer than egg donors—and ask the same questions. Although it's true that the act of donating sperm is a lot easier than donating eggs, it would be interesting to know what men thought about this. After so many decades, after possibly becoming parents themselves, surely these men would have something to reflect on.

A big factor in a donor's subsequent reaction to the experience is disclosure. If everybody knows about your decision to donate eggs, and has had ample opportunity to applaud you or criticize you, it's probably easier to live with it. But if you have kept your gift a secret for many years, what type of impact will that have on your marriage or your own children? Or on your feelings about giving so much but getting so little in return?

It will be interesting in the future to examine the results of such studies. Although my experience over the last 10 years shows that no harm comes to a donor, it's important to check issue this out, and keep checking, as donors get older and become eligible to switch over to recipient status.

WHAT KIND OF WOMAN BECOMES AN EGG DONOR?

In my experience, the women who make this unusual donation are overwhelmingly well-meaning, sincere, and socially conscious. They have high ideals for motherhood, whether or not they themselves have given birth. And, they can certainly use the extra money.

In our practice and in those surveyed for this book, there are no rich egg donors, no women with high-profile, fast-track careers. They may be working toward a Ph.D. or building a business of their own, but right now, they may be struggling a little. These are women who would undoubtedly give back to society in other ways if they could— one day when they are older and more successful, perhaps they will— but for now, donation is one thing they can do that makes them feel fulfilled and useful.

Out-of-work actresses donate so they can go on more auditions and avoid waitressing. College and graduate students do it to get through their degrees faster and avoid having to take a part-time or full-time job. One woman interviewed ran her own jewelry-making business; another was a phone operator. Some are full-time moms who have already had all the children they want or who are between kids. They may have been scheduled for a tubal ligation and have decided that even though they don't want any more children of their own, they would be happy to help someone else who is desperate for them. Some donors have chosen never to have children, but they still want to be represented in the next generation. And some are lesbian women, either partnered or not, who are uncertain about their future as parents but want the opportunity to swim in the communal gene pool.

Many donors we talked to said that they woke up each day so grateful for what God had given them. If they could enable women who didn't have the extraordinary gift of bringing new life into the world, they would do it joyfully.

None of these women were ambivalent—they all felt it was their obligation to do something for someone else. The "inconveniences" inherent in the process seem slight to people who are committed to help humankind. A typical comment, from a donor who was incredibly scared of needles, was that although she was certain she would not be able to inject herself, the first time she tried it, "the needle seemed to slip under my skin all by itself." Another woman, who was so bloated after the aspirations, she had to miss three days of work each time she donated, commented that she was normally so healthy she never took sick leave and it was nice to have a few days off once in a while. Yet another woman, who donated with our practice when she lived in California, was heartbroken when her husband's job took her to Arkansas where there were no egg donation programs nearby. "I always liked going to my appointments back home," she said, "even though I had to drive an hour each way."

Although most of these women got a lot of flak from friends and acquaintances about making this rather uncommon choice, they all stood firm when their position was challenged. "People are so closed off about this," Rachel,* a 27-year-old artist said to me. "They believe it's not right ethically or religiously. But they're not looking at the bigger picture. We have the ability to go beyond our biology; we can pick and choose whether to have kids or stop them with birth control. After all, there was a time when people thought the automobile was weird and dangerous—now it's a given that everyone has a car. So it's the same with reproduction."

There have been some studies that indicate that many donors have some secret in their past that they are atoning for—an abortion, perhaps, or an alcoholic parent, or some unmet psychological need that they feel they can work out by giving their eggs away. In fact, the truth of the matter is that the vast majority of these women are extremely well-adjusted. They realize that they haven't yet been able to give significantly to society in many other ways—they haven't written a symphony or invented a cure for cancer—but they have a special offering that other women can't or won't supply. They are unanimous in stating that

*The names of the donors have been changed.

they are happy to have helped to produce a really *wanted* child whose parents will really appreciate what they've got.

"So many kids are accidents, and their parents treat them like that," one donor related. "I'm interested in a couple or a single woman who has plotted and planned to have a child who is going to be their first priority."

Donating eggs is a mission for many women, a cause they can get behind. And because the donors are young, they still have ideals about parenting and motherhood, and are happy to report that their bodies bounce back fast, so their contribution is not difficult or unmanageable.

None of them—perhaps due to the careful screening of the various practices where they donate—thought of their eggs as children. All of them realized that they were simply giving a gamete that, on its own, would most likely die of attrition in the body. Many of the donors had good friends who were infertile and had gone through years of IUI and IVF procedures. "That has to be the most awful thing," one donor said. "I could probably get pregnant every time my husband touches me— for me it's no big deal. But my two buddies, they've been in crisis about this for at least five years. I really empathize."

Empathy is one thing, but when you feel you can "fix" the problem by giving the ultimate gift, even if it's not to your friend but to a stranger who wants a child, that's quite another. It can make you feel powerful, even goddesslike—the pinnacle of femininity. Clearly one of the strong reasons for participating in this event is that feeling of self-confidence and importance. Some donors are called back when a couple wants a second or third child, so that the first child can have a genetically related brother or sister. This can certainly increase the donor's sense of worth—she wasn't just needed once, but several times.

Of course, the situation changes if you know the recipient of your egg. If you are the sister or cousin or aunt of an infertile woman, your reasons for giving are quite different. Sandra Leiblum, Ph.D., who screens donors for the infertility program at Robert Wood Johnson Medical School in Piscataway, worries about coercion when family members are involved. "The women deny it," she says, "they maintain that they're comfortable with the idea, that they feel responsible for their sibling, aunt, or mother. It's not so much that they want to, but that they feel they should help out their relative. Women can be made to feel guilty [by the entire family] if they don't do the 'right thing.'"

Dr. Leiblum often acts as the buffer for a potential family donor who feels ambivalent about her decision. She finds a way to explain to the recipient that there are medical or psychological reasons that would make such a donation out of the question. "I try not to put the woman in the position of having to say no to her beloved relative. Instead, I make it a program decision, so she's off the hook."

Keeping It Secret

Many of the donors stated that they didn't want their names published—not only did they object to the recipient couple knowing their identity, they also didn't want friends or relatives to know. "I told two of my sisters and my husband; that was all," said Maria, a 35-year-old former donor with three children of her own. "My other sisters would say I was crazy—but they don't have kids, so what do they know about wanting to be a mother? I didn't tell my parents either, because I knew they'd be critical."

Another donor, from a very observant Catholic family, said her mother was in the medical field, so she asked her advice first. Her mom pointed out that the church was against the practice, but said that her daughter should do whatever she thought best.

A lesbian donor interviewed chose not to tell her parents, although she has come out to them and is very open about all her other opinions and decisions. "My mother and I have discussed the topic generally, and she's really anti. She thinks it's not ethical, and that it's messing with nature. So I didn't want her on my back about this." She decided to tell a close friend and her partner—both women were very positive and thought it was an opportunity for her to contribute something of herself to a worthy cause.

But the secrecy doesn't end with the process itself. For many women, it's a conflict to consider never knowing the person who emerged from someone else's body with your genes. There is a lonely cast to the experience—you are so intimately a part of it, and then, within a period of hours, you're out of the loop forever. In a 1991 study, 72 percent of those polled said that they were perfectly content to acknowledge that they had no rights to any child that came from their donation, but they would leave a message for that child even if they could never meet.

WHAT DO THEIR PARTNERS THINK ABOUT DONATION?

We have had women in our program with enormously supportive partners who learn to give them their injections and come to every appointment with them. Then there are some whose significant others don't understand and don't want to.

It almost doesn't matter, because the donors say, "this is my body and I'll do with it what I like," a statement which really can't be refuted.

Imagine a man who is still slightly in awe of the regular monthly event of his wife's menses. She has moods that he can clock by the appearance and disappearance of the Tampax box in the bathroom. She agrees to sex, or initiates it, depending on her "time of the month." And then she tells him that she has decided to participate in a worthwhile and very important cause that involves manipulating this cycle, and actually abstaining from sex during part of it. What is he going to say? He can rant and rave, but it's not his decision. And most spouses want their partners to feel good about themselves—if this is a way to that end, so be it.

"My husband didn't like the idea at first," said Sonia, a 25-year-old secretary with no children who had donated five times. "I had just started my first donation cycle when we met, and I told him about it. He was really annoyed, first because I was seeing a male doctor and he thought the guy had roped me into it. Then he said he was worried that I might use up my eggs too fast, and there wouldn't be any left when we wanted to have kids of our own. Of course I told him that could never happen—as a matter of fact, my mom had her seventh child when she was 48! So he settled down about it eventually."

Nancy, a 29-year old two-time donor who wants to have kids "someday," said that her husband's reaction was, "It seems kinda weird to me, but if you feel it's good to do, then do it." Nancy was very protective of him during her cycles. "I never asked whether he'd give me the shots—I didn't want him to pass out," she explained.

Many men chose not to express an opinion—it was just one of those private "women" things they didn't discuss because it was too embarrassing. Even in rather traditional households where husbands and wives play conventional roles and the men make the major decisions, this is one area where women call the shots.

In lesbian relationships, the choice was still exclusively the donor's although the two women seemed to discuss the topic in a more balanced fashion than in the heterosexual couples. The choice of one of them becoming an egg donor also brought up the issue of which partner would be the one to receive donor insemination in the future, if the two women decided to have their own child.

We all have crucial personal decisions to make that no one can help us with. Whether it's abortion or suicide or joining Alcoholics Anonymous, we must all go through a dark night of the soul in order to make a wise choice. Even when these decisions affect those closest to us, even when we so desperately desire advice and counseling, in the end, we have to do it ourselves. And despite the enormous impact on a donor family, whether this is an anonymous or known donation, whether it's family or strangers, it is finally the donor herself who has to tally up the pros and cons and make the choice.

What If You Could Never Have a Child of Your Own?

Even though follicle stimulation and aspiration seems quite safe and devoid of long-term complications, a donor still has to be a very optimistic person. What if something were to happen that might compromise her own fertility after she had donated? Suppose she was diagnosed with cancer and needed chemotherapy or radiation, which would effectively knock out her ovaries? How would she handle the knowledge that she had helped another couple to have a baby, and could not have one herself?

If a family member or friend has agreed to act as donor, the situation could be even more sticky. Even in the best of all possible high-tech screenings, there can be disasters. Suppose the donor and her sister recipient agree to collaborate, but their parents object for religious or ethical reasons. Will this split the family apart? Suppose the child that comes from such a donation is born with a birth defect or multiple handicaps. Will the recipient blame her friend or family member for this glitch of nature? Or will they support each other to make the best of the situation? And what about the donor's realization that she has helped to create a child with special needs? Will she ever want to have children of her own after this? Would this increase the rivalry between her and her sister?

Although our current understanding of physiology assures us that donors will have as many eggs as they would need for whatever number of children they might desire no matter how many times they go through the procedure, the field is too young to make any definite pronouncements about the absolute safety of egg donation. After completing thousands of superovulations and aspirations, I am clearly confident that there are few, if any, risks to these women. But there's no such thing as a medical certainty—it's the women's own staunch belief in this system that allows them to come back time after time.

One woman smiled when asked what she would do if she were unable to have children of her own in the future. "I'd borrow an egg from someone else, of course." It is a likely assumption that if she were in need, she would find someone to give back to her the gift that she had given to somebody else.

WHAT ABOUT THE MONEY?

If you were told that you could volunteer some of your free hours tutoring illiterate children, would you do it? Well, who has free time anymore? Many people work two jobs and have a house to take care of and a family to support. Volunteering takes a lot of perseverance, and undoubtedly some of the kids you helped study might be less than delighted to receive your assistance. Some of them might be downright threatening and dangerous. Of course, you'd get a big burst of self-esteem for doing it, but on the other hand, polishing your halo when no one can see it shine may not be worth your while.

But suppose you considered your time volunteering as a gift, pure and simple. You enjoy children, you like to see them flourish, and it makes you feel good when one of them actually opens a book and gets something out of it. And in addition, suppose you were paid $50 carfare for every trip you made to the center where you taught. Would that influence your decision? You would obviously get the personal benefits of helping someone who needed you, but you would be compensated for your time and the kids' bad attitudes and any nasty threats that came your way. Wouldn't it be slightly easier to help someone else if you were being helped yourself?

The answer is probably yes. Most egg donors are very happy about the money. The extra few thousand every few months can make a big difference to someone who earns no salary because she's at school or a full-time homemaker, or gets a small salary that must be stretched to pay bills. For young couples who may be saving up to buy a house or a second car, this type of additional income is invaluable.

On the other hand, the actual amount of money is rather arbitrary. In incentive studies done at the Center for Bioethics in Philadelphia, a thousand women were all given different versions of the same questionnaire about the process, and each version quoted a different fee for services. It was found that in order for the donor to feel compensated, she had to receive enough money to offset the actual expected cost of the process and the effects of the drugs that would make her take time off work. Beyond that, however, the amount was irrelevant. Whether the price was $2500, $5000, or $10,000, it didn't increase the number of women who would agree to donate. This confirms the attitude of those who donate organs for transplant—they must see their donation as a gift rather than a service that merits payment.

Although some practices restrict the number of donations possible for any one woman to four or five in a lifetime, others, like ours, have no such arbitrary limitation. Each donation pays $2000 to $5000—this is not a purchase price for eggs harvested, but for the donor's services. The 1993 guidelines put out by the American Fertility Society (now the American Society for Reproductive Medicine) state that "donors should be compensated for the direct and indirect expenses associated with their participation, their inconvenience and time, and to some degree, for the risk and discomfort undertaken."

This means that over the course of several years, a woman might earn from $10,000 to $50,000 from donating her eggs. Not big bucks, but significant for someone on a shoestring budget. Would the women do it if they were not paid?

Some would not. There are women who donate eggs to pay off their credit cards or take a Caribbean cruise. But these are not in the majority. Donors tend to be women who see themselves as fertility specialists—they are just as important as reproductive endocrinologists in promulgating the right of every woman to have a child. If you are really dedicated, you help others out of the goodness of your heart. You are certainly not paid when you donate blood or your bone marrow, so why should you collect for your eggs? In other countries, your position as Good Samaritan is guaranteed by the government. In Sweden, a law was passed forbidding payment of gamete donors; in France, a consortium of sperm banks has forbidden payment; and in England, egg donors may not be recompensed more than 15 pounds or about $30 per cycle. In Israel, the only type of ovum donation allowed is egg sharing—where one woman going through IVF offers her eggs to another going through the same procedure.

In a family situation, it's expected that you would offer up your eggs for free (although in one instance, the recipient gave her sister the deed to a house that she owned in exchange for donating her eggs).

Perhaps the difference lies in the fact that egg donation may really disrupt your life. You are not just coming into a clinic to have one procedure done; rather, you may be tied up for weeks, running back and forth between your home (where you must remember to give yourself injections) and the doctor's office (for your ultrasounds and blood tests.) And then there's the sex restriction.

But money is one of the factors that raises its ugly head in the divisive arguments about whether it's possible to avoid coercion and exploitation in the reproductive technology business. And a business it is—although the outcome is a human one.

The best reasoning for paying egg donors who give so generously is that one good turn deserves another. In order to protect new options for our society, we cannot solely depend on science or medicine; rather, we must rely on human nature. During the past hundred years, we have banned all baby-trading relationships. We know that, despite good motives, it's dangerous to allow anyone to purchase a child because this objectifies human beings and makes them into commodities. But think about private adoptions. They are extremely costly because of legal and other fees, and it's not uncommon for the adoptive parents to help support the birth mother throughout her pregnancy. The connection between the parties is more like that of patron and artist. But it's still supported monetarily.

In recompensing the woman who gives an egg so that a child can be born, we are supporting the woman herself rather than putting a price tag on the gift she gives.

THE DOCTOR AND THE DONOR

It is a strange relationship. The doctor, after all, is looking for healthy young women who will be at his beck and call and will render unto him excellent gametes that can be turned into babies. The doctor quotes an overall fee to the recipient couple, which includes the donor's fee for services. This fee will be paid directly to the donor by the recipients at the end of the process.

It is not surprising that those who are vehemently opposed to egg donation describe this relationship as similar to that of a pimp and a prostitute. Worse, it can be compared to the relationship between a farmer and his prize chickens—who lays the best and the biggest with double yolks? Especially because the donor will be "put out to pasture" when she is too old to come up with good "product."

But these are distortions, fantasies concocted by people who have no comprehension of what really goes on. If they were to spend just a few months in an egg donation program, their view would be entirely different.

The relationship between doctor and donor is symbiotic; one could not provide the required service without the other. In an anonymous donation, recipients have no way to show their gratitude, because the person to whom they owe such a debt never comes forward. Doctors, however, know the donors well, and their gratitude is very obvious. They are generally unstinting in their thanks, which makes the donors happy to be around them. Typically, they want to stay with the doctor's program and come back to donate again—an unspoken secondary gain to the good relationship. It gets harder for the donor to say no when the program calls and asks if she'd do it one more time or do it for a prior recipient who achieved a pregnancy with her egg.

It's for this reason that physicians and donors have to sit down and talk every so often to get their real feelings out on the table. If a woman is burned out from donating, but can't come right out and say so, she may need the encouragement of the physician in order to allow herself to take a break or stop altogether.

THE DANGERS OF EGG DONATION

Most things we do in life carry some risk. All of the donors interviewed for this book shrugged when asked if they were at all concerned about harming themselves in any way by becoming an egg donor. "Everyone says this or that can give you cancer," one woman stated. "If you believe everything you read, you'd go nuts. You know, 'if you eat too many tacos, you increase your risk of cancer. If you breathe the air in California, you get cancer.' It's nonsense. There are so many environmental hazards and pollution, this is a tiny thing to worry about." Again, optimism wins out—most donors said that they took vitamins, ate well, exercised, and, especially when they were getting ready to aspirate eggs, took extra-good care of themselves—almost as if they were the ones who were about to be pregnant and they were concerned about the state of their "baby."

Those who were mothers themselves explained that they would never do anything that would put them at risk for their own childrens' needs—in other words, if they became too exhausted or bloated from donations, and couldn't adequately take care of their own kids, they'd stop donating eggs, despite the fact that it benefited others.

In the early days of egg donation, we worried constantly that we would cause permanent damage to a donor. Whenever you use an invasive technique like inserting a needle into the ovary to retrieve eggs, you run the risk of poking a blood vessel and causing internal bleeding, or introducing bacteria that could cause an infection.

Fortunately, the needle used for aspiration is small, and we can see it quite well on the ultrasound screen so that we are sure to avoid vital structures when we're working. We're incredibly careful about monitoring the donor for several hours after the procedure to guarantee that she's not bleeding internally, and thankfully, the infection issue has never come up. There have been reports of women in IVF programs who develop infections after follicle aspiration and embryo transfer, but these women had underlying pelvic inflammatory disease. In my opinion, their problem was kindled by the transfer, not the aspiration, since during transfer, something is being introduced into the body rather than removing something—and introducing even a small amout of fluid into the uterus, as happens in embryo transfer, can stir up a smoldering pelvic infection. Since donors must have no underlying disease to get into this program, and since they don't have embryos placed inside them, they don't get infections.

Another condition ART programs worry about is *ovarian hyper-stimulation syndrome*, which can, in fact, be dangerous if not accurately diagnosed and treated. After ovulation, substances in the follicle wall that cause blood vessels to proliferate help to turn the old follicle into a corpus luteum, a "yellow body," that secretes hormones. These vasoactive substances (called so because they act on blood vessels) can also open up capillaries and cause fluid to ooze out of them and into the surrounding tissues. Of course, in a stimulated cycle, you have perhaps 20 corpora lutea rather than just one, which means there's a lot more likelihood of oozing from the capillary beds.

In a severe case of ovarian hyperstimulation, up to a gallon of fluid can leak out of the blood vessels, into the abdominal cavity. The patient can be terribly bloated and swollen as the fluid pushes up on her diaphragm, sometimes making breathing difficult. With all the fluid drained from her blood vessels, the donor can become dehydrated. This can cause metabolic disruption or even blood clots in the veins of the lower legs. The danger, of course, is that an errant clot might travel up to the lungs and form an embolism, which could kill.

For this reason, we are vigilant about making sure that donors get enough fluids after their procedure or even hydrating them intravenously when necessary. Luckily, the syndrome only lasts as long as the luteal phase of the cycle, so about two weeks after follicle aspiration, with the arrival of a menstrual period, all the symptoms disappear, including the normal bloating and ovarian tenderness.

But we rarely have to take emergency action—in our program at USC we've never had a really severe case of this syndrome. In the general population of donors, the incidence is less than 1 percent. It's higher in patients who have undergone IVF cycles with their own eggs and subsequently become pregnant, since the hormone hCG which they're now producing can stimulate the ovaries and keep the vasoactive substances just as active as they were after aspiration. But donors are not getting pregnant.

What about the concern for long-term scarring of the ovaries? It's not natural to produce 10 or 15 follicles at a time, so wouldn't this cause trauma to an organ that has to work so hard? Although there are no long-term studies on donors, the various changes that take place in the ovary and the subsequent repair process that happens naturally appear to be the same whether 1 egg or 12 eggs are ovulated. The body just works harder, as it does when it trains for a marathon and the heart has to pump more blood. Surely, nobody expected to make the body function in weightlessness, and yet astronauts do that for months at a time with no ill effect.

Another area of controversy is whether repetitive cycles of super-ovulation using fertility drugs may predispose women to ovarian cancer. Epidemiologists, who are in the business of making cause-and-effect connections to explain disease, reason that if lack of ovulation is protective against cancer, lots of ovulation might cause it. They make this comparison: Chickens, who ovulate daily, run a much higher risk of ovarian cancer than rabbits, who only ovulate several times a year. In humans we know that oral contraceptives and pregnancy are protective against this cancer—and, in both instances, there are fewer cycles and ovulations.

But the trouble is, there are many other factors at play. One pregnancy protects a woman against approximately 30 percent of the incidence of ovarian cancer, even though those nine months average out to about 2 to 3 percent of a lifetime of ovulations. If you take birth control pills for more than five years, you're protected for up to 50 or 60 percent of the incidence of ovarian cancer, even though that accounts for only 10 to 20 percent of all your ovulations. And other situations, like early menopause or late onset of menses, don't protect you at all against this form of cancer. So it's not as easy as cause and effect—ovulation may or may not play a role, but it's by no means the whole story.

At least three studies have contradicted the initial epidemiological investigations tarring fertility medications with the brush of cancer, so the controversy is all but over. It may take another decade to get all the data we need to prove our case. In the meantime, most programs are comfortable telling donors that, although some studies have proposed this unfortunate link, more recent studies have refuted it and, at present, there is no reason to believe that a woman would be increasing her risk of cancer by taking these medications.

THE DONORS SPEAK OUT

"Having kids isn't easy," said Terry, a 30-year-old single donor who works with Alzheimer's patients at a senior-care facility. "I really don't know that I want to do it. But I'd be proud to have had a part in producing a really good child who will grow up to accomplish something."

Another donor who was 29 and unmarried said that she never considered whether the person getting her egg deserved it. "Whether they're homosexual or disabled or older, I don't care," she said. "Being a good parent has more to do with being dedicated and committed and having the ability to love another individual deeply. I really respect these women who've been doing IVF for years—they've sacrificed so much—so they deserve a break. If I can give them that, I will."

"I liked being at the cutting edge of medicine," said Suzanne, 35, who had just left the donor program. "I kept thinking I was part of the reason that reproductive technologies had made so much progress in the last ten years, and that made me feel good."

"This is something I'm blessed with but I'm not using," said Sonia, a 28-year-old unmarried donor. "I believe God intended us to use our gifts wisely. If I had money, I'd to give charity. But I don't. My brother donates platelets every two weeks—he's saving lives. I'm giving life. Even if I were to become infertile in the future, I would never regret what I'd done. I would just hope that in the future, if I need it, there would be someone like me out there willing to give me an egg."

"In the big scheme of things, when you consider what you're contributing to the world, a little pain or a few shots is nothing," said Maria. "After all, the woman who gets my egg is the one who has to carry it for nine months, deliver it, nurse it, and raise it. That's the hard part!"

The admiration and awe of the "real" mother, the one who will play the parent role for the rest of her life, inspires young women who have already given birth and those who are still on the fence. Why else would someone give so generously of her own body? For all the ambivalence in our society about the multiple roles of women at work and at home, there are few individuals who would deny that we need mothers who really want to parent more than ever.

A donor, by osmosis, gets to support and nurture the mothering process. These individuals behind the scenes, who make it possible for new life to begin, deserve our deepest respect.

CHAPTER TEN

SARAH GETS PREGNANT

Sarah was usually a great procrastinator. When she didn't want to do
something, she just put it out of her mind. Of course, with her successful biopsy behind her and a donor just days away from starting a stimulated cycle, it was hard to think of anything else but the baby she might
be having. So she couldn't put it off any longer. It was time to talk to her
mother and sister.

No more excuses, she told herself on the morning of the annual
Girard family picnic. Marilyn and Lillian would just have to sit still and
listen. (Joe's mother already knew and was fine about their impending
pregnancy. As a matter of fact, she had called Joe last night to say she
was already in knitting mode, and she was going for lime green and
burgundy instead of pink or blue.)

But Sarah and her sister were something else. For the past month,
they had been incredibly frosty on the phone, and though they'd
helped move Lillian to the Westchester senior residence together, they
hadn't made any visits to see their mother at the same time, claiming
scheduling conflicts. That was nonsense, of course—they were both
just avoiding potential nastiness between them.

So on this sunny Sunday in December, about a week before
Christmas, Sarah knew she had her work cut out for her. Marilyn

picked them up early so they could get to Lillian and from there, to Joe's mom in Tarrytown.

"I don't know why your mother insists on doing this family thing when it's cold out," Marilyn grumbled as they started up the West Side Highway. "You have so many cousins coming from out of town—suppose it snows or it's five below?"

"It never is," Joe said smugly. "My mother just arranges it that way."

Sarah, sitting in the back seat, listened to their banter with apprehension. She and Marilyn had gotten over bad times quickly in the past, but their angry words about egg donation still rang in her ears. Joe had been pushing Sarah to make up this weekend, and she was feeling sort of conciliatory because everything else in her life was going well. She'd gotten a new account that she'd been hoping for, and the client was really happy with her work. She'd seen Leverton last Thursday, and he was pleased about the ultrasound he'd done in the middle of her biopsy—her endometrium looked really thick, he said, and the biopsy had gone well—he'd probably have the lab results next Wednesday. And to top it all off, she and Joe had had the best sex they'd had in years—twice, in fact, in one week!

Lillian, true to form, wasn't dressed when they arrived, so they sat around in the stately living room of Windswept Pines listening to a large, red-faced man with a big shock of yellowing white hair play Cole Porter songs on the baby grand. For a senior residence, the place was really beautiful, nicely landscaped outside, and filled with light and comfortable furnishings inside. People came and went, talking loudly over the sounds of the piano, most of them wondering when lunch would be served, although it was only 10 A.M. The smells from the kitchen were definitely not institutional steam-table stuff—the heady aromas of garlic and rosemary wafted down the corridor. Lillian had complained steadily since she'd moved in about everything from the food to the beauty parlor, but that was her. Reading between the lines, Sarah thought that she was probably pretty content.

After they'd been waiting for 15 minutes, Marilyn went to the elevator. "I'll see if I can hurry her up," she said impatiently, leaving Joe and Sarah sitting in the large, overstuffed armchairs.

"So when do we move to a place like this? When we can't climb the stairs anymore? Or when you can't get your legs around my neck?" Joe mused.

"Joe! Shh," Sarah grinned. "I put in my vote right now for never moving. I mean, it's perfectly nice, but it's like being back in a college dorm. If you don't like the company, where do you go? Who do you talk to? I hate the idea of our child having to put us in a place like this." She started chewing absently on a fingernail.

"Hey, Lillian put *herself* here. She took her money from the sale of her house and she bought into it. And she gets long-term care if she needs it. It was a very good investment, we all decided that."

"Sure, yes, I know." Sarah scowled. He wasn't reading her real message. "I mean, I feel guilty about putting this on my kid. If I'm not well, or if we don't have the cash for a place as nice as this. Or God forbid that one of us is really sick and she has to be a caregiver. It's one thing to become a parent at 48 when I'm in the peak of health, but what about me at 70?" She shuddered, watching two women with walkers enter the room. "I'd never forgive myself."

"Sarah, guys have heart attacks at 39; women get breast cancer at thirty. And those people would be considered of regular old normal reproductive age. You could die tomorrow walking out in traffic."

"Lillian always said you could drown in a cup of water in the bathtub," Sarah agreed, just as her mother walked into the room on Marilyn's arm. Marilyn was dragging Lillian's huge suitcase on wheels, which Joe immediately snatched from her.

"You certainly can drown in the tub—I thought those guardrails in the bathroom in this place were stupid and would make me feel like an old lady," Lillian interjected, "but I'm thrilled to pieces to have 'em. *You* should get them at home—everyone should have them as far as I'm concerned."

Her mother wanted to smoke in the car on the way to Tarrytown, but Sarah put her foot down. Secondhand smoke worried her as much as too much salt in her food these days, and she'd started on vitamins when she gave up all over-the-counter medications. She was taking a multivitamin with folic acid, Vitamin C, and echinacea to ward off colds, and was drinking lots of water and eating plenty of fiber-rich food. She was going to give this kid a terrific environment, even before the embryo was placed inside her.

"Mom, Sarah has something to tell you," Marilyn blurted out when they were halfway toward their destination.

"Yes. What is it, dear?"

Sarah glared at her sister's back. "What are you talking about?" she asked, knowing full well that Marilyn was trying to provoke her. "You are so out of line," she added in a quiet aside to her sister. Why couldn't she have been the one to bring it up? This was so like Marilyn! Infuriating.

"Are you two girls fighting again? Is that why you haven't come to see me together? Or is it that old-age homes depress you as much as they do me?" Lillian cackled.

Sarah sighed and turned to her mother. "Mom, I really was waiting for a better moment to go into this, but hey, we're all here, trapped in this car, so it's as good a time as any." She took a breath. "I want to let you know that Joe and I are planning to have a baby." She caught Marilyn's eye in the rear-view mirror again, and she saw her sister's eyebrows raise. Obviously, she hadn't expected Sarah to come clean.

"You're adopting a baby?" Lillian gasped.

"No, actually, we're going to have one that comes right out of my body."

Her mother sank back against the seat, staring at Sarah in horror. "You! You know, you must be cracked. You have a perfectly good child, although you never see her or speak to her. What makes you think you need another one? Or is this Joe's insanity? The two of you, honestly. Why do you want this aggravation?" In annoyance, she reached into her purse for a cigarette.

"Is that what Lynnie and I were to you, aggravation?" Sarah asked, really wanting to know.

"You know me, I was never a kootchy-koo idiot about babies. Frankly, I liked you girls a lot better when you'd grown up enough to talk to me. But children are a lot of trouble. And they're worse these days with the crime and drugs and sex." Lillian fumbled with a match, her arthritic hands curled around the task. After she'd tried and failed three times, Sarah decided to yield health concerns to relationship concerns and took the matches, lighting one for her mother.

"We don't see it that way, Lil," Joe said quietly. "Sarah and I are going to be great parents, and if we can't avoid the crime and drugs and sex, well at least it will challenge us to get up off our asses and try and keep our kid safe and sound. Does that make any sense to you? That we would want to bring a person into the world who might live a happy life and do some good and maybe—if I'm not being too idealistic here—help a few other people in her lifetime."

"You really sound like Dudley Do-Right," Marilyn muttered.

"Saving the world by having a baby is bullshit," Lillian said staunchly.

"Mom, he didn't say we wanted to save the world, for God's sake," Sarah interrupted. "Just have a family. Is that so much to ask?"

"All these muggings and the streets coming apart in New York— thank God I don't live there—and the ozone layer and El Niño. I thank God that at 77 I don't have too much of this left to deal with. And even though you're my daughter, and I think you're a smart person, and I generally have a lot of respect for you, this seems half-cocked. Very irresponsible. What do you think, Lynnie?" she asked her other child.

"Well, Mom, since you ask…" Marilyn turned off the highway onto the quiet road that ran along the river. "I thought the two of them were really insane when Sarah first told me, but then I figured I shouldn't have such a closed mind, you know, so I started reading everything I could about lots of people doing this at totally outrageous ages, and every one of them was tickled pink that they'd gotten pregnant and were having a terrific time as parents. The verdict is still out, as far as I'm concerned, as to how they're going to be with teenagers when they're elderly—I mean dealing with a teen has to be hell on earth. Luckily, Joe's going to be marginally close to the kid's age when my sister is doddering."

"I resent that!" Sarah cut in.

"So my answer to you is," Marilyn continued, ignoring her, "that I haven't totally flipped over to their side, but I'm willing to be convinced—that's *if* they can do it, by the way. And it's not easy, from all accounts."

Sarah leaned forward and put her hand on her sister's shoulder. "Thanks for the partial vote of confidence," she said. She was curious that her mother hadn't asked her anything about how she was going to have a baby at 48. She probably didn't need to know.

"Oh, we're going to be successful," Joe said emphatically. "Lillian, please try not to come down so hard with a verdict against this. You know better than I do that if you tell Sarah don't do something, then she will, just to prove you wrong."

"Oh, are you ever right!" Lillian started laughing, then coughing, and Sarah had to take the cigarette out of her hand and pound her on the back to get her to stop. "There was the time she wanted to learn how to scuba dive—that was in college, wasn't it? And your father was livid, but you did it anyway. I remember some other idiot thing you did with land in Connecticut...."

"That was Marilyn, Mom, and it was Massachusetts," Sarah said between clenched teeth.

Marilyn started to whistle.

"Anyhow, you're both adults, and I can't do or say anything that will influence you, I'm sure. But *don't* ask me to babysit!" She leaned across and gave Sarah a glancing peck on the cheek.

"I sure won't, dear," Sarah said, softening a little.

Actually, she had expected Lillian to be vehemently opposed, and she was pleased to see that her mother didn't nag her about it through the party that day. Sarah found herself seated next to her mother at the dinner table, helping her to food from the heavy platters, asking her questions about her new living situation, really listening to her mother as she hadn't in years. It was evident what was going on—Sarah was making comparisons, figuring out what part of Lillian had been the generous, funny, compassionate, objective person that had helped to frame her childhood. There was a lot wrong with her mother—she was irascible and obsessive and could be positively mean and nasty at times, but she had given Sarah a lot. Something to pass on, even if it wasn't her genes.

They stayed over at Joe's mom's that night, sleeping in the double bed in Joe's childhood room, and Sarah had a doozy of a dream. She was back in high school, in Queens, but she was her own age, even though everyone else was a student. And instead of the all-girls' school she'd attended, this one was co-ed. She felt very shy around this one boy Andy, whom she'd had a crush on at 13 in real life. Of course Andy hadn't known she was alive.

As she was leaving school, someone handed her a dish of candies— pink and white M&M's. Actually, they looked just like those coated almonds that you get at Italian weddings, but these were round, like her estrogen pills, and had an *M* emblazoned on each one. She took a few and walked out into the day—but it wasn't Queens as she'd remembered it, it was Paris or Rome, someplace really foreign that she'd only visited once. No one spoke her language, it was rush hour, and she had no idea where she was. She tried asking in French where the residential area was, but the directions she got took her far away from the houses.

She found herself in a cemetery, similar to the one where they'd buried her father. But it was really crowded—people running around, kids playing ball, cars everywhere. She was desperately seeking this one grave (whose was it?) but there was a big hump in the ground that she couldn't get over, and a black car blocked her way.

She woke abruptly, as the morning sun came streaming through the window. "*'M'* for mother," she murmured to herself. And the pieces started coming together—the change in her from the way she'd been in high school—she was now all grown up, able to deal with her sexuality (that's why Andy popped up in the dream), but still feeling like a kid. The candies were supposed to be eaten at a wedding, but she was going to a funeral. Big life events all neatly packaged together, as we conveniently organize them in our dreams. The grave, though, that was a stumper. She thought about it through the day, and then, on the car ride home the following evening, she got an inkling of what it might mean. She was mourning herself as a mother—she hadn't quite gotten over the hump of seeing herself as a failure with Alison, as her own mother had suggested. But she had to give up on that and move on. She could, and would, be a mother again.

They pulled up in front of their apartment about 9 P.M., and she asked Marilyn in for coffee. Joe claimed that he was stiff from so much time in the car and was going for a walk, so the sisters could be alone. They weren't quite as easy with each other as they always had been, but the conversation was okay. Marilyn wanted lots of details about the procedure and the donor, which Sarah gratefully supplied. It helped to talk about it. Even though nothing had happened yet, even though there wasn't a glimmer of a baby inside her, she felt it coming, like a wave about to break.

Her biopsy proved normal, her endometrium in good shape, and all the blanks on her checklist had little X's and initials next to them. She felt unnaturally proud—like she'd just gotten 1600 on her SATs.

"We'll start down-regulating your donor next week" Leverton said, looking at the calendar with her. "The stimulation is scheduled for two weeks after that, and the embryo transfer should fall..." his finger zoomed over the intervening days..."about *here*. How do you feel about that?"

Sarah grinned. "Why are you asking?"

"Because I told you, you can pull out. There's nothing written in stone. Of course, once you begin the cycle, it's more complicated. So I want to give you every opportunity."

But Sarah knew. It wasn't just the dream, or telling her mother and sister. It was time. It was right.

And as the days passed, and Christmas came and went, they were told that the donor was producing lots of great big follicles. Sarah found herself so distracted it was hard to work. Forty-eight hours before the donor's aspiration, Joe went into Leverton's office to deposit a sperm sample. And the next evening, Day 16 of the cycle, Sarah watched the clock at 10 P.M. when she knew the donor would be giving herself her final injection that would trigger the release of the eggs from the follicles.

"I wish I had her phone number. I'd call her now and remind her."

"She *knows*. She's done this before, remember. Don't be a nudge." Joe shook her shoulders lightly.

"Well, I've taken every estrogen pill on time, and I start my prog-esterone the day after tomorrow. I'm holding up my end of the deal, and I wish I knew that she was, too."

"Listen, don't get like this, Sarah. You know that despite the won-derful follicles, and my wonderful sperm, and your perfect uterine lin-ing, things can fall apart. Leverton said, be optimistic, but don't get your hopes that far up."

"Yeah, sure, be a wet dishrag. I believe that this is going to happen."

Thirty-eight hours later, two hours after the aspiration, Leverton called to say that there were 13 eggs, and most of them looked great so it was time for Joe to come in and give another sample. He gave Sarah a kiss, raced for the subway, and went uptown to make his con-tribution. Twenty hours after that, they had word that seven of them had fertilized and there were two more that were really promising. Since they wanted to transfer the best three, they were going to freeze three today and leave four to divide by the next day. The transfer would be done the day after that, and the decision about which three embryos to select would be made just prior to the procedure. Joe would not be needed today, which filled him with relief. Ejaculating on demand was not the easiest (or certainly the sexiest) thing he'd ever done in his life.

Sarah didn't sleep much that night, so the Valium that Leverton gave her before the procedure made her nice and woozy. She fought it, because she wanted to be completely awake and aware.

In her gown, sitting on the edge of the examining table with Joe holding her hand, she felt like an astronaut being readied for a trip to the unknown. No, she was the spaceship—the embryos were the astronauts, voyagers to a distant land. She was in shape, prepared for whatever happened, but since she had no experience with this, it was still kind of scary. Her palms were moist, her mouth dry, and there was a large contingent of butterflies banging around in her stomach. She just hoped none of them would make their way into her uterus. She needed a completely free passage for those tiny embryos.

Leverton and Sirak came in, dressed in burgundy-colored surgical scrubs. Lani poked her head in to wish her luck and Michelle, also dressed in scrubs, came over to give Sarah a little backrub. Another nurse, a young woman she'd never met before, was helping the doctors assemble all the sterile equipment.

The door opened again and Dori, the embryologist, came in to ask how close they were. "This is the moment," Leverton said.

"Good," she responded and gave Joe the thumbs-up sign. "I'll go get the kids."

She was back in a minute with the glass tank that had once been a baby incubator. The "kids," the three fragile cell bundles, were sitting in a petri dish on a stand with a light trained on it. The embryos had now been growing in the lab for the past 72 hours.

"I'm just going to check once more to get the angle of your cervix to your uterus, Sarah," Leverton told her as she lay back and he sat on his small stool in front of her. He draped her belly and legs and flopped down the bottom panel of the table so that he could attach the stirrups. Then he tried adjusting the lamp so that he could get a better view. A large shadow blocked the way. "Joe, I know you want to be in on this, but could you give me a little room?"

Joe jumped back.

"Expectant fathers. What are you going to do?" Sarah joked.

Leverton placed a speculum inside her and used a cotton swab to wipe off her cervix. "When you get up to leave an hour from now, you may feel some fluid trickling out of your vagina. That will be the buffer solution I'm using to clean your cervix right now, not the fluid with the embryos in it."

"Thanks for telling me that. I would have panicked."

Leverton picked up an empty catheter—a cross between a straw and a piece of spaghetti—about eight inches long, thin and floppy at one end, attached to a syringe at the other. He delicately tested it out, easing it slowly and carefully inside her. "You feel anything?"

"Sort of like a tickle," she said.

"Good. Okay." He withdrew it, played with the tip a little to bend it this way and that, and came back for another trial run. "You let me know when you feel it now."

She waited for him to insert it, but nothing happened.

"Well?"

"I don't feel anything."

"Great. That's what I'd hoped you'd say." He looked over at Sirak and murmured to his associate, "You want to try for a soft touch." Then he turned back to Sarah. "The idea is that we don't want the uterus to cramp or react when the embryos go in. So if you don't feel it, we don't get a contraction. Perfect. We're ready to go." He nodded to Dori, the embryologist, that he was ready, then he took a fresh cotton swab, moistened it with buffer solution, and once again, wiped down Sarah's cervix.

But Sarah wasn't paying attention to that. She was completely wrapped up in the glass tank across the room. Dori was loading a fresh catheter. She peered through the microscope on top of the incubator, and placed her arms through the two portholes in the side of the incubator, then opened the top of the petri dish and dipped the catheter into the fluid. Then she removed it, letting in a bubble of air, then dipped it again. Carefully, holding it out in front of her, she handed it off to Dr. Leverton, steadying it between the thumb and first two fingers of each hand and turning it precisely, laterally in space.

For just a moment, Sarah's gaze shifted to Leverton's face, and instantly, she knew why she felt so sure, so right about this whole thing. As he took the catheter and turned toward her, she saw his utter reverence for life—inside that narrow tube between his fingers were three potential human beings. To drop one would be unthinkable. The room was still, hushed, as everyone watched the progress of the catheter right towards her.

"Okay, Sarah," Leverton said, easing the bent tip of the guide inside her. "This is it. Feel anything?"

"No," she sighed, wishing that she did. It seemed like there should be trumpets and bells ringing. "I'm fine," she assured him.

He sat there a minute, poised, waiting for what? For her to change her mind? It was certainly too late for that. Then he pushed down on the plunger very slowly. "Geronimo," he said. "The troops are deployed."

She imagined the three tiny passengers shooting into space on the other side of her cervix, into the hollow of her uterus. It would be dark and warm in there as they groped blindly for their target in the endometrium, a place to rest and grow.

As slowly as Leverton had introduced the catheter, he removed it, once again keeping it horizontal. He handed it back to Dori, who once again put her hands through the holes on the incubator and looked down through the microscope. She sucked up some of the fluid from the dish into the catheter, then using the plunger, she expelled it into the petri dish again. "I see one," she commented. "It must have stuck to the cervical mucus."

"That's going be the kid that gives you the most trouble," Leverton sighed. "Staying out all night, driving fast cars. Well, we can't have this," he joked as the embryologist loaded the catheter again.

The same painstaking journey; the same destination. This time, when he handed the catheter back to Dori and she flushed it, she shook her head. "It's clear."

Leverton pulled the paper drape down over Sarah's legs and pulled up the bottom flap of the table. He took her legs from the stirrups and set them flat on the table. "You just stay there for a while; we'll come get you in about an hour. That'll give the transfer fluid a chance to disperse. Joe, now you can let the circulation back into her fingers, okay?"

Sarah was suddenly aware of Joe's hand clamped down on hers, and her fingertips were about the color of vanilla ice milk. His hands were pretty clammy, too.

"You keep taking those estrogen pills and progesterone suppositories," Sirak reminded her. "And we'd like you to spend the next two days at home, on the couch. No cooking, no cleaning, no shopping, and even though you're lying down, no sex. You can go to the bathroom, take a shower, get up for meals, but we want limited movement and excitement. Maybe you could watch football?"

Sarah scoffed. "Yeah, football would be in the no-excitement category. It would put me right to sleep."

"Fine. That'll do it. Remember, no alcohol, no aspirin or any other drugs, prescription or over-the-counter. This is probably all myth and superstition, but just to be on the safe side, don't do anything that might upset the internal order. We want to give these guys the best chance they could possibly have."

"I promise, I will." Sarah was laughing and she couldn't figure out why. She felt blasted, beatific, as though she could already feel the tug of little hands and hear the peal of childish laughter.

Leverton came over and patted her back. "You've done great; now we just have to wait. In two weeks, we'll give you a blood test and see whether you're making hCG."

"Is that good or bad?" Joe asked.

"It's the pregnancy hormone, sweetie," Sarah reminded him.

"Oh, so it would be good! Incredibly good."

"You two take it easy," the doctor nodded. "See you later."

The staff filed out; Sarah and Joe were alone in the room. He bent over and kissed her lightly on the forehead. "Feel different?"

"No, not at all."

"Hungry?"

"No, why, are you?"

"I could use some pickles and ice cream right now," her husband said.

"We'll pick some up on the way home."

"How do we make it through the next two weeks?"

Sarah shrugged. "The way we always have. Hey!" she shouted, her eyes opened wide.

"What?" Joe sounded panicked. "Are you in pain? Is something wrong?"

"I could swear one of them kicked," she teased him. "Cool it, kid. I feel better than I have in weeks. Just let's take it one minute at a time."

So they did. What else could they do?

CHAPTER ELEVEN

THE PROCEDURE

Timing is everything. Although the donor and recipient may have no contact at all during their superovulation cycle, they are inextricably linked. To achieve a successful pregnancy through egg donation, the donor's ovaries must be chock full of ripe follicles containing viable eggs just when the recipient's uterus is primed, her endometrium thick and ready to receive an embryo.

THE DONOR'S PROGRESS

The donor will start by giving herself Lupron injections for two or more weeks to shut down her own cycle. This will not only be beneficial to the ovarian stimulation that will follow but will also allow her cycle to be synchronized with that of the recipient. The donor will continue with Lupron as she begins taking one of the injectables that contains FSH, just as in any other stimulated ART cycle.

The injections are tough for some women at first. Neither Lupron nor FSH can be taken orally since they are proteins and would be digested in the stomach. Each donor is given an instructional videotape as well as a personal lesson in the office with her partner who may have to give the shots.

Although Pergonal and Humegon had long been the workhorses of assisted reproduction, these medications are now being replaced by the recombinant forms of FSH. Pergonal, Humegon, and the newer medication, Repronex, are forms of human menopausal gonadotropins, and the FSH they contain is extracted from the urine of menopausal women. (Since postmenopausal women have no ovarian function that would keep the reproductive cycle going, their pituitary cranks out large quantities of FSH, which is then excreted in the urine and can be used in fertility medications.) Follistim (Organon) and Gonal-F (Serono), recently approved by the Food and Drug Administration, are genetically engineered forms of FSH, which means they are purer, more uniform physiologically, and much more potent on a gram-by-gram basis. In addition, they are easier to use since they can be given subcutaneously (under the skin) like flu or insulin shots instead of intramuscularly in the hip like the older products. Since it will be possible to mass-produce these natural proteins, just as insulin is now produced for diabetics, there is also a good possibility that the cost of these medications will fall.

The donor takes the FSH injections for an average of 10 days, coming into the office periodically for blood and ultrasound testing. If the donor lives in a different location than the recipient (as is often the case when one sister donates to another), she may get a programmed schedule that bypasses some of the early monitoring. Instead of two weeks of Lupron, she'll take it for three to four weeks with just a single blood test for confirmation that her own hormonal system has shut down. Then she can start stimulation and seven days later, fly in to begin the monitoring of her follicles.

As Lupron suppresses the donor's pituitary hormones, her estrogen, or E2 level, will drop to less than 30 picograms per milliliter before she begins her FSH—low enough to give her mood swings and hot flashes, as though she were menopausal. But as FSH is added to her regimen, her follicles will begin to grow and her E2 levels will rise exponentially. By the fifth day of stimulation, E2 is usually between 200 and 500 picograms per milliliter, and it doubles every two days or so after that. By the time the donor is ready for her final injection of hCG, E2 levels have usually skyrocketed to 2500 picograms per milliliter or higher. By contrast, in a natural ovulatory cycle, E2 levels typically fluctuate from about 40 picograms per milliliter at the time of menstruation to about 300 picograms per milliliter just prior to ovulation.

At each donor visit, the number of follicles in each ovary will be counted and measured. A pointer connected to a beam of light on the ultrasound machine delineates the dimensions of each follicle, and the amount of growth is noted daily. It's very satisfying to donor and doctor (and of course, to the recipient) to count 10 or 15 ripe follicles after 10 days of medication.

The best egg harvest comes from a continual, steady, synchronous growth of follicles in both ovaries, which means that all the eggs are about equally mature. This maximizes the possibilities for fertilization and freezing of extra embryos. On the other hand, if just one or a few follicles grow quickly and are markedly larger than all the rest by day 5, natural follicular selection may kick in and suppress the growth of the smaller follicles. When the aspiration is carried out, these smaller follicles are more likely to yield immature eggs, which tend not to fertilize and, more critically, not to become babies. Of course, in the future, as we learn how to grow immature eggs in better culture media in the laboratory, this will be less of a problem.

THE RECIPIENT'S PROGRESS

The recipient needs no uncomfortable injections or daily ultrasounds. She is the star of the show, and yet, she has little to do but sit home, take her estrogen in order to prepare her uterus, and wait for the call saying it's time for the egg retrieval. It's hard to stay calm, particularly for women who've been through the terrible disappointment of their own unsuccessful IVF cycles. They usually want a play-by-play, or day-by-day report on the donor's progress, while visions of ripe eggs dance in their heads. In the end, all you need is one, but you also want as many backups as you can possibly get.

The recipient does need medication, however. If she's still ovulating, even occasionally, she must use Lupron first to downregulate her pituitary. Otherwise, an unanticipated surge of her own hormones may throw the whole balance of the created cycle off kilter. But if she's postmenopausal, like Sarah, her ovaries are already technically "sleeping," and she can therefore start taking estrogen at any time. We give a graduated dose of oral E2 for two weeks, not to develop follicles, of course (the donor does that), but rather to build up the lining of the uterus so that it will be thick and ready to respond to the progesterone which will make the endometrium receptive to embryo implantation. Estrogen alone cannot prepare the body for pregnancy; rather, it is intended to prime the uterus enough to thicken the endometrium and induce the development of progesterone receptors.

We begin progesterone on the day that the donor's eggs are aspirated. When egg donation first started, we used to give the daily doses of progesterone via intramuscular injection, because we knew that this method of administration would give the most consistent blood levels. But after further study, we switched to vaginal suppositories so that the medication could be given right where it was needed, next to the uterus. It turned out that this method gave lower circulating levels of the hormone in the blood but higher tissue levels in the uterine lining—exactly what's necessary for the window of implantation to open at the right time.

The recipient can have her checkups at our office to be sure that her endometrium is growing nicely, or, if she lives in another state or country, her own gynecologist may be able to monitor her progress. Then, when the donor's eggs are ready for aspiration, the recipient's husband will fly in to give his sperm sample, and the recipient will start the three-day countdown to the embryo transfer.

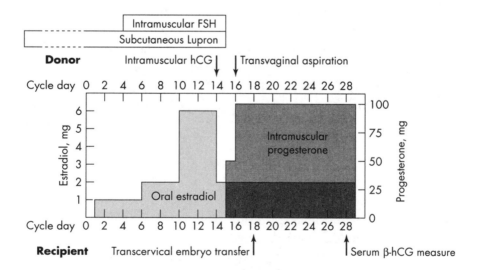

Regimens of ovarian stimulation in the donor and hormone replacement in the recipient.

RETRIEVING THE FOLLICLES

The follicle aspiration procedure is the most dramatic step of the egg donation process. It is also the most fundamental of all of the technical aspects of assisted reproduction, since it was only after doctors figured out how to get the eggs out of the follicles that they started wondering whether fertilization could take place in the laboratory.

Aspiration is a race with the clock. Eggs have to be retrieved at a fairly precise point between the time that they mature and the time that they pop out of the follicle and fall into the peritoneal cavity, from where they will quickly make their way to the fallopian tubes. If we were to allow ovulation to occur naturally, we would have to go fishing for the eggs in the pool of fluid behind the uterus, which would be a terrible job. On the other hand, if we went into the follicle before the LH surge or only a short time after it began, the egg would still be firm-ly attached to the follicle wall, and no amount of poking or sucking on the follicular fluid would convince it to come out.

But when we go into the ovary at the correct time, the egg with its attached cumulus cells will be free-floating and will flow out with the follicular fluid. We can then examine this fluid under a microscope in the laboratory and, just as though we were panning for gold, we can isolate the egg from the fluid.

The window of opportunity for aspiration is about two to six hours before the time that ovulation is scheduled to occur. So we schedule its occurrence, by having the donor give herself an injection of human chorionic gonadotropin (hCG), which acts on LH receptors in the fol-licle. Since we don't want ovulation to actually take place, (which would happen about 38 to 40 hours after the injection of hCG) we schedule aspiration 36 hours after she's had her shot, so that there will be a safe margin of error plus or minus an hour or two to suck out the follicular fluid and the free-floating eggs.

ASPIRATION BY LAPAROSCOPY

When we first started performing IVF, we aspirated follicles by laparoscopy, just as Patrick Steptoe did in the early 1970s. Before that time, the only way you could get inside the abdomen was to make a large incision. Laparoscopy was a major technological advance because it was so much less invasive and allowed the surgeon to enter the body just by making a few small holes. It became a routine procedure in the 1980s and remains a standard diagnostic tool in gynecology—the physician can see just what's going on in the pelvic cavity by peering inside and looking around.

With the patient under general anesthesia, the physician makes a tiny (half-inch) incision right at the navel and places a telescope through the opening into the abdominal cavity. The abdomen is then filled up with about a gallon of carbon dioxide, which gives the physician room to maneuver and makes it possible to visualize the pelvic organs, including the ovaries. Then a second quarter-inch incision is

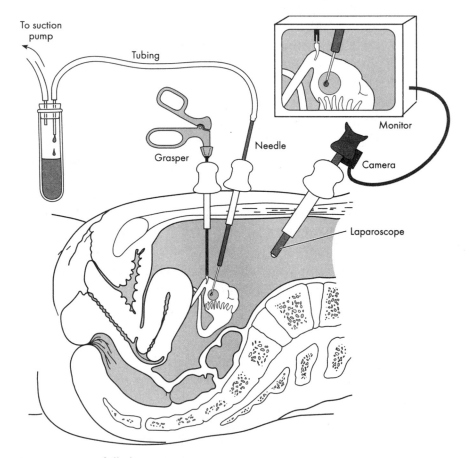

Laparoscopic follicle aspiration.

made in the midline just above the pubic bone and an instrument called a *grasper,* as thick and about twice as long as a ballpoint pen with pincers at the end, is inserted through this incision so that the doctor can hold on to the ovaries. Many gynecologic procedures, such as cyst removal or fallopian tube repair, are now performed by laparoscopy instead of by opening the abdomen. But laparoscopy is rarely used just for follicle aspiration—currently, ultrasound guidance is the preferred method. It is, however, used in certain specific situations.

In laparoscopic egg retrieval, a hollow needle connected to tubing leading to a prewarmed test tube is passed through the abdominal wall directly into each follicle. The doctor can see exactly what he's doing by looking through the telescope placed through the patient's navel. The follicular fluid is collected into the tube, a teaspoon at a time, and the test tube is rushed into the laboratory where it is kept warm until the follicular fluid could be examined under a microscope and the eggs identified. This relay continues until all of the follicles are aspirated.

After the laparoscopy, the husband provides a sperm sample, which is then taken to the laboratory where the gametes are placed together. The couple stays for a few hours in the outpatient surgery center, after which they're allowed to go home.

When it's time for the embryo transfer, the patient is brought back to the operating room. A catheter with the embryos is passed through her cervix and into the uterine cavity in a manner which has remained essentially unchanged from the early pioneer days of this procedure. Today, of course, catheters are soft and pliable, which makes the procedure easier and more comfortable.

IVF was a boon for infertile couples, and it was quickly adapted to all forms of infertility. Although initially, it was designed for women with blocked fallopian tubes, women with normal tubes could also benefit by it. So the question naturally arose, if the tubes ar normal, why not put the gametes directly into them, just as it happens in nature? This led to the development of gamete intrafallopian transfer, or GIFT, which proved to be first of many variations on the IVF theme. An additional benefit of GIFT was that the gametes could meet in the body instead of the laboratory. This made things more palatable for couples who, for religious or philosophical reasons, didn't like the idea of fertilization taking place in an incubator.

In a GIFT procedure, the egg and sperm are deposited at the mouth of the fallopian tube *prior* to fertilization. Since GIFT eliminated the need for embryo transfer, there was no need for two separate procedures—one to remove the eggs, another to return them. The eggs were whisked to the lab for just a few minutes so that they could be identified, mixed with the sperm, and loaded into the catheter, then they were returned immediately to the patient who was still on the operating table.

GIFT remains a successful ART, although it represents the ever-decreasing percentage of ART procedures performed each year. (At its peak, about 25 percent of ART was GIFT, whereas now, it's down to 5 percent.) The reason for this decline is simple—since IVF no longer requires laparoscopy, GIFT is now more traumatic and expensive than an ultrasound-guided procedure. Paradoxically, some medical insurance plans that don't cover IVF may nevertheless approve a GIFT procedure, which they consider "more natural" than IVF. To be a candidate for GIFT, a woman has to have unblocked, normal fallopian tubes and her male partner must produce sperm with normal fertilizing potential.

The only other reason for using laparoscopy with assisted reproduction is to place embryos directly into the fallopian tubes. Early investigators figured that since the embryo in a conventional pregnancy spends about five days in the tube before migrating to the uterus to implant, they might enhance the success of IVF by putting the embryos where they would be if this process had occurred naturally. So, in the 1980s, two new forms of ARTs came on the scene—zygote intrafallopian transfer (ZIFT), where the embryos were replaced in the tube after 24 hours in the lab, and tubal embryo transfer (TET), where the embryos were replaced after 48 hours. As was so often the case with first reports of new procedures, the success rates seemed better than with "conventional" IVF. However, subsequent, carefully controlled investigations confirmed that the new procedures were merely good alternatives, with success rates that were similar to other ART.

When these techniques were first designed, they required two laparoscopies, 24 or 48 hours apart. Today, as in GIFT, egg retrieval is almost always done by the ultrasound route in the doctor's office. ZIFT and TET are reserved for those cases where it would be physically difficult or impossible to transfer the embryos back through the cervix.

Transfer by the cervical route is most successful when it doesn't traumatize the uterus—if it contracts, it may expel the embryo. Some appropriate candidates for ZIFT or TET are women who were exposed to diethylstilbestrol (DES) in the womb. Their small uteri accommodate the transfer catheter easily but are so sensitive that even the thinnest and most flexible of catheters causes cramping, which may prevent implantation from occurring.

Although in the bad old days, the only one who could see what was going on during a laparoscopy was the physician peering through his laparoscope, today, everything is done with video cameras, so the view is broadcast to everyone in the operating room. The patient gets her own copy of the video to take home so that she can watch those precious embryos, traveling in a bubble of fluid, as they make their way into the depths of her fallopian tube.

ULTRASOUND-GUIDED TRANSVAGINAL ASPIRATION

Laparoscopies were really avant-garde when they appeared in the 1970s. But in the late 1980s, ultrasound technology took several leaps forward, and aspiration moved from the operating room to the doctor's office. The method of visualization of the follicles (by ultrasound rather than by laparoscopy) and the placement of the needle (through the vaginal rather than through the abdominal wall) in ultrasound-guided transvaginal aspiration are much easier on the doctor and patient, whether she's an IVF candidate or a donor.

One of the chief benefits is that aspiration is an office procedure. It is very effective in retrieving eggs, have proven to be very safe as far as complications are concerned, saves time and money, and generally causes a relatively low level of discomfort. (When the transvaginal aspiration method was first devised in Europe, no anesthesia or analgesic medications were used. The USC program uses conscious sedation, with intravenously injected sedatives and narcotics. Most U.S. programs use some combination of medications to dull the sensation of the needle.)

The follicles are aspirated through the vaginal wall with a hollow needle small enough to pass into the ovary easily yet large enough to allow free outflow of the follicular fluid and still not hurt the egg as makes its way out of its secure home in the ovary. The idea is to apply just enough suction to ensure that the follicular fluid comes out of the needle rather than leaking around the puncture site. But it has to be sufficiently gentle so that it doesn't damage the egg.

When we first started aspirating eggs this way, a syringe was simply attached to the end of the needle and the doctor would pull on the plunger as though he were drawing blood. This worked to a certain extent, but we got a lot of eggs with cracked shells (that is, a split zona pellucida). Today, we use a controlled suction pump, which produces a very steady, gentle, and constant negative pressure.

In the USC program, as in many others in the country, aspirations are scheduled for the late morning. The donor will arrive in the office

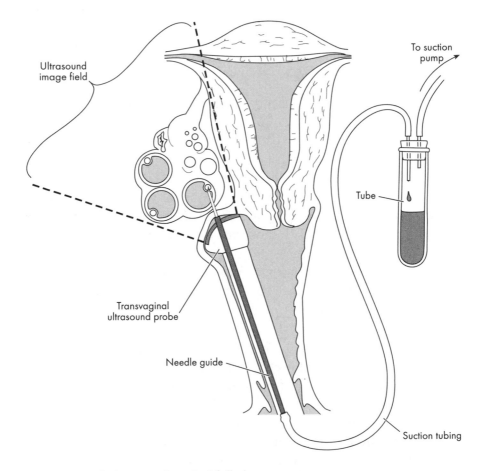

Transvaginal ultrasound-guided follicle aspiration.

an hour or so ahead of time in order to be sure she's comfortable and slightly sedated when the procedure begins. She is given a Valium and an injection of an antinausea medication, which also has a slight sedative effect. She undresses and empties her bladder. As she lies back on the table, a nurse starts an intravenous drip containing a simple saline solution. In the meanwhile, one of the examination rooms is converted to a treatment room complete with sterile drapes, antiseptic solutions, and the capped plastic test tubes that will hold the follicular fluid.

In order to minimize the risk of infection, the physicians are dressed in surgical scrubs, hair covers and masks, and sterile surgical gloves. Two tables are covered with blue sterile surgical drapes—one for the antiseptic preparation of the donor and the other for the containers that will hold the follicular fluid. The ultrasound machine is covered with a sterile plastic drape; the ultrasound probe is sheathed in a surgical Latex condom. When the equipment is ready, everyone takes their places. The nurse brings in the donor who is helped onto the examination table. That nurse will stay by her side throughout the procedure, administer medications, hold her hand, talk to her calmly, and make sure she stays comfortable. One physician focuses on the donor while the second double-checks the equipment. A laboratory technician stands by to receive the tubes when they are filled with follicular fluid.

The donor is connected to electrocardiograph electrodes, a blood pressure cuff is placed around one arm and a pulse oximeter clip is placed on one of her fingers. The pulse oximeter, which looks like a clothespin loosely attached to one of the donor's thumbs, can detect the oxygenation of the blood that flows through that finger. It tells us that the patient is not only breathing normally but also is oxygenating well, and her circulation is carrying oxygenated blood to all parts of her body.

When the donor is connected to all of the monitoring equipment, she's asked to lie back on the table and put her legs into the stirrups, which will hold them up and out of the way even if she falls asleep. A mask or nasal cannula supplies her with supplemental oxygen. The doctor talks to her calmly and quietly, explaining that he's going to begin the procedure.

Through an intravenous line, the donor is now given intermittent injections of a sedative medication that will relax her and will also potentiate the second medication, a narcotic given to block pain. As she begins to drift off into twilight sleep, the doctor places a speculum into her vaginal canal to gain access to the upper part of the vagina, where the aspirating needle will eventually be inserted. So far, the donor, who is now becoming very sleepy, has only a sensation like the one she would have if she were getting a Pap smear.

The doctor takes an antiseptic solution and carefully swabs the upper part of the vagina, especially the area behind the cervix, where the aspirating needle will be inserted. This causes pressure, which wouldn't phase the donor at any other time. But remember that her stimulated ovaries are very large and tender and on the verge of ovulating, so this swabbing can be quite uncomfortable. But her feedback gives the doctor a good idea of how well she's going to tolerate the procedure—if she complains at this point, the physician asks the nurse to inject more sedative and narcotic medication.

The swabbing is done with an iodine-based antiseptic called Betadine that dramatically decreases the number of bacteria that normally live in the vaginal canal. Unfortunately, there is some evidence that Betadine may also be toxic to embryos, so after getting it into the body, we have to get it out. We follow up the cleansing with a large quantity of saline flush. Finally, the vagina is rinsed with a small amount of buffered saline, designed to ensure that even if a small amount of fluid from the vagina should get into the aspirating needle, no harm will be done to any egg that it might come in contact with.

By now, the donor is usually asleep and resting comfortably. Her legs, lower abdomen, and vagina are now covered with sterile drapes which have a small hole directly over the vaginal opening to allow the insertion of the ultrasound probe. The doctor puts on fresh sterile gloves and inserts the transvaginal ultrasound probe.

Everything can be seen on the screen as he eases the probe right and left and up and down. The landmarks are clear—the uterus comes into view, then fades like an image in a kaleidoscope. Replacing it is the bladder, then the right and left ovaries. The doctor, who has been watching the follicles grow over the preceding week, checks them again. Each follicle appears as a large black dot about one inch in diameter on the black-and-white ultrasound screen, and a dotted line on the screen outlines the direction for the aspirating needle. Once again, the doctor talks to the donor, just to reassure himself that she's well sedated so that he can begin the procedure.

The assisting physician hands the primary physician the aspirating needle which is then inserted into the needle guide, firmly affixed to the side of the vaginal probe. The needle is connected by a foot or so of thin plastic tubing to the first of a dozen or so plastic test tubes which will collect the follicular fluid from the aspiration and then be taken to the laboratory for examination. The tubes are held in a heating block, which warms them to the physiologic temperature of 98.6° Farenheit, minimizing any possible thermal shock that the eggs might experience when they are sucked out of their warm, cozy home in the ovary.

The physician inserts the needle into the first follicle. It appears as a bright white line, moving back and forth along the dotted line previously drawn on the screen. The doctor activates the suction pump with a foot pedal, starting the process that draws the fluid into the tubing connected to the needle. As the needle moves into each follicle, one black dot at a time can be seen to decrease in size and gradually disappear on the screen. Simultaneously, amber-colored follicular fluid drips from the tubing into the prewarmed test tube in the assistant's hand. As each test tube is about half-filled, the assistant replaces it with a fresh one and hands the partially filled tube to a laboratory technician, who labels it and carries it to the laboratory. There, it is placed inside a controlled-environment chamber, which will keep it warm until the embryologist can examine the follicular fluid for the presence of an egg.

The doctor is riveted to the screen throughout the procedure, but he's also constantly in touch with the donor (if she's awake) and with the nurse attending her, to learn what her vital signs are. When he has explored both ovaries thoroughly, checking one final time to see that all of the follicles have been drained, he removes the probe. A partial report comes in from the lab. When about half the tubes have been examined and a preliminary count of eggs made. Sometimes, especially with older patients undergoing IVF with their own eggs, the yield is low, maybe only 4 or 5 eggs retrieved from 8 follicles; but with donors, the percentage and overall numbers are a lot better—maybe 14 or 16 eggs out of 18 or 20 follicles.

Then the doctor reinserts the speculum to check for any possible bleeding from a blood vessel in the vaginal wall. He swabs the donor's vagina again, this time to remove any residual blood; then he removes the speculum. He removes her legs from the stirrups and places her feet flat on the examining table. In most cases, not more than 10 or 20 minutes has elapsed from the puncture of the first follicle to the final ultrasound check.

The donor is observed for about two hours as the medications wear off. Her blood pressure and respiration are monitored—it's important to ensure that she not sleep too deeply or experience any unexpected internal bleeding. At the end of this time, she will be alert enough to be taken home to sleep some more. Although some exceptional donors return to work the afternoon after a follicle aspiration, most everyone takes the rest of the day off, and many still feel a little "hung over" the next day. Most women feel some bloating and discomfort in their ovaries, but how much of that is due to the poking and prodding and how much to the ovarian stimulation is unclear.

Because we're concerned about ovarian hyperstimulation, the donors are asked to check in with the office over the next few days. Those who become exceptionally swollen or who become nauseated are asked to come in. Feeling bloated, donors can easily underestimate how much fluid their bodies need. Over the years, we've treated several donors for dehydration by giving them a liter of intravenous saline, which cleared up the problem. It's rare that a donor has any complications, however, and most are feeling pretty good, eager to hear the news about their egg count as quickly as possible.

Sperm Meets Egg

In order to add sperm to the eggs, the spermatozoa must be separated from the sticky seminal plasma that holds them together in the ejaculate. You can do this in several ways, including simple centrifugation and a variety of more sophisticated filtration-type methods. The one that's most commonly used is the density-gradient method, which is based on the greater density of healthy sperm.

When the recipient's husband gives his sample after abstaining from sex for at least 48 hours, the specimen is taken to the laboratory, where it is first allowed to liquefy. After 10 or 15 minutes, we examine a droplet of it under the microscope to assess the approximate count and motility, which gives us an idea of how good the specimen is. Then we layer the rest of the ejaculate on top of a test tube which has been prefilled with a colloidal mixture of proteins. If you will, think of these proteins as microscopic glass beads of different densities. As the tube with the sperm specimen spins at high speeds, the densest and most normal sperm are pushed to the bottom by the centrifugal force, and the least dense, or abnormal, sperm remain on top, along with the white blood cells and other debris.

After we've spun out the specimen for about twenty minutes, we aspirate the most dense, hardy sperm at the very bottom of the centrifuge tube with a thin pipette. We take these fine candidates and mix them with fresh culture medium, then centrifuge them twice more to get them free of the colloidal proteins used in the first centrifugation. The crème de la crème of the ejaculated sperm will be used to inseminate the donor's eggs.

When couples have their original workup, of course, we ask for a sperm sample so that we'll know what we're working with. If we suspect that the sperm may have trouble with fertilization—perhaps because of low count, sluggish motility, or inability to fertilize an egg on previous tries—we ask the husband to provide an additional specimen 48 hours before the follicle aspiration. This specimen is stored in a refrigerator in a special solution called TEST-yolk buffer, which contains special salts and yolk from chicken eggs. The buffer protects the sperm from damage that can take place during cooling. We prepare this specimen at the time of aspiration the same way we did the earlier one, and the two are combined for insemination. Of course, this gives us a double batch of available sperm, but it has another advantage. There's good evidence that the shock of rewarming the sample to body temperature after refrigeration provides an additional "jolt" for reluctant sperm. They may move better and fertilize better, although they may not live as long as their unrefrigerated comrades.

By now, the aspirated eggs have been separated from the follicular fluid and given a "maturity" score, based on the appearance of the cumulus mass around the egg as seen under the microscope. After two to four hours, all but the most immature eggs are mixed with a dose of sperm in a little droplet of culture medium—and a wish and a prayer.

Everything hinges on the gametes coming together. How they find each other—by chance or design, electrical charge or chemical signaling—is unknown. Opposites attract—across a crowded petri dish, teaming with sperm, it's possible to watch under a microscope as one finds his way home.

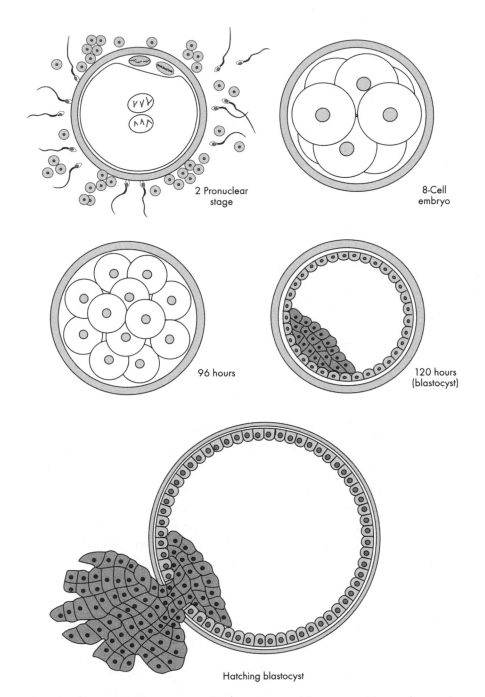

2 Pronuclear stage

8-Cell embryo

96 hours

120 hours (blastocyst)

Hatching blastocyst

Development of embro in vitro from zygote to blastocyst: (Top to bottom) Fertilized zygote, two-pronuclear stage; cleaving embryos 48 hours after follicle aspiration; advanced embryos; hatching blastocyst prior to trophoblast stage.

The little bundles of life are sustained in a culture medium that is designed to imitate the physiologic environment provided by the body in order to meet the metabolic and homeostatic needs of the gametes. Recent changes in the glucose and amino acid content of our media have allowed us to keep more embryos alive, but the basics—temperature, osmolality (the concentrations of salts in solution) and pH (the balance between acid and base)—have remained the same for years. For all of our trial and error in the many facets of assisted reproduction, at least we had that part right.

It takes about 16 to 18 hours after insemination to confirm fertilization; at this point, the one-celled zygote can be seen under the microscope with two polar bodies outside the cell membrane and two pronuclei inside the zygote. A decision is now made as to how many embryos will be cryopreserved. In general, we decide how many embryos we're going to transfer and select those plus one or two extras; the rest are frozen for future use. We cryopreserve them at the zygote stage because they are relatively resistant to the stresses of freezing, since no DNA replication has started; the genes have not even come together to form a new individual. This is important ethically as well as biochemically. At the temperature of liquid nitrogen (−196 degrees Celsius) where no biological activity can take place, the mother's and father's genes are inside the same egg shell, but the new DNA blueprint for the next generation does not yet exist. The cryopreserved zygotes are held suspended in the ethereal limbo between fertilization and the formation of a new individual—a way station in the continuous voyage of life. This means that we are not freezing "people," but only the potential for people.

Once we've frozen our batch of zygotes, we can turn our attention to the fresh ones. We keep an eye on the dividing embryos and remaining eggs, checking them every 24 hours. Even at this late stage, it's not unusual for some of the immature eggs to fertilize, so we may end up with more embryos than we expected.

About 72 hours after follicle aspiration, we place the embryos inside the recipient in a process called embryo transfer. We select the embryos that we think have the best chance at implantation—the ones that have many cells, all of which are round and regular in shape, with little to no fragmentation around the edges.

The less-than-perfect candidates, the ones that that are highly frag-mented or don't have many cells because they haven't divided quickly enough, will be watched for three more days. If these less certain embryos-in-waiting reach the blastocyst stage, they'll be cryopreserved in much the same way as their less-advanced siblings, the zygotes, and stored in liquid nitrogen to be held for a later transfer. If they die or stop dividing, they'll be discarded.

Up until a few years ago, the fertilization process would have been doomed if the recipient's husband's sperm were not up to the job. Sperm quality is nowhere near as age-dependent as egg quality is—it's just sometimes the case that a man has very few sperm, very slow sperm, badly formed sperm which can't make their way into an egg, or no sperm at all. With the great number of things that could go wrong with the little swimmers, it was often necessary to use donor sperm as well as donor eggs.

But times have changed. As long as the male partner has one living sperm, it can be removed from the ejaculate or even from the testis and injected directly into the egg. This is known as *ICSI*, or *intracytoplas-mic sperm injection.*

If a man has no sperm at all, or if he has a genetic predisposition to a disease he would not want to pass on to the next generation, he'll need a sperm donor. But if he has just a little sperm, he's in good shape. Even if a man can't ejaculate, even if he has only a tiny number of mis-shapen and bizarre-looking sperm, he can still become a father. (The incidence of fetal anomalies after ICSI is only slightly higher than the 3 percent rate observed in nature.) Just think of the sperm as a boat and the DNA inside the sperm head as the passenger. The DNA can be perfectly normal even if the boat that transports it is misshapen, can't move forward, or is unable to penetrate the outside of the egg.

ICSI brought about a tremendous revolution in the treatment of male factor infertility in the early 1990s. It was also the first time that micromanipulation was used to inject DNA into an egg and a success-ful pregnancy resulted. And this breakthrough has wider ramifications for new types of ART that are still on the drawing board. The advent of other DNA-injecting techniques involving cytoplasm donation and the movement of egg DNA from one cytoplasm to the other (see the Epilogue) could never have been dreamed of without ICSI.

PREPARING THE EGGS FOR ICSI

The aspirated oocytes are taken to the lab and trimmed of their cumulus with tiny needles, just as a quilter might snip away excess material from a fabric square. The remainder of the cumulus is dissolved with an enzyme. Once this hazy mass has been cleared away, it's possible to see the egg under the microscope. In addition, it's now possible to see the polar body, which means that this is a mature egg. The egg is sucked up with a pipette and washed twice in different culture media, then placed in a fresh drop of medium covered with a layer of sterile mineral oil to protect it from the temperature and atmosphere of the environment.

The sperm are separated from the ejaculate as was described above, except that centrifuge speeds are faster in order to increase the number of sperm we can recover. This is because we're working with specimens that have fewer sperm and more cellular debris, so we have to work harder to get them apart. Even if the sperm that's selected is sluggish and tired, it's going to be injected into the egg and won't have to move on its own.

The performance of ICSI is technically difficult, a watchmaker's nightmare of miniscule moving parts that threaten to run away once assembled. A small amount of sperm is pipetted up and placed in a viscous solution known as PVP (polyvinylpirrilodone), which slows down the fast swimmers. The egg, in a drop of culture medium covered with oil, is placed alongside the sperm drop. As the embryologist peers through the powerful microscope, she introduces the tinniest of pipettes, with a diameter only slightly larger than the sperm head itself. She carefully guides the pipette toward one sperm, sucking it in and blowing it out a few times to confuse it and slow it even further. Then she smacks the sperm tail with the pipette, immobilizing it so that she can suck it in and pick it up by the tail. She then carefully transfers it to the drop with the egg inside it and attaches the egg to another, much larger pipette. She holds the egg so that the polar body is positioned at 6 o'clock or 12 o'clock, which puts it as far away as possible from the injecting needle. This is important because the genetic material of the egg is located adjacent to the polar body. One poke with the needle could disrupt this delicate apparatus and bring the process to a grinding halt.

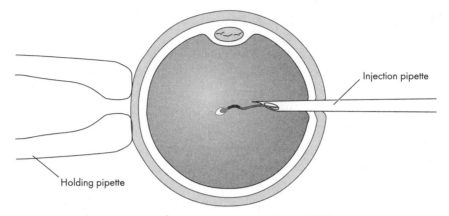

Insemination by intra-cytoplasmic sperm injection (ICSI).

The injection pipette is moved slowly in line with the egg, and is guided surely through the zona pellucida and the oolemma. The egg gives way a little, and the embryologist quickly sucks up a little cytoplasm along with the sperm in the needle. Finally, after the plunger is released, the sperm and cytoplasm are catapulted inside the egg.

In spite of this somewhat unorthodox way of arriving inside the egg, the sperm head decondenses, the sperm aster forms normally, and the remainder of fertilization and embryonic development proceeds just as it does inside the human body. This can be done with as many mature eggs as have been deemed viable for fertilization. Fertilization can be confirmed under the microscope 16 to 18 hours later by the presence of the two pronuclei inside the zygote. These little cell bundles are then kept in an incubator at human body temperature (98.6° Farenheit) for about 72 hours until it's time for the transfer back to the recipient.

EMBRYO TRANSFER

In a best-case scenario, each follicle would give us an egg, and each egg would produce a perfect embryo, but that doesn't happen very often. Typically, we get about 14 eggs from aspirating 16 or 18 follicles, and of those, 10 may fertilize. We transfer up to three embryos at one time in a donor egg situation, as long as the donor is under the age of 35.

One follicle aspiration usually leads to both a fresh and at least one frozen embryo transfer. Once-frozen embryos that have thawed seem to produce pregnancies about two-thirds as often as fresh ones, and this increases the overall success rate per egg retrieval.

The transfer is made on the third day after aspiration, the fourth day of progesterone supplementation. This is the final stretch, and for many, it's the culmination of a decade-long process of trying to have a baby. The patient is given a Valium to relax, but most women are too excited to calm down much. The extraordinarily good numbers on *donor egg* pregnancies give hope to women who have been through years of suffering, trying numerous unsuccessful IVF procedures with their own eggs. So now, as the recipient lies back on the table, her partner in attendance, she is usually more than eager to get started.

The doctor puts on his surgical scrubs and the embryologist goes into the lab to get the incubator containing the embryos that have been growing for the past 72 hours. The specially adapted incubator, originally designed for a premature baby—is wheeled into the room. Inside, instead of a baby, is a lone petri dish. The tiny embryos are suspended in buffered culture solution surrounded by an atmosphere supplemented with 5 percent carbon dioxide to be sure the pH stays at exactly 7.4—not too acid, not too alkaline.

The transfer procedure should be as gentle and painless as possible. This is not just so that the recipient can feel comfortable (which is certainly important!) but also to prevent the uterus from cramping during the procedure. This muscular organ is designed to expel rather than receive. It divests itself of menstrual blood during each monthly period and of babies when their time comes. Putting something into the uterus and having it stay there is another story. If a cramp, or contraction, occurs just after the embryos are placed in the uterine cavity, they may be expelled or moved to another part of the uterus where implantation may be less likely. So getting the uterus to relax is our ultimate goal.

The doctor cleans the outside of the recipient's cervix with a cotton swab to remove as much mucus as possible as well as the remnants of the last progesterone tablet that the patient inserted. He may use a syringe and a thin tube to suck up some of the excess. It's important to have an unblocked entryway—if there's a gob of sticky mucus, an embryo might cling to it and never make its way inside.

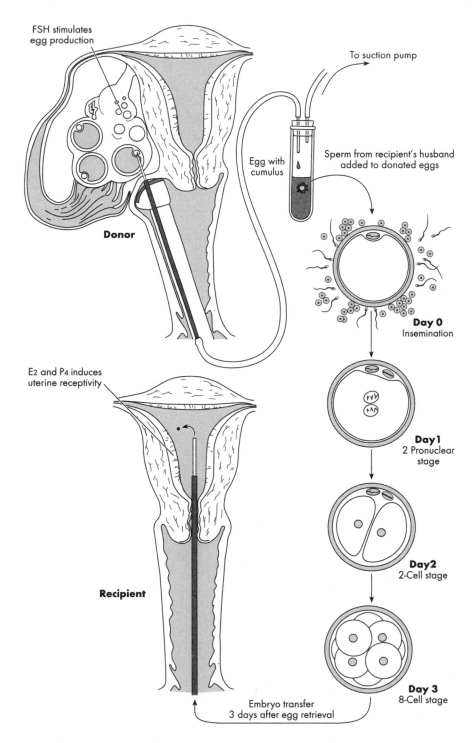

FSH stimulates
egg production

To suction pump

Egg with
cumulus

Sperm from recipient's husband
added to donated eggs

Donor

Day 0
Insemination

E2 and P4 induces
uterine receptivity

Day1
2 Pronuclear
stage

Day2
2-Cell stage

Recipient

Day 3
8-Cell stage

Embryo transfer
3 days after egg retrieval

Egg donation and embryo transfer—participation of donor and recipient.

When he's got a clear view, he tests the angle of the recipient's uterus by passing an empty, soft catheter through the cervix and into the uterine cavity. He has already had a trial run at this—probably during the endometrial biopsy or during the practice cycle—but it's important to double-check to be sure that the angle and configuration of the entry to the cervix haven't changed. Each woman is shaped differently—some have a straight passage from the cervix into the uterus, others are tilted backward. By removing the flexible catheter and bending the tip slightly, the physician can make the passage much easier. His goal is that the uterus not react at all, so he wants the recipient to feel nothing when the embryos are introduced. He has to use a soft touch with complete accuracy—it's like threading a very fine needle.

When the embryologist is satisfied that the transfer will go smoothly, she preloads a fresh catheter with 15 microliters of the culture medium that surrounds and covers the embryos in the petri dish. She lifts the catheter from the solution to let in a little bubble of air. At last, looking through the microscope, she carefully sucks each tiny embryo into the catheter and hands it off to the doctor, who then inserts it into the recipient.

As slowly as the doctor introduced the flexible tube, he withdraws it, and once again hands it off with complete precision to the embryologist. She opens the window ports on the incubator and looks

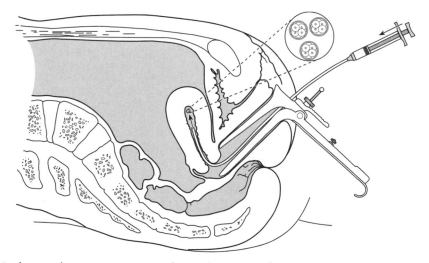

Catheter placement in uterus for embryo transfer.

through the microscope on top. Dipping the tip into the fluid of the petri dish, she sucks a little into the catheter, then flushes it out. If by any chance, one of the embryos has clung to the tip, it will be washed back into the dish. She can then load the catheter again and the doctor will repeat the process, after which another check will take place. These embryos are hard-won; each tiny cell bundle might be the one that implants, so none can be wasted.

When the last check is done, the doctor drapes the patient and pulls up the bottom of the table. He asks her to bend her knees and sets her feet flat on the surface. She will stay in this position for an hour or so to give the transfer fluid a chance to disperse and the embryos a chance to settle in the uterus. They will be held in place by the surface tension between the zona pellucida of each embryo and the small volume of uterine secretions filling the uterine cavity—very powerful forces, considering these microscopic sizes and distances.

The recipient is given instructions to continue taking her estrogen pills and progesterone suppositories until advised to stop, to abstain

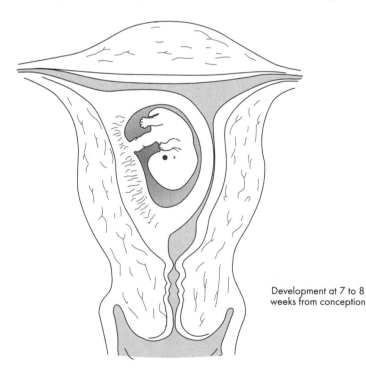

Development at 7 to 8 weeks from conception

Beginning of pregnancy.

from sex until her pregnancy test, and to take no alcohol, aspirin, or other drugs, prescription or over-the-counter. This is such a dangerous time for the tiny lives inside her; they must not be disturbed.

The transfer is not the endpoint of conception. Within two weeks, the patient will return for a blood test to check for the presence of hCG, the pregnancy hormone. If it's a go, there will be more blood tests and regular ultrasounds. As the tiny organism grows, it's possible to see weekly progress—first the gestational sac, then a yolk sac within it, and after four weeks, a fetus with a beating heart.

Of three embryos transferred, the chances are excellent that one or two will make it. The happy recipient will continue taking estrogen and progesterone throughout the first trimester of her pregnancy, and then her own body will kick in and make all the necessary hormones to sustain a baby throughout the next six months.

Now that the pregnancy is launched, no other technological assistance is needed. What was only a dream takes form as flesh and blood and intellect and emotion—a person.

CHAPTER TWELVE

LIFE HAPPENS

Joe took care of her for the next two days like she was a new young plant about to sprout. He brought her her favorite foods, kept up a never-ending stream of juice and bottles of Evian water, rented her videos, played Thelonius Monk CDs for her, and got her a stack of new thrillers to keep her distracted.

"I'm so antsy! I want to go running," Sarah complained, "but I'm afraid to pee. Suppose they leak out."

"The doctors said that couldn't happen. Please relax."

But relaxation was out of the question. Sarah tried breathing exercises, she tried her tai chi meditation and imagined the embryos implanting. None of it worked. When she went back to the office on Wednesday afternoon to catch up on some paperwork, she was in a really terrible mood. The next few days—half-days at the doctor's request—were one hassle after another. Though her assistant, Cecilia, knew enough to keep the worst problems away from her, there were certain things that only Sarah could deal with.

"Sarah, there's a call on line one for you—something about the paper stock for those inserts we're folding into the paper next Sunday—you want to take it?" Cecilia held the portable phone away from her like it was a snakehead.

"Not on your life."

"And the client on the car account wants to see another story-board—and did you promise him a video?"

"Oh, Ceel, I don't know. I think." She was tired and washed out, and when she went out for lunch with her boss the following Monday, she couldn't eat a thing. Her mind raced with possibilities, from losing her job to having a terrible pregnancy, to not getting pregnant at all and having to try another cycle with frozen embryos. And how was all this going to affect her and Joe? She had had a child once, and that had probably satisfied her need to leave some genetic heritage here on earth. Now she wanted a family, a real threesome. But that was such a tenuous goal—how did you create that? It wasn't like getting a couple of gametes to meet in the laboratory. It was more like going on a blind date assuming that eventually it would lead to marriage. A total crap-shoot, all chance, impossible to plan.

The day of her hCG test was cold and clear, a sharp January morning. The office seemed incredibly busy that day—they had to wait about twenty minutes before Sarah could have her blood drawn.

They sat in the waiting room and eavesdropped. There was one young couple—probably using their own eggs, Sarah surmised—about to start another cycle. They had already had four fresh embryos transferred, and then, when those didn't take, four frozen ones. Nothing. There was a pair of sisters, one probably in her late thirties, another in her early forties, chatting about gardening. The younger was going to donate to the older. They haven't started the process yet, Sarah thought, otherwise they wouldn't give a damn about bonsai pruning. But maybe that wasn't true—maybe it was only she who was obsessed, and the rest of the world was sane.

"Mr. and Mrs. Girard?" They were called up to the front and they went in as they had so many times before. Sarah took her accustomed seat in the phlebotomy chair and extended her arm. She didn't even feel the needle anymore, and the bruising on her inner arm from the previous blood draws had almost disappeared in the nine days since the embryo transfer.

Dr. Leverton was darting from one examining room to the next when he saw Sarah in the chair. "There you are! Are you feeling any different? Any breast tenderness? Nausea? I have great hopes for this pregnancy test."

Sarah shrugged. "I'm a little tired, but nothing else, really."

"Well, good luck. My fingers are crossed." Then he disappeared behind one of the examining room doors.

The test results wouldn't be back until three, so they went to their respective offices—more to have somewhere to go than to do any work. Who could concentrate? Sarah wandered over to Joe's office 2:30 and they got on two extensions before calling Michelle.

"It's Sarah Girard," she said, her voice cracking.

"Well, hi!" Michelle said. There was a short pause. Then, "Mrs. Girard, you did it."

"What!?" Joe barked. "We're pregnant?"

Sarah swallowed, then tried to say something and couldn't.

"Your test is positive," Michelle went on, "so congratulations! But it's a little on the low side. We'd like to see your hCG around 20 or more, but it's only 7."

"What does that mean?" Sarah didn't know whether to be delirious or nervous, so she was both.

"Well, sometimes low values mean that the pregnancy may be miscarried. But the most important thing is that it's positive. Could you come back in two days and try again?"

Forty-eight hours later, the blood test reading was 20, and then, two days after that, it was 40. Leverton didn't try to pull any punches. "It's positive. It's not excitingly positive, but there's clearly an implantation. It's just too early to tell whether it's going to turn into a baby. We'll just keep looking at the tests—and you keep taking your progesterone."

By the middle of the next week, the hormone level had risen to 150. Leverton told them that there was no point in doing any more blood tests. "It's rising—you should be happy about that. But we can't be sure of anything until the ultrasound."

"This is the weirdest thing," Joe said. "Like the those embryos haven't made up their mind that they're staying."

Sarah was alternately teary and practical, not wanting to fool herself. She threw herself into work, made plans to take Lillian to Puerto Rico in April, talked to her tai chi teacher about training for a competition in the summer. She wasn't sleeping well, and could barely keep any food down, which she attributed to worry. But then one morning, when she threw up before breakfast, she wondered if by any chance she really was pregnant. She called Leverton and he kind of shrugged over the phone, unwilling to commit himself.

"Just hold your horses—you're at four weeks and five days today, since we count the gestational age of the pregnancy from the date of the egg retrieval—that would have been the date of ovulation in a natural pregnancy. Now we won't see anything on the ultrasound until you're five to six weeks. In the meantime, get yourself some dry crackers and ginger tea," was his rather cut-and-dried solution.

But the ultrasound, too, was inconclusive. They did see a gestational sac, but it was small and hard to find. They couldn't see anything inside it, even though Leverton stared at the screen for so long, he seemed to be hypnotized by it. After an interminable silence, he said, "This is a good sign. We know the pregnancy is in the uterus and not in the fallopian tubes. But I think we can rule out triplets." He explained that some gestations happen more slowly than others, and the visible detection of landmarks on the monitor was not the only criterion. The hCG that afternoon was 2256, and Sarah noted it in her date book. Joe played 22, 56, and Sarah's birthdate, 13, on the Pick-3 on the way home.

Sarah felt miserable, but she didn't let on. Feeling sorry for herself wouldn't help anyone. After all, they had five perfectly good frozen embryos, and they could try again with those. And go through this hell all over again. Her whole body ached; her breasts were sore—which might have been a good sign, but how could she be sure? Before she came in for the next ultrasound at seven weeks, she threw up again, trying to rid herself of hope. She and Joe were pros now, coming in early, having the blood drawn, sitting in the exam room half undressed. Sirak came in to take care of them today, which made Sarah think that Leverton had given up on her.

The doctor turned on the ultrasound and inserted the probe. He turned it to the right, then to the left. Then he cleared his throat.

"Will you just look at that!" he exclaimed. He pointed, but he didn't really have to. There, on the monitor, was a big black spot. Inside it was a white ring. It was there, it was real—no question about it. Sirak pointed to a white dot that was flickering next to the white ring. "Yes, absolutely. We have a fetal heartbeat," he said. "Congratulations, you two."

Sarah was laughing, and Joe was hopping from foot to foot in front of the ultrasound screen as though he were watching the last two minutes of the Superbowl. By the time Leverton came in to confirm the pregnancy, they had switched from laughter to tears.

The white dot kept coming in and out of focus as Sarah breathed, moved, laughed, and cried. But each time it reappeared, they could see that unmistakable, persistent, regular flicker. Leverton stared at the monitor, smiling. "You did it—we can all be proud of ourselves." They could sense his joy, tempered with a kind of cautious hesitation. He put up his finger to the side of his eye, the sure sign that he was really concentrating.

"This is a high-risk pregnancy, you understand. We're not out of the woods yet—you could still miscarry," he warned. "Although the chance is substantially smaller now that we have a heartbeat. I want you to be really careful and good to yourself. Promise?"

They nodded dumbly, still trying to make sense of the news. And it was strange, walking out of the office and down Broadway, understanding that they had achieved what they had so desperately yearned for. That night they held each other close, reminiscing about when they first met, and what had attracted them to each other. "I liked the fact, like Marilyn said, that you won't take no for an answer," Joe said. "I don't know anyone else who could insist that her body do the impossible—like run a marathon, or get an embryo to implant."

In two weeks, Sarah felt too rotten to walk around the block, let alone go running. She was nauseated almost all the time. But the ultrasound showed that the baby (the *baby*!) had grown to more than an inch in length and had a recognizable head, body, even little bumps where the limbs would be. She decided to call Marilyn.

They got through a long discussion about Lillian and the impending trip, and finally, Sarah got up the courage to tell her.

"I'm having a baby, Lynnie," she blurted out.

"Really?"

"Absolutely. Halloween, or thereabouts, is my due date."

"I think that's appropriate." There was a long pause, and Sarah bit her tongue trying to keep from demanding a reaction. "Hey, I wish you all the luck in the world. I think, as a matter of fact, that this is kind of neat. I never really got to be an aunt the last time, and it doesn't look like I'm destined to be a mom, so maybe I'll have fun with this baby."

"Thank you," she said to her sister. "I needed to hear that. Would you help me tell Lillian?"

"Hey, what are sisters for? And what about Alison?"

Sarah had been thinking hard about that one. "I'll tell her myself, but not right away."

Her older brothers, Steve and A.J., with whom she had warm but not terribly intimate relationships, reacted predictably. They were both a little embarrassed, and were certainly not up for hearing any of the gory details, but they told her they were behind her, 100 percent. Both Lolly, her former shrink, and her gynecologist, Susan, who had tried to help her get pregnant years ago, were thrilled. Frankly, Sarah thought they were both having some vicarious reaction to a 48-year-old actually doing this thing, but she didn't much care why they were happy for her, just that they were.

They did have a few scares. Sarah started bleeding early in the third month, and Leverton sent her back to bed for a week. If she had to stay there for the whole pregnancy, she decided, she would do it. She had her laptop and a fax machine and a phone, and she'd work it out. When she called to ask her boss permission, she got a very cold shoulder, and Sarah was all set to get a lawyer when the woman demanded whether she would be back after her maternity leave. But it turned out to be a moot point, because the bleeding tapered off and she was given the okay to return to the office.

She got a few strange looks as she started growing larger by the day, but her accounts were doing so well, no one dared to say boo. One woman in another department asked how old she was, and she had the oddest reaction—it was like when she was in college and got carded for the first time in a bar. For a second, she was tempted to lie and say that she was 38 instead of 48, but she stopped herself in time. "I'm old enough to know what I'm doing," she said simply, giving the woman a radiant smile. And that was the end of it.

Her mother was the toughest nut to crack. Lolly had always said that Lillian was a total baby and needed everyone to rally around her, which meant that loving a real baby was out of the question. And true to form, Lillian didn't want to talk about it. It was as if the pregnancy wasn't happening at all. Sarah hadn't expected a great deal of enthusiasm, but she was kind of disappointed in her mother's nonreaction.

But Joe's mom, Nancy, and all the Girard crew made up for it. They threw her a shower in her fourth month, right after the amniocentesis that showed they were having a healthy baby girl. Joe's youngest cousin, Chloe, one of the Virginia Girards who had three kids of her own, came up and put her arm around Sarah.

"You know, Joe and I used to spend summers together when we were kids, and I have a very special feeling for him. You and I haven't had the chance to get to know each other well because we live so far away, but I hope you'll take this in the right spirit, not that I'm out of line or anything. Well, I'd like to be your baby's godmother, and if anything ever happened to you and Joe, I'd be there. Okay? I've got these three of my own, and I can tell you how precious they are, and it's important to know you have family that can be a support if you need it. God willing, you'll never need it! So you two just think about it, all right?"

Sarah had tears in her eyes as she embraced the other woman. So this was what family was all about. Making another person a priority, even though you weren't bosom buddies and didn't live that close. Giving of yourself because you could. She nodded her acceptance.

But it made her think more about Alison. Why was she so hesitant? What was she looking for? She didn't really expect that her daughter was going to hop on a plane and race to her side. Or that this baby would heal the wounds that had kept them apart for years. She wanted her approval, sure, but she told herself to grow up. Never would she beg for scraps. And when she told her—and she was going to tell her soon—she would simply be reporting the news. There wouldn't be anything emotional handed out or demanded back.

In her fifth month, when she was gigantic, she and Joe called the lawyer and accountant and made appointments to make new wills and living wills, and to set up a trust fund. They arranged for Chloe and her husband to be their daughter's legal guardians. They took out a medium-sized box in their bank's vault, and deposited all their new papers inside it. Just like grownups, Joe said. Not marriage, nor buying the co-op had ever made them get so organized. But Claire, as they had chosen to name their daughter, helped them to put all the pieces together.

In their sixth month, they started thinking about redecorating. They had to carve out a space for the new inhabitant of the apartment, but didn't want to go overboard tearing things apart in the loft. They decided to take down the hammock temporarily and use the area that had been designated as the office for a nursery.

Sarah was just coming back from picking up the wallpaper samples and some fabric for curtains when she heard the phone ringing. She felt so clumsy these days, especially when she'd been walking a lot and her big feet were particularly swollen. But she couldn't make it inside the apartment by the fourth ring, and she grunted in disgust as she let her packages fall to the floor. She was about to Star-69 it when the phone started ringing again.

"Hello," she gasped.

"Hi, Mom."

There was a moment when she thought it was a wrong number, but that deep throaty voice could only belong to one person. "Alison?"

"Hi. You sound out of breath."

"You sound ... my goodness it's nice to hear from you." She sank down into the chair beside the phone table, fanning herself lightly with a magazine that was sitting there. She was having a hot flash because her daughter had called.

"It's so early here, the sun's not really up. I helped out in a bad fire last night—haven't been to bed yet."

"Are you okay?"

"Hey, me? I'm made of asbestos, remember?"

"Good, you stay that way." She was itching to say it, desperate to tell her and completely frightened. Maybe it was that talking to Alison reminded her of all the mistakes she had made as a parent. And undoubtedly, despite her experience and her good intentions and having Joe along for the ride this time, she would make more.

"Yeah, I'll be fine. Hey, Mom?"

"What?"

"Marilyn says you're pregnant. You should have called." There was no regret in her voice, just slight surprise that she hadn't been included.

"I know I should have. I've told myself every single day that I was going to do it, and then, well, as you see, I'm a coward when it comes to you."

"I haven't been the greatest daughter—I've known for two months, but maybe I was just a little jealous. And holding on to see if you'd make the first move."

Sarah laughed. "The two of us; we're like each other that way—too stubborn to bend, too pigheaded to back down."

"But not stupid. You gave me some real smarts, Mom. I have to hand it to you. And if you want this baby—well, that's dumb, obviously, you're really gung-ho on this baby—I want you to have the best one ever."

"Oh, Alison, it means so much to hear you say that." Sarah was beyond tears, just savoring the sound of her daughter's words.

"Yeah, so do you know what flavor you're getting?"

"It's a girl. We're calling her Claire."

"Um-hmm."

Sarah thought she sounded unimpressed. True, Alison had made the call, but she wasn't making it in the spirit of reconciliation or recognition of Sarah's choice or anything like that. No matter—she could live with it.

"So look, if you guys are ever out here, come on over, ah, I guess after the baby's born. I just hope it won't give Jason any ideas. You know he actually asked me if I'd ever reconsider not wanting to have a baby. I said, no way, but if he brings it up again, can I have him call you so you can tell him what I'm all about?"

"Absolutely." She would do whatever her daughter wanted. There was a connection here, albeit a tenuous one. "Alison, I'd love to come see you."

"That'll be good. Talk to you later, Mom."

And then she was gone. Sarah was left feeling strange, just the way she had when she'd tried to insist on Alison going to college after high school and not getting a job first. She had a feeling that once out of academia, this kid would never go back. And she was right. They'd argued a little about it from time to time, but Alison was so happy doing what she liked, and wasn't that interested in money, so what was a mother to do?

The hardest part about having children, Lolly had once told her, is that when we first get them, we have to hold them so close that they can't be touched by danger. And then, when they're ready to leave, we have to open our arms and let them fly. If we do that, they'll always be able to come back when they want to. Not when we want them to.

The baby was growing so fast, and Sarah's blood pressure was elevated, so the obstetrician decided to induce her at 38 weeks, two weeks shy of her due date. But after prostaglandin injections and eight hours on Pitocin, her cervix wasn't even dilated enough to get an instrument through to break her waters. So they decided on a caesarean.

"It's better this way, sweetheart," Joe said as they prepped her for the operating room.

"Better for who? All that recovery, and what about my bikini line?" Sarah grumbled about it, but she wasn't surprised. Leverton had told her that most women over 45 who had babies didn't deliver them vaginally.

She didn't want to be out completely, so they gave her an epidural and some drugs to relax her, and when her tawny-headed daughter was lifted out of her, she was awake and aware enough to mumble a small prayer to the universe for making this extraordinary event happen.

She watched her husband take their daughter in his arms, and waves of love for both of them swept through her. Of course it was too soon to say, but to her eyes, they looked so much alike, except for their coloring. Sarah watched Joe's rapt attention on their child. He had lost that unfocussed look he sometimes had, as though Claire's birth had shocked him out of the banalities of life into what was really important.

In a month, she was taking Claire for long walks along the West Side piers in the afternoons. Kids were rollerblading, messengers zooming past on bicycles, and New York had never been so lovely. Every day she would stop at a sidewalk cafe and buy herself an Orangina, watching life happen. People would always comment on Claire—on her lovely smile, her startling brown eyes, her golden curls.

One day, an elderly woman pushing a shopping cart stopped and threw her head back and laughed at Sarah. "I don't believe it," she said.

"Don't believe what?"

"You are too young to be a grandma," she said decisively.

"You're so right," Sarah smiled.

"So this is not your grandbaby?"

"No she most certainly is not."

"Well, bless me. And bless you. May your tribe increase, and may you have many more." The old woman kept walking.

Sarah stared after her, wondering briefly what it would be like when she was this lady's age, and Claire was a young woman. The world would be different, and the people in it much more tolerant of choice and change. It might even be mainstream to wait to have babies until you were in your late fifties. Maybe people would see the wisdom in waiting to bear children until you'd lived long enough to know their worth. So many possibilities lay on the horizon.

When her daughter was 13 and starting puberty and she was 61 and collecting social security (if that still existed), they'd have a big party to celebrate the fact that they both belonged to the sisterhood that makes new life appear. And one day, Sarah hoped, she would be a grandma, so she could see what happened with the next generation.

If she lived to be 100, maybe she'd have some answers. And maybe she wouldn't. Things had worked out well up to now; she had to assume they'd continue to do so through her lifetime, and her daughter's, and all the generations that flowed from them.

CHAPTER THIRTEEN

THE ETHICAL CONUNDRUM

In a perfect world, we would all know right from wrong. You would champion the causes that made my heart beat faster; you would abhor and revile any person, place, or idea that I felt strongly against. Good and evil would be obvious, even to tiny children. The solutions to any moral or ethical problems would be acceptable to all, and there would be no dissenters.

As a group, we acknowledge that certain things are wrong. In our society, no one applauds cannibalism, nor do they countenance incest, necrophilia, or serial murder. But what about good things? Is charity good, or does it make people dependent on the government? Is public education good, or does it ignore ethnic and cultural differences that may be beneficial to a child's well-being? The subtleties and vagaries of human endeavor distinguish us from other species. Just when you come up with a bright idea to revolutionize society—bingo—somebody tells you that it will hurt as many individuals as it helps, that it will sabotage what really works in our existing system, that it's downright dangerous to the further development of the planet.

That, of course, is the current situation with reproductive endocrinology. What used to be a completely personal choice—having a baby—has been extended to the community at large, and what the

233

individual desires is often in conflict with what the group wants.

It seems impossible, therefore, to achieve a consensus about any of the following issues:

- how best to protect the welfare of the unborn child
- how best to protect the donor from possible coercion or exploitation
- how to reconcile the fact that recipients tend to be rich and donors tend to be poor, which makes high-tech baby-making an upper-class activity
- the fact that having a child using any IVF technique is not "natural," and having babies after menopause using a third-party donor is even less so
- what to do with frozen embryos that no one wants
- whether it should be legal to test embryos prior to implantation with the intention of discarding them if they have chromosomal abnormalities
- why vast sums of money and scientific resources should be spent on creating children when the world is already overpopulated and there are so many orphans who might be adopted
- whether intergenerational gamete donation is harmful to the family structure
- whether posthumous reproduction, using the eggs or sperm of deceased family members to carry on a line, is unethical
- who is the final arbiter on fit parents? on fit doctors?
- how to set the limits of selective baby-making. If in the future, we can eliminate certain undesirable traits with genetic engineering, if we can pick the gender and skills and personality of our children, what will we be erasing from the human race? And who is to say what is undesirable?
- where do we go from here?

This is a viper's nest of problems to which there are no easy solutions. But in order to start sorting feelings from thoughts; in order to make clear-headed sense of the conundrums that face us in reproductive medicine, we have delegated experts known as ethicists. If we can hear their various opinions with open minds, it may help us to settle our own consciences. Or maybe just start us thinking along lines we haven't yet considered.

What Is an Ethicist?

We may say that the concept of "morality" deals with personal conduct—it is some type of behavior that can be judged good or evil in terms of certain principles deemed right or wrong by society. "Ethics" takes those principles and attempts to make them into a discipline, a standard of behavior by which we can all judge ourselves and the world we live in. The Greeks, by the way, didn't separate ethics from aesthetics—so that everything right or good was also a thing of beauty.

The more specialized field of bioethics arose in the 1960s, when science and medicine had made stellar leaps ahead, but society had not yet caught up. Organ donation, psychosurgery, screening individuals for inherited diseases, and the whole field of death and dying needed some arbiters, and so an interdisciplinary band of experts from the fields of theology, law, medicine, nursing, philosophy, psychiatry, and sociology set to work.

Van Rensselaer Potter, Hillsdale Professor of Oncology, Emeritus, at the University of Wisconsin, invented the concept of "bioethics." He felt that biology imposed obligations on humans—that the "continued degradation of the planet and the international population explosion that contributes to it are matters that concern every scientist." His assertion that human values were intimately connected to the realm of science gave researchers pause. If the human species was to survive in what Potter termed "a civil society," investigators would have to examine their actions and understand that science can no longer function in a vacuum—it had to concern itself with long-term human survival. That meant that there had to be a dialogue between science and religion, and a healthy balance between growing technological achievement and making the world a better place to live in.

But Potter had only scratched away a bit of the thin veneer that overlays most bioethical problems. The question changed and deepened as it became evident that humans may count for less and less as technology grows unchecked. When science wants to take over, who puts on the brakes?

So the next wave of interest in bioethics came during the Kennedy administration, when Sergeant Shriver got together with Dr. Andre E. Hellegers, an obstetrician with an interest in protecting the rights of the children he brought into the world. Collaborating with Eunice

Kennedy, they set up Georgetown University's Kennedy Institute for the Study of Biomedical Ethics in the early 1970s in order to improve treatment of the mentally retarded and to discuss population issues. In recent years, their work has included discussion of fetal tissue transplantation and the rights of preembryos.

Over the last two decades, no less than 278 worldwide organizations have emerged that are devoted to the study of bioethics. Ethicists are hanging out shingles right around the corner from clinics and laboratories. Who are these high-minded individuals, these pundits who like to tell us what's right and wrong? They come from many walks of life—they are to be found in hospitals, universities, and humanistic think tanks. They are the philosophers of our day, and they are also educators, taking apart the complex issues that confront us all and explaining them so that they can be digested and considered logically. Most important, they are supposed to be highly practical, responsible people—they want to come up with clear-headed ways out of the fog of media and personal opinion that generally obscures the truth.

Ethicists try to come up with the rational choice. The intention of most bioethical centers is to develop a certification process for people who go into the field. Whether they be doctors, lawyers, or shamans, they should be able to make rational recommendations based on a set of common principles that would be free of emotion or bias.

Why should we listen to ethicists? Can't we make up our own minds about crucial issues that touch the deepest core of human endeavor? Surely everyone reading this book has his or her own ideas about where we draw the line when it comes to generating new life. Certainly, each instance is so specific as to bring up a myriad of "what if's." And that's where standardization of policy becomes both a blessing and a curse.

Because advanced technology lies on such a slippery slope, we are in peril of falling over the edge. How far do we go with human experimentation? with assisted suicide? with cloning? These problems may test ethical standards, but they don't break any laws. So how do we regulate these decisions? If you violate a law, you've hurt society and you get in trouble and have to pay for it. Now here we come to the hardest question: What is it that would so disrupt ethical standards that a law might be necessary?

Every hospital has an ethics committee, so that life-and-death issues can be discussed in an open forum. Most controversial or experimental procedures must go through this committee, which will decide whether or not it should be carried out. And yet the power of these committees ranges widely. In addition, particular state or local laws may supercede the guidelines established by hospitals. So in many instances, doctors are flying blind when it comes to the type of medicine they might practice. This speaks to the need to get ethicists increasingly involved in the day-to-day working of programs similar to ours at USC. It is essential to have a path to follow at the beginning, so we can't get lost along the way.

ESTABLISHED GUIDELINES HELP US TO MAKE CHOICES

The Ethics Committee of the American Society for Reproductive Medicine (ASRM), has established guidelines to protect the rights of all involved in the new world of high-tech reproduction. This rotating group of 10 individuals from all over the country, representing the fields of obstetrics and gynecology, reproductive endocrinology, law, political science, and ethics has set down guidelines for all practitioners to follow. The most salient of the recent recommendations are:

- Cryopreservation of embryos: Each couple must set down in writing their wishes about the disposition of extra embryos produced during IVF or ovum donor cycles. The committee considers the embryos abandoned when no decision is made about their disposition if more than five years have passed since the doctor has had contact with the couple.
- Oocyte donation to postmenopausal women: Although the committee discourages pregnancy in women past natural reproductive age because of possible medical hazards to an older woman, they point out that women generally live longer than men, who are never prohibited from fathering children at any age. They recommend that doctors and patients decide if this is appropriate on a case-by-case basis.
- Embryo splitting for infertility treatment: The practice of dividing an embryo and saving one-half of it for a future pregnancy comes as close to cloning as any that currently exists, and it opens the door to possible abuses of technology. When more than one child can be born with identical genomes, the integrity of personal

identity is at stake. The committee has urged caution with this practice, although it did not recommend that it never be used.

- The use of fetal oocytes in assisted reproduction: The committee came out against this practice, as have most religious and governmental groups, because it involves collecting fetal eggs from newly aborted or miscarried fetuses. It is obviously not possible to get informed consent from clusters of cells that are only potential children, and the dangers of creating fetuses specifically for this purpose complicate things even further.

- Posthumous reproduction: This practice would only be used between partners, when one was suffering from a life-threatening disease. If sperm was collected from a partner who was about to undergo chemotherapy or radiation, gametes could be stored until after his or her death. This way any child that resulted from mixing these gametes with the living partner's would be genetically linked to both parents.

Clearly, this is not a complete list. New, thorny problems arise daily, and professional committees meet infrequently and agree on issues even less frequently. So physicians are left with a lot of autonomy and case-by-case head-scratching. It is incumbent on every reproductive endocrinologist to consult the opinions of ethicists who can be objective, as they are not involved with patients the way physicians and therapists tend to be.

PROCREATIVE LIBERTY

In America, we are told that life, liberty, and the pursuit of happiness are gifts we are given at birth. And although there is no provision in the U.S. constitution related to giving life, procreative liberty is assumed to be a fundamental human right. Since the Supreme Court has granted protection for the right not to procreate (using contraception or abortion), it is a given that the U.S. government legally stands behind the ability of each individual to bring forth new life.

In our country, we cannot sterilize a criminal or mentally troubled person, no matter how severely challenged he or she might be, and we can't prevent anyone who chooses to use contraception or have an abortion from doing so. This means that we tacitly approve of people taking charge of their own reproductive future.

John Robertson, professor of law at the University of Austin, states that for most individuals, "reproduction—and the parenting that usually accompanies it—is a central part of their life plan, and the most satisfying and meaningful experience they have. It also has primary importance as an expression of a couple's love or unity. Its denial— through infertility or governmental restriction—is experienced as a great loss, even if one has already had children or will have little or no rearing role with them" (Robertson, *Children of Choice*, p. 24). The recent uproar over the right to clone humans caused 19 European nations to ban the practice in January 1998. But Americans are nervous about governmental restrictions, especially of any developing technology that might be helpful to those who might really need it. Robertson notes that a couple whose child is dying of leukemia might hope to clone the child in order to match his bone marrow. He also points out that we are at least 10 years away from having to make such ethical choices, since we currently don't have the ability to clone a human.

The emerging legal position appears to be that some, if not all, assisted reproductive technologies have protected constitutional status and that even if we are not sure about the future ramifications of what ART could mean to society, we cannot restrict this fundamental freedom of choice (Robertson, 1984 and 1986). (In "American law and assisted reproductive technologies," *Fertility and Sterility*, Supplement, Vol. 62, No. 5, November 1994.)

We take a strong stand for individual liberty in this country—the right to "life, liberty, and the pursuit of happiness," says it all. In order to be happy, most individuals feel a need to carry on their line and their family traditions. And there is nothing in writing that prohibits them from doing this if it requires the assistance of a third party. But being free to act is one thing; taking that action is another, and there are almost always other considerations. Consideration is doing harm to others: How "good" is ART for the child, donor, recipient, couple, or any other involved parties? Next we have to ask whether an individual's autonomy is more crucial than any of society's strictures. A third consideration is whether justice is being done.

These three principles often come into conflict, and this contention is what makes the line between law and ethics so fuzzy. For example, suppose we allow a handicapped older single mother with a minimal support system to have a baby with a donor egg. We have protected her right to reproduce, and we have partially served justice, which asks that each individual be given his or her due; but aren't we coming up short on the issue of harm being done to the unborn child? If this mother is not able to care adequately for her new baby, is society at fault for allowing this birth to take place?

So we come down to a second distinction. The legal right to reproduce is ours any time we want it, but the moral right may need some restrictions placed on it. Most ethicists agree on three moral grounds for not reproducing and some maintain that there are six. The first three are:

- *transmission of disease to the offspring*—of course, this situation makes a good argument for using donor eggs to save the day;
- *unwillingness to provide proper prenatal care*—as when a mother drinks, takes drugs, or is repeatedly exposed to toxic chemicals;
- *inability to rear children*—if you can't provide food, clothing, shelter, education and health care for your child, you shouldn't have one.

The next three moral objections are dicey, because there's actually no way to prove that they are harmful to the child, the parents, or society:

- *psychological harm to the offspring*—can ART leave a residue of emotional damage? We really don't yet know the answer;
- *overpopulation*—in some countries this is relevant, when there aren't sufficient resources to care for new babies. As of this date in America, of course, we are blessed with all that we need to offer our children. Worldwide, ART procedures account for about thirty thousand births annually, or about 0.03 percent of the more than one hundred million births that occur naturally each year;
- *nonmarriage*—fewer and fewer people feel that traditional marriage between a man and woman is essential to proper childrearing. However, many religious groups still hold to this standard as the moral "norm."

These six concerns speak to our discomfort with letting every person do whatever they please. We have an urge to draw a line, not just for the good of individuals, but for society as a whole.

For this reason, there are certain restrictions placed on those who would offer reproductive services. States impose licensing requirements on all doctors, including those offering gamete donation, as well as laboratories and facilities where ART procedures go on.

There are also restrictions placed on those who would become parents. Doctors must give clients full and accurate information about all risks and benefits of the treatments they receive, they must honor legal duties of privacy and confidentiality, and they must enter written agreements with clients about the course of treatment, the disposition of preembryos, and the nature and price of services provided. There are federal and state regulations that requires disclosure of any and all experimental or research procedures.

In vitro procedures, oocyte aspiration, and pregnancy are all stressful events with potential physical, emotional, and social problems for many different individuals. So we have to weigh the moral considerations more heavily than the legal ones when we're making choices about the ethics of any ART procedure.

FIRST, DO NO HARM

All physicians take the Hippocratic oath when they dedicate themselves to the healing professions. They are enjoined not to do anything that would endanger a life or the quality of a life that is at least status quo. There are legal regulations controling research ethics, thanks to the tragedy of the Tuskegee study that began in 1932 and withheld treatment for syphilis from infected black men. Because of this inhumanity to a select group, Congress enacted regulations requiring informed consent from all participants in any medical procedure.

But no regulation or statute regarding informed consent can overcome downright deception or fraud. Consider the case of Cecil Jacobson in Virginia who used his own sperm to impregnate infertility patients who believed that they were getting the sperm of their previously selected donor. Or consider the black eye dealt to the entire infertility field by the disaster at the University of California at Irvine in May of 1995. Doctors there apparently took eggs from IVF patients without their consent and used them to create pregnancies in other recipients. They explained to the unsuspecting donors that unfortunately, they had retrieved fewer eggs than expected during their follicle aspiration process. In truth, they had absconded with part of the harvest. As many as sixty couples are thought to have been involved in the donation without consent, and it's unlikely that the full extent of the scandal will ever be unraveled, since the recipients may fear that their children will be taken away from them.

As the dreams of reproductive technology become actual protocols, the notion of "doing harm" becomes less clear-cut. We may agree that it's wrong to conceal the truth about whose embryo is whose. But go back a step: Is it harmful to generate life in a mother who may not live to see her child graduate from college? Is it harmful to implant more embryos in a uterus than you anticipate becoming fetuses? If they all do implant, is it harmful to the mother to carry five babies at once? Is it harmful to the babies? And if the choice is in favor of the mother's health, is it harmful to exercise the right of selective reduction and destroy one or more of those embryos?

Right now, it's the job of the physician and her or his colleagues to make a reasonable judgment, and to help patients decide whether harm is being done to the recipient or the donor of the egg because of the drugs they take and the procedures they undergo. Even then, most individuals would agree that if all parties involved are acting under informed consent, they are making a personal decision that is basically their own business.

Some groups take exception to that stance. If you listen to the American Life League, who maintains the Pro-Life Forum on the on-line Eternal Word (EWTN) Website, anything beyond natural conception and gestation is harmful. They say that "ethics and morals, along with judgment, have been sacrificed in order to advance the mad dash for knowledge. This philosophy has destroyed all limits, so that now the rule is, quite simply, if it can be done, it must be done, and damn the consequences." (*From the Pro-Life Activist's Encyclopedia,* The American Life League, 1996.) This group feels that harm will be promulgated in situations like embryo splitting, (where a woman could conceivably give birth to her own identical twin sister) or a gestational carrier who wasn't even human—would you want to have an ape or a cow give birth to your child? Another group that wishes to protect the mother's rights consists of those feminists who see reproductive technology as a way to keep women barefoot and pregnant until their dying day. It's their contention that the predominantly male medical community has conned women into giving consent when they are actually helping to ruin their lives and putting them in harm's way.

Harm, of course, is relative. According to John Robertson, the greatest harm is never being born at all. Even if a child is born to a woman of 60 who becomes senile and dependent at 75, the child is still in good shape because that child exists and has the potential to make something of her life. And the woman has achieved her fondest wish— to bring new life into the world.

SELECTIVE REDUCTION

When we try to initiate a pregnancy with any of the ARTs, we have to hedge our bets. Even with egg donation, the most successful of the ARTs, embryo implantation rates are at best 20 to 25 percent per embryo, and they're considerably lower with IVF, and lower still as the women—and their eggs—get older. Since our intention is to give the recipient the best possible chance of having a baby, we need to increase the number of embryos transferred to the uterus, with the hope that at least one will implant. The more embryos replaced, the higher the probability that at least one will take. Unfortunately, along with this increased chance of pregnancy comes the increase in the probability of multiple gestation.

Of course with egg donation it doesn't matter how old the recipient is—pregnancy rates with donor eggs are only dependent on the age of the donor. But pregnancy rates with IVF and other ARTs are very age-dependent. Multiple gestations are rare in women over the age of 40 going through IVF with their own eggs, even if five embryos are replaced at once. For younger women, we use fewer embryos—as of this writing, we are transferring four embryos to women between the ages of 36 and 39 and three embryos to women age 35 or under. Recipients of egg donation get no more than three embryos. And so sometimes we get three for three, even in a woman of advanced reproductive age.

The request for more embryos is patient-driven rather than physician-driven. If a woman is around 40 and has failed one or more ART procedures in the past, she may assume that her probability of pregnancy is low (and her time is running short). She naturally wants as many embryos transferred as possible to increase her chances.

It's hard to carry four babies to term, no matter how old the mother is. Quadruplets are at substantially increased risk of prematurity and all the health risks that come with it, including long-term disability. And carrying quadruplets at the age of 50 would be a real feat. So if technology works perfectly and all the embryos implant, as is very often the case in egg donation, then what do we do?

We arrive at the depressing prospect of selectively reducing the number of embryos after implantation has taken place. We usually wait until 10 or 12 weeks of gestation, near the end of the first trimester, because spontaneous losses are quite common prior to that time. It's also easier to detect some fetal anomalies at this stage, which may help decide which of the fetuses will be selected out.

Fortunately, we have had only a handful of patients who have had to make this difficult choice. But I will never forget the few I've had to participate in; each one is engraved on my memory and makes me think twice, every time I transfer four or five embryos into an infertile woman.

The first time I had to refer a patient for this procedure, I felt responsible and quite guilty. Her uterus was too small to accommodate the triplets she was carrying, and she was emotionally overwhelmed at the prospect of raising three children at once; she made the decision to reduce them to twins. I went with her to the hospital and stayed with her throughout the procedure.

The physicians who perform selective reduction are specialists in obstetrics, experts at amniocentesis. The same expertise that allows them to pass a needle into the amniotic sac without harming the fetus is the one that allows them to target the fetus precisely without harming the remainder of the pregnancy.

The patient had to meet with the Ethics Board at the hospital before she could have this procedure, but there was no objection. The board's stance was that this was not an abortion but rather a life-preserving procedure for the remaining fetuses. I watched as the physician performing the procedure located the most appropriately positioned gestational sac at the top of the uterus and inserted a long, thin needle under direct ultrasound control through the sac and into the heart of the fetus. Then he injected a very small amount of potassium chloride, which causes an electrical imbalance in the heart muscle. The tiny heart stopped.

The mother was distraught; the physician quiet and competent, and the two other fetuses went right on, unaffected. Over time, their sibling would simply be absorbed back into the flux and flow of the uterine environment. The tissue would eventually be expelled months later with the debris that is cast off with the placenta.

I have never gotten over the image of the reduction. Nor do I really want to. Whereas I am a strong proponent of reproductive freedom, including free access to all forms of contraception and abortion, I believe that reproductive endocrinologists must maintain their ultimate respect for life. Selective reduction is currently a necessary evil and should be used judiciously to protect the well-being of the mother and that of the other siblings (intentionally proceeding with a septuplet pregnancy is positively foolhardy). But if we practice responsible medicine and exert control prior to gestation, we will only have to use this procedure in the rarest of cases. By limiting the number of ovulating eggs in IUI cycles and enhancing the per-embryo implantation rate in ART cycles, we can keep the number of embryos transferred to a minimum. In so doing, we can prevent others from having to make the difficult choice of selective reduction.

Not quite contraception, not quite abortion, selective reduction leaves us with a strange taste in the mouth. Having chosen life, we must figure on just how many lives are safe and productive. Once again, we have an ethical dilemma with few easy answers.

BUT IT'S NOT NATURAL

There are ethicists who feel that the only ethical way to have a child is the old-fashioned way: one man and one woman of reproductive age, creating life through procreation. Willard Gaylin, M.D., director of the Hastings Center for Bioethical Research in Briarcliff Manor, New York, writing for the Scripps-Howard chain right after Arceli Keh's child was born, said that "there are some natural limits to human engineering that need not and ought not to be tested." Gaylin feels that "medical advances designed to cure disease ought not to be available for reasons of convenience. One ought not be free to always do one's one thing even in this most narcissistic of times." It is inappropriate, he feels, for a postmenopausal woman to have a baby.

Of a similar opinion is Evelyne Shuster, Ph.D., Medical Ethicist for the Veterans Administration Medical Center in Philadelphia and a member of the ethics committee of the ASRM. She is concerned that an industry controlled by men is calling the shots, turning women into baby machines even at impossible ages. When babies are "produced" by the system instead of generated naturally, she says, they turn into commodities, and this downgrades the integrity of each child. It is as unnatural for young women to be paid for their eggs as it is for women in their fifties to carry babies. She does not totally object to men having children in their seventies, because physically, they can—they don't need drugs and procedures to do it. She points out that men don't have to go through the arduous process of labor and birth so their health is not at risk, and for the most part, they aren't the ones who wake up in the middle of the night to feed the child. Women, on the other hand, naturally lose their procreative ability at menopause, which is the marker she would set (whether it occurred at age 38 or age 54) as the cutoff to be allowed into donor-egg programs.

But age is a completely relative thing. There's no ethical argument to being a mother over the age 50 or even 60, but there is an aesthetic one. (Remember, though, that the Greeks lumped beauty and correctness together.) Gaylin, quoted in the *New York Times* after the oldest-known mother, Keh, had her baby at 63, said, "'I do feel we have a responsibility to the symmetry of life and to some rules of nature.'" He wasn't playing gender favorites either. "'I do not think it's attractive for a 70-year-old man to have a child,'" he said. Dr. Gilbert C. Meilander Jr., an ethicist and theologian, agreed with Gaylin. "I'm reluctant to use right-wrong language," he stated, and then added, "[but] it just doesn't seem fitting." The choice of words—*symmetry, attractive, fitting*—point up how ill at ease people get when something doesn't feel comfortable. We think bathing suits look fine on the beach; but we would look askance at people walking into an office building in the same attire. We smile indulgently when we see a twenty-year-old with a belly as big as a watermelon, but we are put off by a gray-haired woman in the same condition. One is "natural," the other is not.

I feel that Gaylin and Shuster's arguments fall short because they aren't looking at the bigger picture. After all, nature is capricious; what's "natural" isn't always in perfect balance or symmetry. I am more in agreement with Alex Capron, professor of law at the University of

Southern California Law School. Capron points out that nature has a few glitches of her own in the reproductive arena. On the up side, consider parthenogenesis, where an egg reproduces itself and offers an evolutionary advantage to many species. On the down side, think about cancer, which is natural growth gone haywire.

It's the job of scientists to mess with nature—certain people have naturally high blood pressure or high cholesterol, but we've developed medications to take care of that. We can bypass a blocked artery with an operation; we can get the HIV virus down to undetectable levels in the blood with protease inhibitors. So why shouldn't medicine do something to ameliorate the reproductive process?

Capron points out that in centuries past, it was natural for an elderly man, (usually a widower because his former wife had died in childbirth) to select a young wife who was a good breeder. The idea was economic—he needed offspring in order to keep his line alive and keep his monetary and property holdings intact. Today, many older women select a young husband because they have more in common with them than with men their own age. And they may wish to consolidate that relationship with a child they can raise together. There really aren't that many women in their sixties who anticipate having a child—as far as we know, there have only been three in the world. Most women of advanced reproductive age, in their late forties or early fifties, fall into the description of "young middle age." And if we're going by "natural" as a criterion, what about the 57-year-old woman in California who had a baby with no assisted technology at all? Should she be penalized for not having passed through the change of life when society said she was supposed to?

Our criteria for using egg donation at USC is that the mother be healthy enough to withstand the rigors of pregnancy, labor, and birth, and that she show that she can adapt physically and psychologically to the type of lifestyle she will have to lead with a young child. Finally, she must have a good support system around her so that if something should happen to her, there will be others waiting in the wings to help her or to take over care of that child completely, if necessary.

If we were to set a cutoff age for donor eggs, Capron suggests, menopause would be a meaningless timeline since most women live at least thirty years past the change of life. "If life expectancy is the essential criterion," he states, "we ought to prevent all women with potentially fatal health problems from having babies." A 30-year-old in remission for breast cancer or a 35-year-old whose parents both died prior to age 50 of heart attacks should also be suspect.

FAMILIES IN CRISIS

I have always asked women who want a child and can't because they have no viable eggs if they would first ask for a donation from a family member, such as a sister or a cousin. The closer you stay to your family ties, the more genetic integrity you retain. But many couples who have no siblings have looked to other generations for their donations. And this presents a thorny problem. If your Mom gives you an egg, is your child really your sister? If your father donates sperm, is he the grandfather or the father of your child, or both? What about posthumous donation?

A year or so ago in Florida, a pair of newlyweds went through an intersection that was missing a stop sign and suffered a terrible car crash. The husband was killed and the wife asked that his sperm be collected because she wanted to carry his child. The hospital did as she requested and froze the sample for her, which she then stored for a year. In the meantime, she met and fell in love with another man. She was about to thaw and destroy the sperm when her late husband's mother came forward and offered to carry her son's child herself. She would get an egg from a stranger to mix with her son's sperm and have the resulting embryo implanted inside her. In memory of her son, she would raise his child.

Are we ready for this child born of a postmenopausal pregnancy who would effectively have no living genetic parents? Since his grandmother would be playing the role of his mother, he would also have no grandparents. Is this right for the child? Is it right for the grandmother who has become the surrogate? And for the new bride who, but for a vandalized stop sign, would have been a mother—though not of this particular child, since her egg would have made an entirely different baby? Makes your head spin, doesn't it?

A lot of programs have stipulations against intergenerational donations. They bring up all sorts of Oedipal questions that are too confusing for most people to handle. But innovation is born out of confusion. In the future, technology may change the way we view our relationships to family members. After all, for centuries we had extended families who lived together in compounds or communities, and over the course of the last century, we evolved into smaller units known as nuclear families. Along the way, we've had experiments such as the kibbutz in Israel where children born to two biological parents became property of the group. Or nineteeth-century Utopian communities like those founded by Proudhon or Owen, where the leader was allowed conjugal freedom with any or all of the female members and was the progenitor of most or all of the offspring. These half-hearted attempts at bringing up baby in the best way possible had to be scrapped, but human beings are inventive, and have come up with lots of unique alternatives.

So today, thanks to ART, our thoughts about the family unit are changing again. Now, when you could conceivably have a child who is the product of donor sperm and a donor egg, carried by a surrogate, and raised by two people of either gender who are life partners, there are five individuals who serve as parents. What we have always believed about the family unit is in a state of flux.

It's anybody's guess what could happen if procreative liberty runs amuck. But where do we stop it? And how? And should we tamper with such basic rights?

GIVE ME NO REGULATION—OR GIVE ME DEATH!

The heart of the matter is how we as a society view the importance and urgency of parenting. If we were really scrupulous about investigating people's motives for having children, and if we had a regulatory system to tell us who could and who couldn't have them, there would be a lot fewer children in the world. After all, why pick on older couples? They're the ones who've lived long enough to know what they want. And what they want—desperately—is a child they can love and cherish. Many younger people have children but don't much care to raise them. Undoubtedly there would be less child abuse and neglect if we were all monitored by some higher authority. But who would that authority be? And what would be their criteria for selecting appropriate parents? Would there be a waiting period? Would you have to have some sort of financial check, or an assurance of backup help in case you were unable to serve as parent? Would a government official come into your home from time to time to see how you were doing? The likely board of admissions set up by the Department of Health and Human Services wouldn't know the first thing about who should and who shouldn't be a parent. And if you were denied the right to reproduce, how would this be enforced? The ramifications are unthinkable.

It is doubtful that this could happen in our country because most of us loathe the idea of the government sticking its nose into our bedrooms—we are champions of procreative liberty, even when it appears to go overboard. Of course, the free-market model we're using right now leaves the profession open for a lot of criticism. And yet, at the moment, we're not ready to move to a regulatory model. "Right now, we have a happy couple and a happy doctor," says George J. Annas, professor of law at Boston University's School of Public Health. "I think it's bizarre for women over sixty to have children, and it's unusual and strange for women over fifty, but we don't have any motivation to draw any lines until disaster happens or the public thinks these programs have gone too far."

Most people say that all humans have a fundamental right to reproduce. Even a 14-year-old who has no intention of raising her own child does the deed, and no one stops her. Why shouldn't an unthinking teen be subject to the same type of testing and therapy that an older mother is required to have?

The answer to this lies in our American standard of freedom of choice. As we decided in the abortion debate of the 1970s (which still goes on), if the government can't interfere with your termination of a pregnancy, they certainly can't interfere with your inception of one—by any means possible.

The means, of course, have expanded. We used to rely on coition to generate new life, now we have other possibilities. Realistically, however, there's no way we are ever going to abandon old-fashioned sexual contact as a way to make babies. Most people can't afford to do it any other way, and they enjoy it too much to stop trying. On the other hand, if we fear that laboratory reproduction takes something out of human beings, we are extremely short-sighted. As Dr. Joseph Fletcher, a bioethicist at the Institute of Society, Ethics and the Life Sciences in Hastings-on-Hudson, New York wrote in the *New England Journal of Medicine,* "with our separation of baby-making from love-making, both become more human because they are matters of choice, and not chance."

SOCIETY'S BARGAIN: YOUNG, POOR WOMEN HELP OLDER, RICH WOMEN

Margaret Atwood, in her powerful novel, *The Handmaid's Tale*, pictures a future world where one class of women will service a higher class of women by bearing children for them. (In this scenario, where a younger woman not only provides the egg but also the uterus in which the fetus will grow, we have a more blatant example of class distinction when it comes to motherhood.) There are slaves and there are masters, and childbearing is a lower-echelon activity relegated to the poor masses.

In our own society, we tend to have a rather schizophrenic view of motherhood. On the one hand, most of us see parenting as a civic duty, a way to keep the kids off the streets and instill in them the family values that will inspire them to be great parents. On the other hand, many think that women who stay home with the kids are little more than bums, mooching off their husbands. Motherhood is usually considered a second-class career when compared with becoming a doctor or lawyer, although these days the pendulum is swinging backward, and it's chic once more to be a mother. That, also, is too simplistic and wrongheaded a way to look at it. Being a mother, like being a father, is a combination of guts, hard work, and blinding flashes of insight and compassion.

To bring these diverse opinions into some kind of accord, we have developed a system where women can establish their primary career (a paying job), and then, when it's up and running, can depend on the resources available in the rest of society to start in on their secondary career (motherhood, a nonpaying job). They can do this only with the participation of younger women who can supply the means to their end.

If our civilization is to thrive for many more generations, we have to do many jobs well. We can't just settle for being accountants or social workers; we also must be thinkers, feelers, lovers, and parents; also, chauffeurs, cooks, mechanics, and home designers. The stuff of our life becomes one commodity after another—if we can negotiate a business deal, we can also negotiate third-party reproduction. And as childbearing becomes a later priority, one that we can tackle when we've proved ourselves in other arenas, our feelings about egg donation will change.

One of the criticisms leveled at reproductive technology is that the baby becomes a product—highly desired, very expensive, and difficult to get. In a system that uses money as an evaluation of what things are worth, it is hard not to wonder whether we are evolving into a culture that pays hard cash for everything good, and pities the poor individual who can't participate because she doesn't have the means. Whether the prize is a deluxe Caribbean cruise or a heart transplant, a Porsche or a late-life baby, you have to put your money where your mouth is. And this clearly puts a restriction on such luxuries. If you don't come from wealth or achieve wealth or have wealth thrust upon you, you're out of the game.

This in no way means that having children becomes a lower priority than having a money-making job. But it does divide those who *are able* from those who *enable,* which of course isn't fair. The consolation is that the young donor who needs that $2500 fee for her services right now, may in a couple of decades be the older successful woman who remembers and therefore understands that it's now her time to pay $2500 (it will probably then be more like $25,000) to another young woman.

IS ADOPTION A MORAL OBLIGATION?

The number of unwanted and abandoned children in the world is staggering. There are those whose parents have been killed in wars or on the street, and those who are left to die because the parents have no home or food to feed themselves, let alone another mouth. There are children who were carelessly conceived and are as carelessly thrown out, by people of all ages who have no awareness of the value of human life. And there are those who are scorned because of their gender or a congenital condition or handicap. We in the United States think of ourselves as extremely generous and compassionate toward the needy, but there are homeless kids wandering our land who would refute that.

So why wouldn't a 50-year-old woman who couldn't have a child of her own adopt? Doesn't she have a moral obligation to do so? If she is that desperate to be a parent, why can't she parent someone else's child?

When we make a decision, we have certain ideals in mind. None of us is completely without bias or prejudice. If we're going to expend at least 18 years and who knows how many thousands of dollars on the upbringing of an individual, we ought to have some say in who that individual is. Family ties, as we know, can be the strongest. Our inner feelings toward a person who is connected in some way, even if it's just through one partner's genes, will for some people be a lot more potent than those we might have for a stranger. Many people feel they could not love a child who did not look or feel like them, and for that reason, they would not feel comfortable adopting a child from a foreign country or of a different race. And those are about the only choices for older couples who want to adopt.

Is comfort an issue? Doesn't morality supercede everything? Shouldn't we just bite the bullet and take the children who are out there, waiting, before producing one that's in accord with our tastes? Probably not—and there is no law saying that we have to. We may turn out to be better parents if we have some say in what we like and don't like about the process and the people involved. And though that seems selfish, well, parenting and establishing a family are self-directed activities. We might just as easily argue that couples who aren't infertile should forgo natural reproduction and adopt needy children.

PREEMBRYOS AND EMBRYOS

If we were at all clear as to what we owe to children who have already been born, maybe it would be slightly easier to figure out our debt to those cells who are not yet children but have some status as genetic confabulations—the mixture of male and female elements. No one can actually decide when life begins, so it's hard to say what that life is worth until it's established. The Catholic Church says life begins at the moment of fertilization, when egg and sperm unite; the Muslim faith, on the other hand, believe it starts at 40 days after conception. There is no consensus among Protestant or Jewish groups. In truth, the formation of a new organism is a drawn-out process rather than a one-shot deal.

When does life begin? It's really quite arbitrary. For example, we could consider the entry of the sperm head into the interior of the egg as irreversible joining of male and female. But you recall from Chapter 4, even though the sperm is inside the egg, the gametes haven't united yet. So it's not fertilization.

Is it syngamy, when the chromosomes align and a new, complete genetic complement is formed? Probably not, because up until the eight-cell stage, theoretically, each cell of the embryo could be placed into individual human eggshells and form eight new individuals. It's probably also at this stage that the genome is activated—the fetal DNA is actually transcribed to make new proteins. Prior to this point, the embryo is functioning on autopilot, using only the building blocks that were already present in the egg at the time of ovulation.

But we're still not at the magic moment of personhood because the potential for splitting the embryo continues beyond the point of implantation. Even when the blastocyst has made a successful landing in the wall of the uterus and its cells begin to interweave with those of the mother, identical twinning could still occur. It is only when the embryonic plate forms, about 14 days after ovulation, that we know for certain how many individuals will come out of that implanting embryo.

The Ethics Committee of the ASRM has chosen to designate this point as the foundation of life, the stage formally called "embryo." All stages prior to this point, from fertilization to blastocyst to early implantation, are referred to as the "preembryo."

So it's clear that life is not an all-or-nothing phenomenon, but rather a continuum. The most accurate markers we have are when the gametes are joined (somewhere between fertilization and syngamy) and when a new individual is formed (at about the formation of the fetal plate).

But does this preembryo qualify as a "person"? American law says no. Preembryos have no legal rights and therefore, their "owners," or those who have donated the gametes that created them, get to make decisions for them. This is not a happy solution, because since slavery was abolished, "ownership" applies to things rather than people. We may call the position of embryo donors "guardianship," but that seems to be fudging the distinction. Since these organisms can't speak for themselves, their creators must take responsibility for them and grant them a certain amount of consideration. (In other words, two gamete donors shouldn't produce an embryo in order to sell it to another couple.) Like dead people, severed limbs, or surgically removed organs, preembryos are respected by virtue of the fact that they don't have a voice. This is the respect they deserve—they are human "parts." But they are not independently human.

WHAT DO WE DO WITH THE FROZEN EMBRYOS?

After a couple achieves a pregnancy, they tend to forget about all the difficulties that went into accomplishing their goal. And it's hard to keep your mind's eye on those unused embryos, sitting in liquid nitrogen in the laboratory—tiny Sleeping Beauties frozen against the possibility that one day, the couple will want another. And if they don't, they must eventually decide whether to destroy these bits of tissue or give them generously to another couple who might want to use them.

There is a great need for the professionals in the field to take charge of the theory and practice of embryo donation. If we don't do it, we leave ourselves at the mercy of less-informed governmental regulators with axes to grind and taxpayers to please.

In an ad hoc committee on embryo donation that I set up with several other physicians and a lawyer at the Society for Assisted Reproductive Technologies (SART), we proposed a set of guidelines for programs choosing to offer embryo donation. We suggested that these programs must first have an established embryo freezing program. They may charge a fee to a potential recipient for embryo thawing and transfer, although a price could not be set on an embryo. A quarantine period of six months, similar to that set for frozen sperm, should be set before transfer so that potential donors could be tested for infectious disease. In the advent of the death of one partner, the other partner would remain the conservator of the frozen embryos.

Other countries have taken a hard stand on regulation. In July 1996, the hourglass tipped over on more than three thousand embryos in storage in Great Britain. British law states that embryos must be claimed within five years or the gamete donors forfeit their rights to them. These tiny entities had outstayed their limit, and therefore the 33 clinics with all this potential life on their hands were now allowed to destroy them. It's hard to keep track of anyone over a five-year period—after so much time has elapsed, it's not surprising to find that many have moved, are no longer married, or want nothing more to do with the cold little cell bundles.

So the word went out that within a week, the embryos would be thawed and sprinkled with alcohol, which would kill them. Then they would be incinerated.

The Catholic church and international right-to-life organizations were up in arms. Surely this "prenatal massacre" could not occur. A group of Italian doctors offered to "adopt" the embryos and find suitable Italian women, desperate for children, who would have them implanted. But British law deemed this impossible. They would need informed consent of both the sperm and egg donor to pass the embryo along to another individual. And since it was impossible to find these negligent nonparents, the storage facilities were mandated to accomplish their task.

Do these clusters of cells, which the Catholic church persists in calling the "preborn," have rights? Do they have a say in their disposition? After all, the likelihood is that they never will be born. The reason that people stockpile so many embryos is that current technology can't guarantee that one egg plus one sperm making one embryo necessarily guarantees a successful pregnancy. So we have thousands of extras waiting around, most of which will never see the light of day.

It is interesting, in this climate of concern about who's really responsible for reproductive decisions, that even potential parents themselves get shut out. In 1992, in France, a woman whose husband had been killed in a car accident came forward to claim two of the embryos that the couple had previously frozen. The hospital refused her request, and she took them to court, assuming that since one of the gametes involved belonged to her, it was her choice to initiate a pregnancy. She lost the case. In July 1994, France passed a law prohibiting embryo transfers after a partner's death without that person's prior consent.

If you could store your embryos in your home freezer next to the ice cream and salmon steaks, it would be your call when to turn opportunity into a laughing, breathing child. But when you put yourself and your embryos in the hands of technology, you lose your autonomy. You paid the doctor to do the IVF procedure and paid the lab to mix the egg and sperm and freeze it and store it. The hospital or commercial storage facility is regulated by the state. (Actually, Louisiana, Minnesota, and Illinois have gone further than any other states and have each enacted legislation that protects the rights of the preembryo.)

When you choose to put part of your money in the bank, you must abide by bank rules. Since you must pay a storage fee for your frozen embryos, and make provisions for them whether you decide to use them or give them to another couple or abandon them, you are tacitly agreeing to this new system that allows people to "make" babies rather than simply have them.

There are currently thousands of frozen embryos in cryopreservation tanks throughout the United States. Many are just waiting to be claimed by their owners when they are ready to have another child; others, however, have been abandoned. Each year, owners are sent a notification and a bill for the next years' storage, but many people just vanish, cutting out on their obligation to pay and, more, on their commitment to making a choice.

Although five years is a suggested time limit for storage, many clinics don't want to get involved. So in our country, these orphaned embryos could conceivably stay in suspended animation indefinitely.

Let's face it: Nobody would go through the time, agony, and expense of producing embryos and then simply lose track just because they'd moved or gotten a divorce. The truth of the matter is that most of us would rather not have to make big decisions like this one. We'd rather procrastinate and avoid than come down on one side or another of the issues.

FREEZING EGGS INSTEAD OF EMBRYOS

It's possible that we will be able to avoid this big ethical dilemma if technology improved and we didn't have to overproduce. If every embryo created had a home to go to, we could rest easier. But one of the biggest hitches of the oocyte donation scenario is that thousands of embryos will be created that will never be used. If you have aspirated 20 eggs from a donor, and 10 of them turn into perfectly viable embryos, you transfer 3 and freeze the rest. Suppose, however, that all three implant and develop into fetuses. After being overwhelmed with triplets, you might never want more children. The leftover frozen embryos could be donated to another couple, and to some, this may be greatly preferable to destroying potential new lives.

These are all huge decisions that could be made much less complex if it were the egg rather than the embryo being frozen. And this, in fact, is one of the new reproductive innovations that could change the future of egg donation.

You can see what an incredible benefit it would be if you had the foresight to freeze your own eggs when you were young and healthy. If you should be diagnosed with cancer in the future, or if you went through premature menopause, you could still have your own genetic children.

You wouldn't need a donor, and this would eliminate the ethical quandry of the procedure. If you had IVF using your own eggs and too many were retrieved, some could be frozen prior to fertilization. If you didn't get pregnancy on the first try, you could still go back, claim your eggs, fertilize them, and have the resulting embryos transferred.

You would also take care of religious qualms about unused embryos. Currently, the church and right-to-life groups strenuously object to keeping "preborn" individuals in limbo, frozen for future use or destruction. But if you're only freezing a gamete, it's not yet a potential person. It's more like freezing a piece of a lung or a kidney for later use when the entire organ is damaged or needs a boost.

As of this writing, it is too soon to say how well we will make use of frozen eggs. A great deal more research is necessary before frozen eggs become the norm. However, it is hard to argue with the idea of freezing eggs now in the hope that within 5 or 10 years, the technology will allow us to use all the eggs all the time.

FOR THE GOOD OF THE CHILD?

All of the other issues pale beside this one: What are we doing to the next generation of kids by manipulating the elements of their lives? Is an egg donation baby child born to a 48-year-old mother a disadvantaged child?

The field is too new to go around to all the donor-egg kids and ask whether having an older parent has messed up their lives. But certainly, they can testify to plenty of natural situations that have done them great harm. Consider the terrible situations that children are prey to: broken homes, irresponsible teen parents, living homeless or in poverty, or being constantly abused. Children born out of wedlock to 14-year-olds bear a much greater burden than those born to middle- and upper-class 50-year-old women. Teens who have babies because they are able to do so have no life experience, no parenting skills nor the desire to master them. Their babies are commonly cared for by grandparents or other relatives while the biological parent goes to school or to work.

In some ways, children born to older parents have got it made. The people who choose to "produce" children when they can't have them naturally are by far more stable, sophisticated, mature, and dedicated parents than the norm.

So maybe asking whether older mothers having egg-donation babies is good or bad is the wrong question. Glenn McGee of the Center for Bioethics in Philadelphia suggests that instead we should ask, What does it mean to be a mother or a parent? Does it mean giving the very best that you can personally, financially, emotionally, socially to the person you bring into the world? Right now, parents and physicians are in the drivers' seat—and they are working under the tyranny of choice. There are so many options, we feel we have to have it all, and there's the rub. When do we stop? The system allows us to get a sperm donor, an egg donor, a gestational carrier, and even remove one cell from an embryo and examine it for genetic glitches if we want preimplantation diagnosis.

A child who is loved and cared for usually does very well indeed. And in future, as more children come into being with a little help from technology, there will be less stigma on not looking just like your parents or having parents who are the age of most grandparents. Ethics will eventually catch up with science. But what do we do in the meantime? In order to protect the next generation, there has to be some form of internal regulation.

Who Should Make Policy?

So the next question is, who makes the system possible? Should we come down on the side of privacy and leave all these options in the hands of parents and physicians—or is that too one-sided a perspective? Or should there be a team effort on the part of lawyers, ethicists, school administrators, hospital administrators, and others to oversee the extraordinary possibilities we have at hand? A lot of forethought should go into any choice we make for our kids, because they're the ones who will have to live with it.

Glenn McGee suggests that one ethically sound option would be to use the model of adoption for egg donation. These two situations are totally different at the outset—in adoption, the adoptive parents are agreeing to take a child that has been abandoned by his birth parents; in a donation procedure, the parents desperately want the child that will be the result of selected gametes. After that, however, the situations become quite similar: There's a child to be raised and cared for.

In any adoption, the potential adoptive couple must have a session with a psychologist, a home visit to examine the environment the child will grow up in, and a court visit to meet with a judge or magistrate to demonstrate adequate personal and financial resources. There is oversight here from all directions. In the egg donation situation, right now, we're probably too lenient. Since we have the opportunity to act in the best interest of the child, we should do so. Physical health and family history should certainly be valid criteria, as should stability of the potential parent or parents. But it gets problematic when you start thinking about putting together a board comprising legal, medical, psychological, and ethical experts. Who would select these individuals? Who would be the ultimate authority?

WHERE DO WE DRAW THE LINE?: MIX-AND-MATCH GENES

In addition to following guidelines set by a professional organization such as ASRM, groups of doctors and ethicists come together on a regular basis to review and update the practices in the field. In April of 1996, a symposium on the ethics of ART took place at the University of California, Irvine, on the heels of the fertility clinic scandal mentioned earlier. I was asked to chair a workshop that focused on professional guidelines for the clinical practice of oocyte and embryo donation. In this work, as in that of most other ethics committees, there is never complete consensus. But we were able to get the issues on the table and make everyone aware of the ramifications of their actions. We were hoping to establish a framework for other programs around the country to adapt and use according to local norms of professional practice and ethical standards. Our goal was, as we put it in our guidelines, "to simultaneously maximize individual and reproductive freedom attempting to minimize individual risks ... to minimize coercion and exploitation while allowing maximum freedom to participate in assisted reproduction, whether as a recipient or as a donor."

We wanted to match requirements for egg donors with the more established recommendations for sperm donors. And rather than set an upward limit for the number of cycles a donor might engage in, we suggested that oocyte donation might be done with unstimulated cycles, circumventing the repetitive use of fertility medications. Most programs allow from three to five stimulated cycles, although some permit more. We proposed a list of donor's rights, including informed consent, full disclosure about the information revealed about them to the recipient, the right to know the results of all their medical tests, the right to information about what becomes of their unused donated gametes, and the right to medical care for any complications resulting from the procedures.

Our workshop did not recommend an upward age limit on recipients since none are set for men, although we recognized that programs should be free to set their own arbitrary limits. We chose not to come up with a number of embryos to be transferred to minimize the number of multiple gestations, although most participants agreed that three seemed like a reasonable number. We also established that children born of gamete donation should have the right to nonidentifying information about the donors who had supplied the necessary egg or sperm. And we formally recognized the professional autonomy of programs that would allow physicians to match their own specifications for donors and recipients with prevailing local norms or individual moral beliefs.

There are other, newer reproductive technologies on which we will have to make decisions in the near future. Do we want to give parents the right to select the gender of their child? Or to abort a baby who carries the BRCA-1 mutation for breast cancer or the apo-E2 gene for Alzheimer's? Or will we keep the problematic embryo and alter it, inserting new genes or deleting abnormal ones? What about altering the cytoplasm of the egg and leaving the genes intact? Then, of course, there's the newly charged cloning debate. There is so much interest in this new technology that it's difficult to say what forms it will take in the next few years. Who knows what other uses it might have in improving human life?

Because the possibilities for reproductive technology are multiplying at warp speed, it is essential that we stay on top of both the technology and the ethical questions it raises. There is no doubt that the great philosophical and ethical questions of our day should be debated constantly and fervently. But if the doctors don't throw themselves into the fray and express themselves adequately, we risk the danger of outside influences that might very well quash the next flurry of brilliant innovation in medicine.

Yes, our primary job is to help women to have children. But we must never lose sight of why we're doing it. Everyone in the field of reproductive technology must take the awesome responsibility for the generation of new individuals within the great sea of life. We can't just surf on the current wave of technology and hope that no one will notice when we overstep some bounds. Let's look at those children waiting to be born. We owe it to them to act responsibly and decisively.

Epilogue

The extraordinarily rapid advances in reproductive endocrinology are dizzying—there is so much on the horizon that will alter the way we look at motherhood. Only 10 years ago, it was strange and bizarre to think of assisting reproduction in a laboratory; today it is commonplace. And 10 years from now, the field will have undoubtedly made strides ahead that will overshadow the small, stumbling steps we have taken up to now. When Sarah's daughter wants to conceive, she might be able to choose among dozens of options that right now are still on the drawing board.

Someday soon, we will freeze eggs instead of embryos, giving young women the option of holding in reserve their own oocytes for some still-unforeseeable time when they're married or ready to reproduce. Someday soon, we'll be able to restructure the interior of an egg, using a woman's original genes but housing them inside a younger woman's cytoplasm. We may be able to "fix" damaged chromosomes, and allow couples to repair various medical problems that might endanger the new individual before implantation.

Naturally, there are potential dangers to the freedom we'll have. Already, some couples may be tempted to become pregnant using "designer embryos," finding egg and sperm donors on the Internet or through private programs that will cook up an embryo with just the right hair and eye color, just the right athletic ability or personality trait that they admire. Of course, regardless of the assurance of two donors' exceptional genetic makeup, the offspring can turn out completely different. Remember that lots of traits skip a generation.

But there's really no imminent threat of becoming a society that chooses to engineer "perfect" children. Most couples want their own genetic offspring; short of that, they want a child who seems a little like them but is mostly a brand new merger of nature and nurture. It is highly unlikely that we will ever choose to produce children in the image of what we feel is right for them. And thank God for that. We will use technology to improve what we've already got—to strengthen our eggs and sperm and embryos so that they can at last achieve their reproductive potential.

THE NEWEST TECHNOLOGIES

Egg Aging and Cytoplasmic Transfer

We used to think that the body worked as one unit, that eggs and sperm and hearts and livers all basically aged at the same rate. But as scientists discover the physiologic principles governing reproduction, they are finding that there are many different steps involved in the aging process. For example, at 50, you will have "elderly" eggs but a potentially youthful uterus, if it is properly stimulated hormonally. The egg and the uterus can be separated and controled independently—the egg coming from a young woman, the uterus from an older one. An older uterus and a younger egg can together achieve a perfectly fine pregnancy.

What is it that happens in the egg to make it "older"? Like any other cell in the body, the egg is a miniature factory complete with power generators, assemblers, and repair shops for various components, from the smallest to the largest. The blueprint for all of these components, as in any other cell, lies within the nucleus, a small portion of the egg that houses the DNA. The factories and workshops that take care of development and reconstruction are outside this nucleus, suspended in a clear, gelatinous, protein-loaded material called the cytoplasm. It is the cytoplasm that directs the development of the embryo right after it's fertilized.

So what ages more rapidly, the DNA or the supporting machinery in the surrounding cytoplasm that makes growth and development possible?

Let's look at the DNA first. It is well known that you are more likely to have a child born with some genetic abnormality if you're over 35.

This is the reason that older mothers-to-be are advised to have amnio-centesis when they're pregnant—to rule out Down's syndrome (an extra chromosome 21 in the fetus) and other chromosomal anomalies. As you get older, the incidence of such anomalies increases exponentially, and you're more at risk not only for children born with birth defects but also for miscarriages (the rate for women over 40 is 50 percent or higher). Unfertilized eggs from IVF procedures have a high incidence of chromosomal anomalies—evidently, it's not the process of IVT but the eggs used that are defective. Not surprisingly, this incidence jumps dramatically in groups of older patients.

Why does the DNA deteriorate so drastically over time? To try and discover the reason, we must go back to the womb, before the female child is born. Inside her mother's uterus, the eggs of a baby girl fetus undergo rapid multiplication. In her fifth month of gestation, she may have 8 million to 10 million eggs in her two developing ovaries. But at birth, only about two million eggs remain, every one of them held in their first meiotic prophase. The egg, encased in its primordial follicle, surrounded by a single layer of helper cells, lies dormant for years, waiting for puberty to start up the hormonal engines. Right now, it has all its chromosomes suspended in a small amount of cytoplasm, but at this stage, it is not capable of ovulation, fertilization, or further development.

If this egg ovulated when its owner turned 40, it would have spent 40 years in its dormant state. During this time, its chromosomes would have been exposed to background radiation and many other toxins. It seems reasonable to assume that this exposure to environmental hazards might play some role in the deterioration of the DNA, but it seems insufficient to explain the dramatic increase in genetic anomalies observed as women cross over the 40-year threshold.

But now let's recap the development of the egg during the month or so prior to ovulation. In response to signals not yet understood (or perhaps by simple random chance), the primordial follicle enveloping the sleeping egg gradually develops into a primary follicle. The number of helper cells increases, and the egg starts to expand in size in preparation for its exit from the ovary. Since no DNA replication has yet taken place, all of the increase in the egg's volume represents an increase in the volume of the cytoplasm. In the last two weeks before ovulation, the granulosa cells surrounding the egg begin secreting fluid which eventually coalesces into a follicle.

You will recall that the pituitary communicates with the ovary by sending a chemical message (follicle-stimulating hormone, or FSH), and the follicle grows, starting up its production of estrogen, when it encounters sufficient levels of this hormone, which it does during a natural ovulatory cycle, or in response to fertility drugs.

As the pituitary sends out its next foray of hormone—this time LH (luteinizing hormone)—the follicle will release its egg. It is the LH surge at ovulation that causes the egg to put out its first polar body, containing half of the the DNA. Any error in the first meiotic division— which, you may remember from Chapter 4, occurs more frequently in an older egg—can happen only at this point or later. And when the second polar body is cast off after fertilization, the egg gets a second opportunity to make a mistake.

Do genetic abnormalities occur because the DNA has been knocked around and poisoned with external pollution and radiation for 40 years? Or is it because some factor in the cytoplasm fell down on the job? Is it perhaps possible that the DNA was perfectly normal, but the energy stored within the cytoplasm was insufficient to align the chromosomes properly and separate the DNA into equal parts? At that critical moment when the chromosomes needed to separate, did the tired old egg lack sufficient strength to push them far enough apart? If that were the case, one of the chromosomes might have gotten left behind.

Let's consider the egg's function for a moment. The human egg is very much like a chicken egg: The embryo stays in its shell for a given period of time and then metamorphoses into another state of being. In the case of a chicken, the fertilized zygote within the egg gradually consumes and transforms the egg yolk and egg white into the muscles, bones, and feathers of the chicken. And in both chickens and humans, the DNA blueprint must be replicated many times as the embryo increases from one cell to several hundred inside the egg shell, whether it's the covering of the chicken egg or the zona pellucida. Each time another cell division takes place, the cytoplasm splits in two, but the DNA must be replicated in its entirety. This takes energy and building materials—and those must come from the cytoplasm.

The human embryo is different from a chicken embryo in that its zona pellucida does allow the influx of some nutrients such as glucose to enter from the bloodstream. But large molecules cannot get through the hard outer covering, which means that at the time of ovulation, the egg must contain within itself many of the building blocks for that difficult week prior to implantation. Hatching from the zona pellucida and implanting in the endometrium are also energy-demanding processes that may well fail if the cytoplasm doesn't have the necessary resources to nurture and guide them.

So the cytoplasm is really important. The embryo just can't do much, isolated and trapped within the zona. All it can manage is the transport of small molecules and products of respiration. Only through the various nutrients and repair workshops in the cytoplasm can it actually survive and grow. So the older the egg, the older the cytoplasm, and the less efficient it is at assisting in reproductive function.

The technique of *cloning*, for example, involves the separation of nuclear material and cytoplasm. In the case of Dolly, the famous Scottish sheep, the nuclear material came from a cell that was not an egg at all. This genetic material was specially prepared and then inserted into an egg whose own nuclear material had been removed, leaving only the cytoplasm and the eggshell.

Now if you can separate out these components, you may be able to enhance the development of the fertilized, growing egg by altering its cytoplasm. Hatching and implantation may be quite for a depleted egg whose cytoplasm is no longer functioning on all cylinders. So, if you were to give that egg an influx of young cytoplasm, you might retain the old genetic material intact. The major hitch of egg donation is losing your ability to pass on your genes to your child. Cytoplasmic transfer will change all that.

In 1997, Jacques Cohen's team from the Institute of Reproductive Medicine and Science of St. Barnabus Medical Center in Livingston, New Jersey, reported a successful birth after cytoplasmic transfer in a younger woman who had had recurrent failures with IVF. Their technique simply involved taking some of the cytoplasm from a donor egg and moving it into the (presumably poor-quality) egg that the patient had produced, thus improving its quality and subsequent function, leading to successful implantation and birth.

Dr. Cohen synchronized the cycles of the egg recipient and the egg donor by keeping them on fertility drugs for one cycle. Both women grew multiple, large follicles, which he then aspirated right before ovulation. At this point, Cohen took about 5 percent of the cytoplasm from the donor's egg (about the amount contained in five red blood cells) and injected it along with one sperm from the recipient's husband, into the recipient's egg. This technique so far has resulted in two pregnancies in previously infertile women.

Cohen also tried a second technique. He pinched off a portion of the donor's cytoplasm still wrapped in part of the oolemma—sort of like portioning off a part of a soap bubble. Then he slipped it under the zona pellucida of the recipient's egg. He used electrical stimulation to fuse them and afterward, performed intracytoplasmic sperm injection

(ICSI) on the revamped egg. So far, this method has not resulted in a pregnancy.

A more intriguing option might be to use the cloning technology to help older eggs. For example, an older egg might be allowed to fertilize and combine its genetic material with that of a sperm. The resulting new genetic blueprint could then be removed from the cytoplasm of the old egg and moved into a young egg that has had its nucleus stripped out, using the technology of cloning. The resulting individual would have the genes of both the father and the (older) mother, yet the egg would have a high chance of implanting because of the young cytoplasm. Of course, whatever genetic errors might have occurred when the first or second polar bodies were cast off during fertilization would already be present.

A second alternative, therefore, is to move the nuclear material from an older immature egg into the cytoplasm of a younger egg. The nuclear maturation of the genetic material from the older egg would then take place within the cytoplasm of the younger egg, which we must assume would be able to separate chromosomes normally. This technique, which I'll call "oocyte improvement," avoids the stigma of cloning. Subsequent fertilization would take place using ICSI, to get around the difficulties in traversing the zona pellucida after all this manipulation of the egg. The DNA from the injected sperm would be able to comingle with the female DNA inside a new, improved egg. Subsequent embryonic development and implantation would proceed as it does in a young egg. Dr. James Grifo, at The Cornell Medical Center, has recently reported getting to this first step—moving the nucleus of an immature oocyte into an enucleated recipient oocyte and observing the completion of meiosis.

As of the writing of this book, these technologies are still in their very early experimental stages, and the advantages they might offer are as yet unproven. We really have no idea what may crop up as we start experimenting with cytoplasmic transfer. One interesting twist we can foresee in this type of treatment lies in the fact that mitochondria, small energy factories within the cytoplasm, contain their own DNA. In the case of cytoplasm donation, the DNA within the mitochondria would be that of the cytoplasm donor and not that of the nuclear donor. So children thus born with the help of this technology will have the DNA of three separate individuals: the mother, the father, and the cytoplasm donor.

The ramifications of cytoplasm donation are tremendous. First, it would replace the majority of egg donation cycles, since they are per-

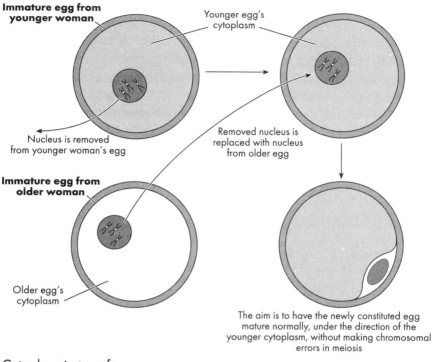

Immature egg from younger woman

Younger egg's cytoplasm

Nucleus is removed from younger woman's egg

Removed nucleus is replaced with nucleus from older egg

Immature egg from older woman

Older egg's cytoplasm

The aim is to have the newly constituted egg mature normally, under the direction of the younger cytoplasm, without making chromosomal errors in meiosis

Cytoplasmic transfer.

formed in women who have residual ovarian function and thus an adequate supply of eggs to act as the source of genetic material. Over the long term, it might justify the practice of freezing pieces of ovaries from young women as a hedge against reproductive failure later in life. A small strip of the ovarian cortex might be removed from a young woman during a diagnostic laparoscopy and preserved in liquid nitrogen. This piece of tissue might contain hundreds or even thousands of primordial follicles and immature eggs. The nuclear material from these immature eggs could then be used in the future, along with cytoplasm donation, to generate new, "reconstituted" eggs. And in the future, no matter the age or fertility of the woman, she would still be able to have a baby with her own genetic input.

Frankly, although what has just been described seems like science fiction, it's been a perfectly viable option for men for years. A young man can store any number of vials of sperm for future use. So all the potential future applications of immature oocyte cryopreservation and cytoplasmic transfer just level the playing field for women.

Egg Freezing

The world of animal embryology was way ahead of the game when it came to the freezing of reproductive tissues. Long before doctors ever froze a human embryo, they realized that they could achieve some spectacular results with rabbits and sheep. It was quite common to allow animals to mate, then retrieve the blastocyst by uterine flushing, and freeze the embryo for later use. Cryopreservation of animal blastocysts after in vivo fertilization had been practiced for many years before human IVF appeared on the scene.

So it was natural to adapt the animal experience to the human embryo, and the first human birth after embryo freezing was reported in 1985 by the Australian team led by Alan Trounson, Ph.D., whose background was in animal embryology.

The following year, Richard Marrs' group at USC achieved the first human birth after embryo cryopreservation in the United States. I was fortunate enough to have been a junior member of the program at this time. Our approach was imprecise and extremely experimental—we really didn't feel sure of ourselves when we set out to use the excess embryos we had left over from IVF procedures.

Our research facilities were at the university campus, several miles away from the clinical center where IVF was being practiced. This meant that we had to transport the embryos designated for freezing by hand to the research facility. The little cell bundles would often spend many hours en route while waiting to be frozen. It's not surprising, with this haphazard system, that it took many attempts to achieve that first success, which in retrospect, I have to attribute to a combination of perseverance and good luck.

Embryo freezing became more technologically advanced over the next few years. Better cryoprotectants (the fluids added to the culture medium to protect the embryo during the freezing process) were developed, with superior results. A better understanding of embryo physiology caused us to freeze the cells earlier. Whereas we had previously waited until the more advanced cleavage stages, we moved the time of freezing back to the 2-pronuclear stage, which appeared more resistant to damage during the cryopreservation process. As of this writing, pregnancy success rates with cryopreserved-thawed embryos are approximately two-thirds of those with fresh embryos.

You can freeze sperm, and you can freeze embryos, but no one cared much in the 1980s about freezing eggs. (There was one successful live birth in 1986 with a previously frozen egg, but the technology stalled after this.) There were several good reasons not to pursue this course: The only reason for oocyte retrieval at that time was to get pregnant immediately, which meant immediate fertilization in vitro. If any excess embryos were left over, they could be frozen for another attempt when a couple decided to expand their family. So why bother with freezing eggs?

But in the 1990s, many women who were about to undergo chemotherapy or radiation therapy for cancer and lose ovarian function began asking their doctors if it would be possible to freeze their eggs. If you already had a partner, you could freeze your embryos. But suppose you were in your twenties and hadn't yet met your mate; or you were divorced, in your thirties or forties. You'd need to save eggs, not embryos. If a woman was not in a stable relationship, she would have a choice of donor sperm or nothing.

The success rates for freezing eggs were really low. The major problem was that fertilization tended not to occur in a frozen-and-subsequently-thawed egg. This was very discouraging. Why bother with a technology that wouldn't allow you to get past the first step of embryo formation? But when ICSI came along, the rules changed. As in the case of so many other scientific breakthroughs, allied technologies had to be rethought in light of this one new discovery.

During egg freezing, the zona pellucida hardens in much the same way it does after being fertilized, in order to prevent more than one sperm from entering the egg. This hardening during the freezing process is enough to prevent fertilization. The ICSI technology, developed to help weak sperm get through the zona pellucida, could now be used to help otherwise normal sperm to penetrate the hardened zona of a frozen-thawed egg. The egg would now fertilize and the remainder of the embryo process, including cell division, DNA replication, and subsequent implantation, could proceed normally.

Right now, egg freezing is still a lot less efficient than embryo freezing. The egg appears to be more sensitive to the freezing process due to the fact that the chromosomes are held by a sensitive spindle apparatus, quite different from the fertilized embryo's more hardy chromosome alignment. Additionally, the ICSI technology is still somewhat traumatic to the egg, and 10 to 20 percent of eggs die immediately upon being injected. Nevertheless, it is now clearly a viable option. A successful twin pregnancy resulting from a frozen-thawed egg donation was reported in October 1997 by Dr. Michael Tucker, an embryologist at Reproductive Biology Associates in Atlanta.

Egg freezing may once again change our concept of motherhood—and the restrictions we put on it. If in the future, a young woman doesn't know if she'll ever want to have children, or she's been told that she has a condition that might prevent her from doing so, she can opt to have her young eggs aspirated and cryopreserved. Held in suspended animation at the temperature of liquid nitrogen, these eggs may last for years, even decades, until she is ready to make use of them.

About Designer Embryos

It is possible, although not common, that both partners might have something wrong with their gametes and both egg and sperm will have to be provided by donors. If the woman is in her late forties, for example, and her husband had a prior vasectomy that can't be reversed, then their options will be extremely limited. They could use a donor egg and ICSI, if the husband had a minor surgical procedure to extract the sperm directly from his testicle. But suppose the male partner has no sperm at all. In that case, both egg and sperm would have to be donated and an embryo produced in the laboratory. This may be considered "pre-implantation adoption."

This couple might also choose to adopt a frozen embryo originally produced in another couple's ART cycle. If the donor couple has successfully become pregnant with an embryo from this batch and don't want additional children, they might be delighted to find recipients who could give their unused embryo a home. Such frozen embryos have very good pregnancy potential.

But there are other reasons that couples decide to adopt embryos, even when they don't both have deficient gametes. Maybe they're uncomfortable with the idea that only one of them will have genetic input into their child, so they both opt not to contribute any DNA to their offspring. The partner with a functional gamete bows out unselfishly, so that the couple can start their child's life on equal footing.

In some cases, couples borrow gametes just to save time and money. If they've already been through many unsuccessful ART procedures, they may feel that frozen embryo transfer, particularly using an embryo from another couple's successful ART cycle, will get them to their goal more quickly. In these instances, the incremental cost to the program of transferring such frozen embryos is very low and thus the cost to the "adopting" couple (about $2500 or $3000) is also relatively low compared with an egg donation or adoption of a child, which currently ranges from about $10,000 to $20,000.

I don't think that most couples are really interested in taking "designer embryos" to the max—that is, practicing a form of eugenics in order to produce a specific child with specific physical and mental characteristics. People who come right out and say that they want "perfect" children really mean that they would like attractive, intelligent, caring, competent, talented and coordinated offspring who otherwise resemble themselves. In all the years I've been helping couples to achieve pregnancies, their first wish is that their children, as much as possible, be products of their own genes. The desire for optimal physical and mental characteristics pales when compared with the longing to keep one's DNA in the family.

Sperm donation has been available for many years in this country. If there were truly a desire for perfectly engineered children, why wouldn't millions of men freely admit that they weren't up to the snuff, say, of a Nobel prize winner or an Olympic athlete? The vast majority of the population finds this line of reasoning ridiculous. Remember the argument about genetic variety. There would not be a lot of variation in the gene pool if every child was a product of, say, Michael Jordan and Marie Curie, or of Mother Theresa and Bill Gates. If you recall what happens to the errant strands of DNA during meiosis and mitosis, you'd have an incredibly tiny chance of ever getting the combination you planned for. And although there will always be a few misguided couples who will try for a child who has the mind of a Ph.D in physics, the body of glamorous movie star, and a compassionate but assertive personality, most just want a really great kid who's a little like them.

As a matter of fact, there has been a movement away from donor gametes as more and better reproductive treatments become available. The purpose of technology in medicine is to restore function where function has failed. So what we're aiming for with ART is to help a failing gamete, to restore a failing gonad, and to find new ways to permit the comingling of DNA. Designer embryos, no matter how perfectly selected, will necessarily always remain a second choice.

This is not to say that embryo adoption will disappear, or that there is something inherently wrong with it. There will always be instances of missing gonads and absent gametes that will require double donation. Assisted reproduction and donor gametes have simply expanded the options and possibilities for couples and individuals. Eugenics is just as unlikely to be practiced in the future as it has been in the past.

Preimplantation diagnosis

Imagine a time when a woman conceives naturally, then comes to her doctor's office five or six days after ovulation and fertilization for an exam. The physician will be able to flush out the blastocyst before it implants in the endometrium, and will be able to biopsy and analyze it for chromosomal abnormalities. If he finds a problem—a missing chromosome or one too many—the mother may choose not to put the blastocyst back. This is a lot nicer than undergoing prenatal testing and having an abortion when the pregnancy is several months along and the fetus is well-formed.

In the future, if an error in the DNA is detected, the doctor may be able to alter it through gene therapy—removing the deficient piece of DNA and splicing in a good piece that has the correct code for the correct protein. Life-threatening conditions or others that may predispose us to cancer or disability may be circumvented prior to implantation.

After working on whatever needs to be fixed, the doctor will replace the blastocyst in the mother's uterus with minimal damage.

The Next Ten Years

Well, what else could happen to the institution of motherhood? More significantly, what do we, as a society, want to happen?

The goal of assisted reproduction is to allow all adult human beings who so desire to reproduce, regardless of the physical limitations nature gave them. And eventually technology will overcome all the glitches that we've had in fertility. Egg donation was a big leap ahead for women who couldn't use their own gametes; ICSI made fatherhood possible for men who had previously only dreamed about it. But cytoplasmic donation will make egg donation largely obsolete. And, if we are smart enough, we'll come up with a synthetic cytoplasmic replacement, so that the cytoplasm donors will not have to undergo the soon-to-be primitive process of ovarian superovulation and follicle aspiration.

Maybe, one day we'll be able to achieve meiosis in the laboratory. So let's imagine taking an intestinal cell from a man without testicles, who currently can't produce sperm and therefore can't pass his genetic information along. If we can achieve meiosis from this cell, we could generate a gamete artificially which could be used for sexual reproduction. And a woman with no ovaries, and therefore no eggs, could also take a cell from another part of her body and have it reduced by meiosis in vitro to generate the genetic component of her gamete. These two artificial gametes would be accurate genetic reflections of the two parents. They could be injected into an enucleated egg or artificial cytoplasm, and a new genetic individual could be formed, leading to the birth of a baby whose characteristics would resemble those of the parents. It would be just the same as if fertilization had taken place in the conventional way. It wouldn't make any difference what gender the parents were.

Right now, meiosis in the laboratory is pure science fiction. In addition to this amazing technology, we'd also need to work on post-fertilization events within the egg. Somehow, we'd have to be able to create a *centrosome,* the organizing hub of the mitotic spindle that allows the chromosomes to align properly, and which is carried by the sperm. I have no idea right now how that could happen. But I'm not ruling out the fact that it might.

Once we get such advanced technology going, we can forget all about the ethical issues that currently trouble us the most, including intergenerational gamete donation, families in flux, and coercion of donors versus freedom to donate. But at the same time, entirely new ethical dilemmas will appear as we adapt to the new technology.

That's life. There's no way to stop the progress of knowledge, which brings with it lots of head scratching and soul searching. Technology is inherently neither good nor bad. The same science that gave us the hydrogen bomb will one day give us an inexhaustible supply of energy that will permit us to live in the cleanest of environments and perhaps travel to the stars. The revulsion of cloning will be overshadowed by the possibilities of restructuring cells in the human body that will eradicate disease. The same fledgling steps in assisted reproduction that will allow all adults to have babies will also permit the development of the perfect contraceptive. And that will solve another major problem of humanity—population control.

The experts and ethicists will never stop debating or offering guidelines. Nor should they. Broad guidelines and institutional oversight of local practice standards and ethical behavior are appropriate. But until the technology stabilizes, it's unrealistic to expect that we will be able to apply them over any appreciable period of time. So even though our current system of making decisions on a case-by-case basis seems disorganized, random, and sometimes dangerous, it doesn't really seem that we have much in the way of alternatives. Look back for a minute to where we were only 10 years ago, when a woman of 63 having a baby was unbelievable. Then it will be easier to imagine the perspective we'll have 10 years from now, when we can wonder at our earlier narrow-mindedness.

Life Beyond the Womb

The last thing a plant does before it dies is to send out seeds, to propagate a new tender organism. Human beings clearly wish to do the same. At midlife, as we look, Janus-faced into the past and the future at the same time, we can put forth a germ of our own immortality. The seeds we plant will blossom as we nurture them, and then blow away, far from our influence, taking with them all the devotion and care we've lavished to make them grow healthy and strong.

What better inheritance could medical science offer? By assisting the delicate coupling of egg and sperm, male and female, we can insure that a portion of all individuals will still be here if they want to be, centuries after their own demise.

We carry on our traditions, our heritage, by tracing our lines in the sand.

Resource Guide:
IVF Clinics in the United States

If you're interested in IVF and egg donation, you won't have to go far to find a facility and a physician who can help you. The following list is the most current available, compiled from a 1995 survey by SART (Society for American Reproductive Technology) and the Centers for Disease Control and Prevention.

We have adapted the list to exclude those programs that do not offer egg donation. Those starred with an asterisk do not offer egg donation if the recipient is over the age of 36.

EASTERN UNITED STATES

CONNECTICUT

Hartford Fertility and Reproductive Endocrinology Center, P.C.
100 Retreat Avenue, Suite 900
Hartford, CT 06106
Phone: (860) 525-8283
Fax: (860) 525-1930

Yale University School of Medicine
In Vitro Fertilization Program
Department of OB/GYN
333 Cedar Street, Dana 2
New Haven, CT 06510
Phone: (203) 785-4708
Fax: (203) 737-4093

New England Fertility Institute
1250 Summer Street
Stamford, CT 06905
Phone: (203) 325-3200
Fax: (203) 323-3130

DELAWARE

Reproductive Endocrine and Fertility Center of Delaware
4745 Stanton-Ogletown Road, Suite 111
Newark, DE 19713
Phone: (302) 738-4600
Fax: (302) 738-3508

DISTRICT OF COLUMBIA

Columbia Hospital for Women
Medical Center ART Program
2440 "M" Street, N.W., Suite 401
Washington, DC 20037
Phone: (202) 293-6567
Fax: (202) 778-6190

George Washington University
IVF Program
2150 Pennsylvania Avenue, N.W.
Washington, DC 20037
Phone: (202) 994-4614
Fax: (202) 994-0815

FLORIDA

Fertility Institute of Boca Raton
875 Meadows Road, Suite 334
Boca Raton, FL 33486
Phone: (561) 368-5500
Fax: (561) 368-4793

Arnold Palmer Hospital Fertility Center
23 West Copeland Drive
Mail Point 127
Orlando, FL 32806
Phone: (407) 649-6995
Fax: (407) 841-3367

Center for Infertility and Reproductive Medicine
3435 Pinehurst Avenue
Orlando, FL 32804-4002
Phone: (407) 740-0909
Fax: (407) 740-7262

Reproductive Medicine and Fertility Center
615 East Princeton Street, Suite 225
Orlando, FL 32803
Phone: (407) 896-7575
Fax: (407) 894-2692

University of Miami IVF Program
601 North Flamingo Road, Suite 205
Pembroke Pines, FL 33028
Phone: (800) 550-4405
Fax: (954) 430-5223

Center for Advanced Reproductive Endocrinology
4100 South Hospital Drive, Suite 209
Plantation, FL 33317
Phone: (954) 584-2273
Fax: (954) 587-9630

Northwest Center for Infertility and Reproductive Endocrinology
2825 N. State Road 7, Suite 302
Margate, FL 33063
Phone: (954) 972-5001
Fax: (954) 972-6310

Tampa IVF Center
University of South Florida College of Medicine
Harbourside Medical Tower, Suite 529
4 Columbia Drive
Tampa, FL 33606
Phone: (813) 254-7774
Fax: (813) 254-0940

Women's Health Care and Reproductive Services
12611 World Plaza Lane
Fort Myers, FL 33907
Phone: (941) 275-8118
Fax: (941) 275-5914

Park Avenue Women's Center
Shand's Hospital University of Florida
807 N.W. 57th Street, Suite C
Gainesville, FL 32605-6400
Phone: (800) OB-GYN-UF
Fax: (352) 392-6204

First Coast Assisted Fertility
3627 University Boulevard, Suite 450
Jacksonville, FL 32216
Phone: (904) 391-1149
Fax: (904) 399-3436

Florida Institute for Reproductive Medicine
836 Prudential Drive, Suite 902
Jacksonville, FL 32207
(Phone: (904) 399-5620
Fax: (904) 399-5645

South Florida Institute for Reproductive Medicine
6250 Sunset Drive, 2nd Floor
Miami, FL 33143
Phone: (305) 662-7901
Fax: (305) 662-7910

GEORGIA

Reproductive Biology Associates IVF Program
5505 Peachtree Dunwoody Road, N.E., Suite 400
Atlanta, GA 30342
Phone: (404) 843-3064
Fax: (404) 257-0792
or 256-1528

MARYLAND

Center for Advanced Reproductive Technology at the
    University of Maryland
405 West Redwood Street
Baltimore, MD 21201
Phone: (410) 328-2304
Fax: (410) 328-8389

The GBMC Fertility Center
6569 North Charles Street, Suite 406
Baltimore, MD 21204 Phone: (410) 828-2484
Fax: (410) 828-3067

The Johns Hopkins Hospital
Department of OB/GYN
Houck Building, Room 249
600 North Wolfe Street
Baltimore, MD 21287-1247
Phone: (410) 955-6883
Fax: (410) 614-9684

The Union Memorial Hospital Assisted Reproductive
    Technology Program
201 East University Parkway
Baltimore, MD 21218
Phone: (410) 554-2632
Fax: (410) 554-2900

Center for Human Reproduction of the Mid-Atlantic
10215 Fernwood Road, Suite 303
Bethesda, MD 20817
Phone: (301) 897-8850
Fax: (301) 530-8105

Shady Grove Fertility Center
9707 Medical Center Drive, Suite 230
Rockville, MD 20850
Phone: (301) 340-1188
Fax: (301) 340-1612

MASSACHUSETTS

Brigham and Women's Hospital
IVF Program
75 Francis Street, ASB1+3
Boston, MA 02115 Phone: (617) 732-4455
Fax: (617) 232-6346

Faulkner Center for Reproductive Medicine
1153 Center Street
Boston, MA 02130
Phone: (617) 983-7379
Fax: (617) 983-7305

Boston IVF
One Brookline Place, Suite 602
Brookline, MA 02146
Phone: (617) 735-9000
Fax: (617) 566-3024

Fertility Center of New England
20 Pond Meadow Drive, Suite 101
Reading, MA 01867
Phone: (617) 942-7000
Fax: (617) 942-7200

Boston Regional Medical Center for Reproductive Medicine
3 Woodland Road
Stoneham, MA 02180
Phone: (617) 979-4700
Fax: (617) 665-9386

Reproductive Science Center of Boston
Deaconess—Waltham Hospital
Hope Avenue
Waltham, MA 02254
Phone: (617) 647-6263
Fax: (617) 647-6323

NEW JERSEY

East Coast Infertility and IVF
200 White Road Suite 214
Little Silver, NJ 07739
Phone: (908) 758-6511
Fax: (908) 758-1048

Institute of Reproductive Medicine
Saint Barnabas Medical Center
94 Old Short Hills Road
Livingston, NJ 07039
Phone: (201) 533-8286
Fax: (201) 533-8890

Cooper Center for IVF
8002 Greentree Commons
Marlton, NJ 08053
Phone: (609) 751-5575
Fax: (609) 751-7289

Diamond Institute for Infertility
IVF Program
89 Millburn Avenue
Millburn, NJ 07041
Phone: (201) 761-5600
Fax: (201) 761-5100

Robert Wood Johnson Medical School ART Program
303 George Street
Suite 250
New Brunswick, NJ 08901
Phone: (732) 235-7055
Fax: (732) 235-7318

IVF New Jersey
1527 Highway 27, Suite 2100
Somerset, NJ 08873
Phone: (732) 220-9060
Fax: (732) 220-1122

NEW YORK

Brooklyn Fertility Center
980 East 12th Street
Brooklyn, NY 11230
Phone: (718) 258-5880
Fax: (718) 951-9460

Montefiore's Fertility and Hormone Center
20 Beacon Hill Drive
Dobbs Ferry, NY 10522
Phone: (914) 693-8820
Fax: (914) 693-5428

Advanced Fertility Services
1625 Third Avenue
New York, NY 10128
Phone: (212) 369-8700
Fax: (212) 534-5873

Columbia University College of Physicians and Surgeons
Division of Assisted Reproduction
622 West 168th Street, PH-1630
New York, NY 10032
Phone: (212) 305-9175
Fax: (212) 305-3869

Cornell University Medical College
Center for Reproductive Medicine
505 East 70th Street
New York, NY 10021
Phone: (212) 746-3173
Fax: (212) 746-8996

New York Fertility Institute
1016 Fifth Avenue
New York, NY 10028
Phone: (212) 734-5555
Fax: (212) 734-6059

New York University Medical Center
Program for IVF, Reproductive Surgery, and Infertility
317 East 34th Street, Fourth Floor
New York, NY 10016
Phone: (212) 263-8990
Fax: (212) 263-7853
or 263-8827

Long Island IVF
625 Belle Terre Road, Suite 200
Port Jefferson, NY 11777
Phone: (516) 331-7575
Fax: (516) 331-1332

Strong Infertility and IVF Center
601 Elmwood Avenue
P.O. Box 685
Rochester, NY 14642
Phone: (716) 275-1930
Fax: (716) 756-4146

NORTH CAROLINA

North Carolina Center for Reproductive Medicine
400 Ashville Avenue, Suite 200
Cary, NC 27511-6676
Phone: (919) 233-1680
Fax: (919) 233-1685

University of North Carolina ART Program
Department of OB/GYN
CB 7570, Old Clinic Building
Chapel Hill, NC 27599-7570
Phone: (919) 966-5288
Fax: (919) 966-5214

Institute for Assisted Reproduction
200 Hawthorne Lane, Dept. 6A-IVF
Charlotte, NC 28233
Phone: (704) 384-5800
Fax: (704) 384-4604

Program for Assisted Reproduction at Carolinas Medical Center
1000 Blythe Boulevard
Charlotte, NC 28203
Phone: (704) 355-3153
Fax: (704) 355-1941

Reproductive Diagnostics Center
for Reproductive Medicine
330 Billingsly Road, Suite 200
Charlotte, NC 28222 Phone: (704) 372-4600
Fax: (704) 624-3841

Duke University Medical Center ART Program
Department of OB/GYN
Box 3143
Durham, NC 27710
Phone: (919) 684-5327
Fax: (919) 681-7904

Bowman Gray School of Medicine
Wake Forest University
Department of OB/GYN
Medical Center Boulevard
Winston-Salem, NC 27157-1067
Phone: (910) 716-3778
Fax: (910) 716-0194

Abington Memorial Hospital
Toll Center for Reproductive Sciences
1200 Old York Road
Abington, PA 19001
Phone: (215) 576-2349
Fax: (215) 576-7550

Reprotech IVF Program
440 South 15th Street
Allentown, PA 18102
Phone: (610) 437-7000
Fax: (610) 437-6381

Reproductive Gynecologists, P.C.
Keating Building, Suite 120
1 Bale Avenue
Bala Cynwyd, PA 19004
Phone: (610) 664-6550
Fax: (610) 660-0199

Advanced Fertility Institute
507 Delaware Avenue
Bethlehem, PA 18015 Phone: (610) 868-0661
Fax: (610) 868-1115

Family Fertility Center
95 Highland Avenue
Bethlehem, PA 18019
Phone: (610) 868-8600
Fax: (610) 868-8700

Geisinger Medical Center/Fertility Center
Division of OB/GYN
100 North Academy Avenue
Danville, PA 17822-0116
Phone: (717) 271-5620
Fax: (717) 271-5629

Pennsylvania State University ART Program
Department of OB/GYN
500 University Drive
P.O. Box 850
Hershey, PA 17033
Phone: (717) 531-6731
Fax: (717) 531-6286

Hospital of the University of Pennsylvania ART Program
3400 Spruce Street
106 Dulles Building
Philadelphia, PA 19104
Phone: (215) 662-2981
Fax: (215) 349-5512

Pennsylvania Reproductive Associates
IVF Program
Spruce Building, Room 786
8th and Spruce Streets
Philadelphia, PA 19107-7705
Phone: (215) 829-5095
Fax: (215) 829-7210

Thomas Jefferson University In Vitro Fertilization Program
834 Chestnut Street, Suite 300
Philadelphia, PA 19107
Phone: (215) 955-4018
Fax: (215) 923-1089

University Women's Health Care Associates
Magee Women's Hospital
300 Halket Street
Pittsburgh, PA 15213
Phone: (412) 641-4726
Fax: (412) 641-1133

Reproductive Endocrinology and Fertility
Crozer Chester Medical Center
1 Medical Center Boulevard
Upland, PA 19013-3995
Phone: (610) 447-2727
Fax: (610) 447-6549

Reproductive Science Center of Greater Philadelphia
950 West Valley Road, Suite 2401
Wayne, PA 19087
Phone: (610) 964-9663
Fax: (610) 964-0536

PUERTO RICO

Pedro J. Beauchamp Reproductive Endocrinology and Infertility
Centro Medico San Pablo
Edif. Dr. Cadilla, Suite 503
Paseo San Pablo 100
Bayamon, Puerto Rico 00959
Phone: (787) 798-3310
Fax: (787) 740-7250

Fertility Center of the Caribbean
Torre San Francisco, Suite 606
369 Dediego Avenue
Rio Piedras, Puerto Rico 00923
Phone: (787) 763-2773
Fax: (787) 763-2773

RHODE ISLAND

Women and Infants Hospital
Division of Reproductive Endocrinology
101 Dudley Street
Providence, RI 02905
Phone: (401) 453-7500
Fax: (401) 453-7598

SOUTH CAROLINA

Reproductive Endocrinology and Infertility
Greenville Hospital System Center for Women's Medicine
890 West Faris Road, Suite 470
Greenville, SC 29605
Phone: (864) 455-8488
Fax: (864) 455-8489

Southeastern Fertility Center
IVF Program
1375 Hospital Drive
Mount Pleasant, SC 29464
Phone: (803) 881-3900
Fax: (803) 881-4729

VIRGINIA

Dominion Fertility and Endocrinology
46 South Glebe Road, Suite 301
Arlington, VA 22204
Phone: (703) 920-3890
Fax: (703) 892-6037

Eastern Virginia Medical School
The Jones Institute for Reproductive Medicine
601 Colley Avenue
Norfolk, VA 23507
Phone: (757) 446-7116
Fax: (757) 446-8998

Medical College of Virginia
IVF Program
P.O. Box 9800034, MCV Station
Richmond, VA 23298
Phone: (804) 828-0810
Fax: (804) 828-0573

Richmond Center for Fertility and
Endocrinology Ltd.
7603 Forest Avenue, Suite 301
Richmond, VA 23229
Phone: (804) 285-9742
Fax: (804) 285-9745

WEST VIRGINIA

West Virginia University Center for Reproductive Medicine
830 Pennsylvania Avenue, Suite 304
Charleston, WV 25302
Phone: (304) 342-0816
Fax: (304) 342-0828

CENTRAL UNITED STATES

ALABAMA

ART at Birmingham
Women's Medical Plaza, Suite 508
2006 Brookwood Medical Center Drive
Birmingham, AL 35209
Phone: (205) 870-9784
Fax: (205) 870-0698

University of Alabama-Birmingham
IVF Program
Kirklin Clinic
Sixth Avenue South
Birmingham, AL 35294
Phone: (205) 801-8225
Fax: (205) 934-0914

ARKANSAS

University of Arkansas IVF Program
Freeway Medical Tower, Suite 705
5800 West Tenth Street
Little Rock, AR 72204
Phone: (501) 296-1705
Fax: (501) 296-1711

ILLINOIS

Center for Human Reproduction
IVF Program
750 North Orleans Street
Chicago, IL 60610
Phone: (312) 397-8000
Fax: (312) 397-8399

IVF Illinois
836 West Wellington
Chicago, IL 60657
Phone: (773) 296-7090
Fax: (773) 528-8704

Prentice Women's Hospital
Northwestern University Medical School
333 East Superior, Suite 1576
Chicago, IL 60611
Phone: (312) 908-8244
Fax: (312) 908-6643

Rush-Presbyterian-St. Luke's Medical Center
1653 West Congress Parkway
Chicago, IL 60612
Phone: (312) 942-6609
Fax: (312) 942-4043

University of Chicago IVF Program
Department of OB/GYN, MC 2050
5841 Maryland Avenue
Chicago, IL 60637
Phone: (773) 702-6642
Fax: (773) 702-5848

Midwest Infertility Center
4333 Main Street
Downers Grove, IL 60515
Phone: (630) 810-0212
Fax: (630) 810-1027

Highland Park Hospital Fertility Center
750 Homewood Avenue, Suite 190
Highland Park, IL 60035-2497
Phone: (847) 480-3950
Fax: (847) 480-2608

Oak Brook Fertility Center
Reproductive Endocrinology/Infertility
2425 West 22nd Street, Suite 102
Oak Brook, IL 60523
Phone: (630) 954-0054
Fax: (630) 954-0064

Center for Fertility and Reproductive Medicine/Lutheran General
  Hospital
1775 Dempster, 1 South
Park Ridge, IL 60068
Phone: (847) 723-8785
Fax: (847) 723-8219

Rockford Health Systems Departmentof Reproductive Medicine
Rockford Memorial Hospital
2350 North Rockton Avenue, Suite 408
Rockford, IL 61103
Phone: (815) 971-7234
Fax: (815) 971-7425

INDIANA

Advanced Fertility Institute
201 North Pennsylvania Parkway, Suite 205
Indianapolis, IN 46280
Phone: (317) 817-1300
Fax: (317) 817-1316

Indianapolis Fertility Center
IVF Program
8081 Township Line Road
Indianapolis, IN 46260
Phone: (317) 875-5978, ext. 3060
Fax: (317) 872-5063

IOWA

University of Iowa Hospitals and Clinics
Center for Advanced Reproductive Care
Department of OB/GYN, Bldg. MRF
Room 565
Iowa City, IA 52242
Phone: (319) 356-8483
Fax: (319) 353-6659

Mid-Iowa Fertility
3408 Woodland Avenue, Suite 302
West Des Moines, IA 50266
Phone: (515) 222-3060
Fax: (515) 222-9563

KANSAS

Reproductive Resource Center of Greater Kansas City
12200 West 106th Street, Suite 120
Overland Park, KS 66215
Phone: (913) 894-2323
Fax: (913) 894-0841

The Center for Reproductive Medicine
Reproductive Medicine Laboratories
2903 East Central
Wichita, KS 67214
Phone: (316) 687-2112
Fax: (316) 687-1260

KENTUCKY

Alliant Health System Fertility Center
Women's Pavilion Health and Resource Center
315 East Broadway
P.O. Box 35070
Louisville, KY 40232-5070
Phone: (502) 629-8157
Fax: (502) 629-7004

LOUISIANA

Fertility and Laser Center IVF Program
4720 I-10 Service Road, Suite 100
Metairie, LA 70001
Phone: (504) 454-2165
Fax: (504) 888-2250

Fertility Institute of New Orleans
6020 Bullard Avenue
New Orleans, LA 70128
Phone: (504) 246-8971
Fax: (504) 246-9778

Center for Fertility and Reproductive Health
Louisiana State University School
of Medicine
150 Kings Highway
Shreveport, LA 71130
Phone: (318) 632-8276
Fax: (318) 632-8275

MICHIGAN

University of Michigan Medical Center
Division of Reproductive
Endocrinology IVF Program
1324 Taubman Center
1500 East Medical Center Drive
Ann Arbor, MI 48109-0718
Phone: (313) 763-4323
Fax: (313) 763-7682

Oakwood Hospital Center for
Reproductive Medicine
Oakwood Medical Building, Suite 109
18181 Oakwood Boulevard
Dearborn, MI 48124-4092
Phone: (313) 593-5880
Fax: (313) 593-8837

Wayne State University IVF Clinic
Hutzel Hospital
4707 St. Antoine
Detroit, MI 48201
Phone: (313) 745-7547
Fax: (313) 745-7037

Center for Reproductive Medicine
2 Hurley Plaza, Suite 101
Flint, MI 48503 Phone: (810) 257-9714
Fax: (810) 762-7040

Grand Rapids Fertility and IVF
1900 Wealthy Street, S.E., Suite 315
Grand Rapids, MI 49506
Phone: (616) 774-2030
Fax: (616) 774-2053

West Michigan Reproductive Institute, P.C.
885 Forest Hill Avenue, S.E.
Grand Rapids, MI 49546
Phone: (616) 942-5180
Fax: (616) 942-2450

Sparrow Hospital Fertility Center
1215 East Michigan Avenue P.O. Box 30480
Lansing, MI 48909-7980
Phone: (517) 483-2700
Fax: (517) 483-2837

FIRST, Inc., IVF Program
5400 Mackinaw Suite 2400
Saginaw, MI 48604
Phone: (517) 792-8771
Fax: (517) 792-3377

Henry Ford Medical Center
IVF Program
1500 West Big Beaver, Suite 100
Troy, MI 48084
Phone: (248) 637-4050
Fax: (248) 637-4025

Ann Arbor Reproductive Medicine Associates
Ann Arbor Office Center, Suite 100
4990 Clark Road
Ypsilanti, MI 48197
Phone: (313) 434-4766
Fax: (313) 434-8848

MINNESOTA

Center for Reproductive Medicine
and IVF Minnesota
Abbott Northwestern Hospital
2800 Chicago Avenue, South, 3rd Floor
Minneapolis, MN 55407-1320
Phone: (612) 863-5390
Fax: (612) 863-2697

Midwest Center for Reproductive Health
Oakdale Medical Building, Suite 550
3366 Oakdale Avenue, North
Minneapolis, MN 55422
Phone: (612) 520-2600
Fax: (612) 520-2606

University of Minnesota
Women's Health Clinic
Department of OB/GYN
Box 395 UMHC
Minneapolis, MN 55455
Phone: (612) 626-3232
Fax: (612) 626-0665

Mayo Clinic Assisted Reproductive Technology
200 First Street, S.W.
Rochester, MN 55905
Phone: (507) 284-4520
Fax: (507) 284-1774

Reproductive Health Associates
360 Sherman Street, Suite 350
St. Paul, MN 55102
Phone: (612) 222-8666
Fax: (612) 222-8657

MISSISSIPPI

University of Mississippi Medical Center
IVF Program
2500 North State Street
Jackson, MS 39216-4505
Phone: (601) 984-5330
Fax: (601) 984-5965

MISSOURI

Advanced Assisted Reproductive Technology Program
Washington University School of Medicine
Department of OB/GYN
4444 Forest Park Avenue
St. Louis, MO 63110
Phone: (314) 286-2459
Fax: (314) 286-2455

Infertility Center of St. Louis at St. Luke's Hospital
    IVF and GIFT Program
224 South Woods Mill Road, Suite 730
St. Louis, MO 63017
Phone: (314) 576-1400
Fax: (314) 576-1442

NEBRASKA

Nebraska Methodist Hospital Reproductive Endocrinology and
    Assisted Reproductive Technologies Laboratories
8111 Dodge Street, Suite 237
Omaha, NE 68114
Phone: (402) 354-5210
Fax: (402) 354-5221

University of Nebraska IVF Program
600 South 42nd Street
Omaha, NE 68198-3255
Phone: (402) 559-4214
Fax: (402) 559-4520

OHIO

Akron City Hospital IVF Program
525 East Market Street, Suite 410
Akron, OH 44309
Phone: (330) 375-3585
Fax: (330) 375-3986

Fertility Unlimited, Inc.
Northeastern Ohio Fertility Center
468 East Market Street
Akron, OH 44304
Phone: (330) 376-2300
Fax: (330) 376-4807

Bethesda Fertility Center/Infertility Unit
619 Oak Street
Cincinnati, OH 43506
Phone: (513) 569-6086
Fax: (513) 569-6098

Center for Reproductive Health
University Hospital, Inc.
Eden and Bethesda Avenues
Cincinnati, OH 45267-0456
Phone: (513) 558-2730
Fax: (513) 558-8916

Greater Cincinnati Institute forReproductive Health
   at the Christ Hospital
2123 Auburn Avenue, Suite A44
Cincinnati, OH 45219
Phone: (513) 629-4400
Fax: (513) 629-4595

University Hospital of Cleveland
IVF Program
11100 Euclid Avenue
Cleveland, OH 44106
Phone: (216) 844-1514
Fax: (216) 844-8619

Ohio Reproductive Medicine
4830 Knightsbridge Boulevard, Suite E
Columbus, OH 43214
Phone: (614) 451-2280
Fax: (614) 451-4352

Miami Valley Hospital Fertility Center
One Wyoming Street
Dayton, OH 45409
Phone: (937) 208-2327
Fax: (937) 208-2450

Fertility Center of Northwest Ohio
2142 North Cove Boulevard
Toledo, OH 43606
Phone: (419) 479-8830
Fax: (419) 479-6005

OKLAHOMA

Henry G. Bennett, Jr., Fertility Institute
IVF Program
3433 N.W. 56th Street, Suite 200
Oklahoma City, OK 73112
Phone: (405) 949-6060
Fax: (405) 949-6872

Center for Reproductive Health
1000 North Lincoln Boulevard, Suite 300
Oklahoma City, OK 73104
Phone: (405) 271-9200
Fax: (405) 271-9222

TENNESSEE

Appalachian Fertility and Endocrinology Center
2204 Pavilion Drive, Suite 305
Kingsport, TN 37660
Phone: (423) 392-6400
Fax: (423) 392-6053

University Fertility Associates of
UT Medical Group, Inc.
909 Ridgeway Loop Road
Memphis, TN 38120-4020
Phone: (901) 767-6868
Fax: (901) 683-2231

Center for Assisted Reproduction
Centennial Medical Center
2400 Patterson Street, Suite 319
Nashville, TN 37203-1546
Phone: (615) 321-4740
Fax: (615) 320-0240

Vanderbilt Center for Reproductive Medicine
Vanderbilt University, C-1100 MCN
Nashville, TN 37232-2515
Phone: (615) 322-6576
Fax: (615) 343-4902

WISCONSIN

Women's Endocrine Clinic
University of Wisconsin Hospital
600 Highland Avenue
Madison, WI 53792-6188
Phone: (608) 263-1201
Fax: (608) 263-0191

Marshfield Clinic Fertility Center
1000 North Oak Avenue
Marshfield, WI 54449-5777
Phone: (715) 389-3103
Fax: (715) 389-3808

Advanced Institute of Fertility
Sinai Samaritan Medical Center
2000 West Kilbourn Avenue, Suite C462
Milwaukee, WI 53233
Phone: (414) 937-5437
Fax: (414) 937-5446

Reproductive Specialty Center
2315 North Lake Drive, Suite 501
Milwaukee, WI 53211
Phone: (414) 289-9668
Fax: (414) 289-0974

WESTERN UNITED STATES

ARIZONA

Fertility Treatment Center
3200 North Dobson, Suite F-7
Chandler, AZ 85224
Phone: (602) 831-2445
Fax: (602) 897-1283

Arizona Institute of Reproductive Medicine, Ltd.
2850 North 24th Street, Suite 503
Phoenix, AZ 85008
Phone: (602) 468-3840
Fax: (602) 468-2449

Arizona Center for Fertility Studies
8997 East Desert Cove Avenue, 2nd Floor
Scottsdale, AZ 85260
Phone: (602) 860-4792
Fax: (602) 860-6819

Reproductive Endocrinology and Infertility
1501 North Campbell Avenue
Tucson, AZ 85724
Phone: (520) 626-3943
Fax: (520) 626-2768

CALIFORNIA

Alta Bates In Vitro Fertilization Program
2999 Regent Street, Suite 101-A
Berkeley, CA 94705
Phone: (510) 649-0440
Fax: (510) 649-8700

West Coast Infertility and Reproductive Associates
250 North Robertson Road, Suite 403
Beverly Hills, CA 90211
Phone: (310) 285-0333
Fax: (310) 285-0334

Central California IVF Program
6215 North Fresno, Suite 108
Fresno, CA 93710
Phone: (209) 439-1914
Fax: (209) 439-3936

West Coast Fertility Centers
301 West Bastanchury Road, Suite 175
Fullerton, CA 92835
Phone: (714) 446-1234
Fax: (714) 446-9163

Werlin and Zarutskie Fertility Center
4900 Baranca Parkway
Irvine, CA 92604
Phone: (714) 726-0600
Fax: (714) 726-0601

Reproductive Sciences Center
4150 Regents Park Row, Suite 280
La Jolla, CA 92034
Phone: (619) 625-0125
Fax: (619) 625-0131

University Infertility Associates
701 East 28th Street, Suite 202
Long Beach, CA 90806-2759
Phone: (562) 427-2229
Fax: (562) 933-7895

Century City Hospital Center for Reproductive Medicine
2070 Century Park East
Los Angeles, CA 90067
Phone: (310) 201-6619
Fax: (310) 201-6657

UCLA Fertility Center IVF Program
10833 Le Conte Avenue, Room 22-177 CHS
Los Angeles, CA 90024
Phone: (310) 825-7755
Fax: (310) 206-3670

University of Southern California IVF Program
1245 Wilshire Blvd.,Suite 403
Los Angeles, CA 90017
Phone: (213) 975-9990
Fax: (213) 975-9997

NOVA In Vitro Fertilization
1681 El Camino
Real Palo Alto, CA 94306
Phone: (415) 322-0500
Fax: (415) 322-5404

· Huntington Reproductive Center
301 South Fair Oaks Avenue, Suite 402
Pasadena, CA 91105
Phone: (818) 440-9161
Fax: (818) 440-0138

Center for Advanced Reproductive Care
510 North Prospect, Suite 202
Redondo Beach, CA 90277
Phone: (310) 318-3010
Fax: (310) 798-7304

Northern California Fertility Medical Center
406 1/2 Sunrise Avenue, Suite 3A
Roseville, CA 95661
Phone: (916) 773-2229
Fax: (916) 773-8391

Pacific Fertility Center at Sacramento
2288 Auburn Boulevard, Suite 204
Sacramento, CA 95821
Phone: (916) 567-1302
Fax: (916) 567-1360

IGO Medical Group
9339 Genesee Avenue, Suite 220
San Diego, CA 92121
Phone: (619) 455-7520
Fax: (619) 554-1312

Reproductive Endocrine Associates
6719 Alvarado Road, Suite 108
San Diego, CA 92120
Phone: (619) 265-1800
Fax: (619) 265-4055

Sharp Fertility Center
IVF Sharp-Mary Birch Hospital for Women
3003 Health Center Drive
San Diego, CA 92123
Phone: (619) 541-4949
Fax: (619) 541-4165

Astarte Fertility Medical Center
450 Sutter Street, Suite 2215
San Francisco, CA 94108
Phone: (415) 773-3413
Fax: (415) 837-1155

Pacific Fertility Center-San Francisco
55 Francisco Street, Suite 500
San Francisco, CA 94133
Phone: (415) 834-3000
Fax: (415) 834-3099

San Francisco Center for Reproductive Medicine
390 Laurel Street, Suite 205
San Francisco, CA 94118
Phone: (415) 771-1483
Fax: (415) 771-6974

University of California-San Francisco
IVF Program
350 Parnassus, Suite 300
San Francisco, CA 94117
Phone: (415) 476-5405
Fax: (415) 502-4944

Fertility and Reproductive Health Institute of Northern California
2516 Samaritan Drive, Suite A
San Jose, CA 95125
Phone: (408) 358-2500
Fax: (408) 356-8954

Center for Reproductive Medicine
San Ramon Regional Medical Center
6001 Norris Canyon Road
San Ramon, CA 94583
Phone: (510) 275-8255
Fax: (510) 275-8336

California Fertility Associates
IVF Program
1245 16th Street, Suite 220
Santa Monica, CA 90404
Phone: (310) 828-4008
Fax: (310) 828-3310

The Fertility Institutes
18370 Burbank Boulevard, Suite 414
Tarzana, CA 91356
Phone: (818) 776-9892
Fax: (818) 776-8754

COLORADO

Colorado Springs Center for Reproductive Health
1625 Medical Center Point, Suite 290
Colorado Springs, CO 80907
Phone: (719) 636-0080
Fax: (719) 636-3030

Colorado Reproductive Endocrinology
3600 East Alameda Avenue, Suite 220
Denver, CO 80209
Phone: (303) 321-7115
Fax: (303) 321-9519

University of Colorado Health Sciences Center
Department of OB/GYN
4200 East Ninth Avenue
Campus Box B-198
Denver, CO 80262
Phone: (303) 315-7128
Fax: (303) 315-8889

Colorado Center for Reproductive Medicine
799 East Hampden Avenue, Suite 300
Englewood, CO 80110
Phone: (303) 788-8300
Fax: (303) 788-8310

Conceptions Women's Health and Fertility Specialists
7720 South Broadway, Suite 580
Littleton, CO 80122-2624
Phone: (303) 794-0045
Fax: (303) 794-2054

NEVADA

Fertility Center of Las Vegas
8815 West Sahara, Suite 100
Las Vegas, NV 89117
Phone: (702) 254-1777
Fax: (702) 254-1213

University Institute for Fertility
820 Shadow Lane, Suite 100
Las Vegas, NV 89106
Phone: (702) 384-5645
Fax: (702) 384-7712

Northern Nevada Fertility
75 Pringle Way, Suite 803
Reno, NV 89502
Phone: (702) 688-5600
Fax: (702) 322-3603

NEW MEXICO

Reproductive Endocrinology and Infertility Associates of New Mexico
Presbyterian Professional Building
201 Cedar Street, S.E., Suite 207
Albuquerque, NM 87106
Phone: (505) 247-0000
Fax: (505) 224-7476

Southwest Fertility Services
1720 Wyoming, N.E.
Albuquerque, NM 87112
Phone: (505) 271-9651
Fax: (505) 332-2103

OREGON

Northwest Fertility Center
1750 S.W. Harbor Way, Suite 200
Portland, OR 97201
Phone: (503) 227-7799
Fax: (503) 227-5452

University Fertility Consultants
Oregon Health Sciences University
1750 S.W. Harbor Way, Suite 100
Portland, OR 97201-5164
Phone: (503) 418-3774
Fax: (503) 418-3757

TEXAS

Center for Assisted Reproduction
1701 Park Place Avenue
Bedford, TX 76022
Phone: (817) 540-1157
Fax: (817) 267-0522

National Fertility Center of Texas
7777 Forest Lane, Building C-638
Dallas, TX 75230-2517
Phone: (972) 788-6686
Fax: (972) 566-6670

University of Texas Southwestern Medical Center at Dallas
Southwestern Fertility Associates
5323 Harry Hines Boulevard
Dallas, TX 75235-9032
Phone: (214) 648-7642
Fax: (214) 648-2813

Baylor ART Program
6550 Fannin Street
Houston, TX 77030
Phone: (713) 798-8484
Fax: (713) 798-8431

The Center for Reproductive Medicine
3506 21st Street, Suite 605
Lubbock, TX 79410
Phone: (806) 788-1212
Fax: (806) 788-1253

Fertility Center of San Antonio Methodist Plaza
4499 Medical Drive, Suite 360
San Antonio, TX 78229
Phone: (210) 692-0577
Fax: (210) 692-1210

South Texas Fertility Center
Methodist Women's and Children's Hospital
7703 Floyd Curl Drive
San Antonio, TX 78284-7836
Phone: (210) 567-6121
Fax: (210) 567-4958

UTAH

Utah Center for Reproductive Medicine
50 North Medical Drive
Salt Lake City, UT 84132
Phone: (801) 581-4838
Fax: (801) 585-2231

WASHINGTON

Washington Center for Reproductive Medicine
1370 116th Avenue, N.E., Suite 202
Bellevue, WA 98004
Phone: (425) 462-6100
Fax: (425) 635-0742

Olympia Women's Health
403 Black Hills Lane, S.W.
Olympia, WA 98502
Phone: (360) 786-1515
Fax: (360) 754-7476

Seattle Fertility and Gynecology Clinic/Swedish Hospital
1229 Madison Street, Suite 1220
Seattle, WA 98104
Phone: (206) 682-2200
or 682-9935
Fax: (206) 682-5434

University of Washington Fertility and Endocrine Center
4225 Roosevelt Way, N.E., Suite 101
Seattle, WA 98105
Phone: (206) 548-4225
Fax: (206) 548-6081

Virginia Mason Fertility and Reproductive Endocrine Center
1100 9th Avenue, Mailstop X8-OB
P.O. Box 900
Seattle, WA 98111
Phone: (206) 223-6191
Fax: (206) 625-7274

GLOSSARY

Acrosome reaction: The chemical and physical changes in the membrane on the head of the sperm that allow it to penetrate an egg.

Ampulla: The wide distal end of the fallopian tube where the sperm must meet the egg in order for fertilization to take place.

Anovulatory cycle: A menstrual cycle that takes place even though ovulation has not occurred—common in perimenopausal women.

Aspiration: A procedure for collecting eggs from the ovaries done by passing a hollow needle into each fluid-filled follicle. The fluid is sucked out ("aspirated") and the egg separated from the fluid under the microscope in the laboratory. An aspiration can be performed laparoscopically or, most commonly, under ultrasound guidance by the transvaginal route.

Assisted hatching: A technique done in the laboratory whereby a small opening is made in the zona pellucida of the embryo in order to facilitate implantation.

Assisted reproductive technology (ART): Any treatment that involves the manipulation of human gametes in order to assist a pregnancy. Types of ART include IVF, GIFT, ZIFT, and TET, as well as egg or embryo donation, cryopreservation, and surrogate birth.

Blastocele: The fluid-filled cavity in the middle of the blastocyst.

Blastocyst: The stage of embryonic development that is reached about one hundred and twenty hours after fertilization. At this stage, a fluid-filled cavity (the *blastocele*) develops in the center of the embryo and cells begin to specialize. Some of them will go on to become the fetus, some will become the placenta.

Blastomere: One of several dividing cells that make up the preembryo—a new mitotic division takes place approximately every twelve hours after fertilization.

Capacitation: A change in the sperm cell, causing hyperactivity and faster swimming, that enables the acrosome reaction and penetration of the egg. It takes place after the sperm has passed through the cervical mucus of the female reproductive tract or when prepared for insemination in the laboratory.

Centrosome: A hollow structure within the cytoplasm of the cell near the nucleus, closed on one end and open on the other, that contains two centrioles which organize the mitotic spindle, then separate during mitosis, each becoming part of the two new daughter cells.

Cervical mucus: The secretion produced by glands in the cervical canal which changes throughout the cycle from watery and slippery at the time of ovulation to crumbly and dry right afterward.

Cervix: The opening of the uterus at its lowest end; essentially, it is a narrow canal that connects the vaginal canal with the uterine corpus where implantation takes place.

Chromosome: The structure within a cell's nucleus that holds the DNA. Each cell has 46 chromosomes, except for the gametes which have 23.

Cloning: Growing cells in a laboratory that are exact replications of one another.

Corpus luteum: The yellow body that is formed from the collapsed follicle after it releases its egg. The corpus luteum produces progesterone as well as some estrogen after ovulation, in order to prepare the lining of the uterus for implantation of an embryo.

Cortical granules: Tiny vesticles which line the outside of the oolemma of the mature egg. When a sperm successfully binds to the oolemma, indicating that fertilization has taken place, chemicals from these granules are released into the space beneath the zona pellucida, hardening it so that no other sperm can enter the egg.

Cryopreservation: Storing tissue or cells by freezing them in liquid nitrogen.

Culture medium: The fluid solution used in the laboratory to grow cells in vitro.

Cumulus: The sticky white cloudlike clump of cells that develops around the egg just prior to ovulation and which accompanies it during and after ovulation or aspiration.

Cytoplasm: The protein-rich gelatinous fluid surrounding the nucleus of a cell that contains microscopic structures that guide cell development and function.

Deoxyribonucleic acid (DNA): The long, strandlike molecule in each cell's nucleus that contains the genetic code.

Dominant follicle: The largest follicle that develops in one female cycle containing the egg that will ovulate

Donor egg: An egg retrieved from one woman which will be inseminated in vitro. The resulting embryo will then be transferred to another woman.

Donor embryo: An embryo formed from a dual donation of both egg and sperm which will be transferred, in a process called embryo transfer, to a recipient in order to achieve a pregnancy.

Donor insemination: Insemination with sperm other than that of the recipient's partner.

Downregulation: The process by which the natural female cycle is halted with a GnRH agonist, like Lupron, in order to stop the pituitary from producing the gonadotropins FSH and LH and the ovary from developing follicles and producing estrogen.

Ectopic pregnancy: A pregnancy that implants outside the uterine cavity, most commonly in the fallopian tube.

Egg retrieval: Retrieval of eggs from the ovary. See also *Aspiration.*

Ejaculate: The seminal fluid that emanates from the penis during sexual climax and carries the sperm cells out of the male reproductive tract.

Embryo: A fertilized egg that has gone through one or more cell divisions. Also, the stage of human development that is marked from the time of fertilization through the eighth week of pregnancy. See also *Zygote.*

Embryo transfer: The replacement of one or several embryos back into the female reproductive tract; usually understood to mean transcervical embryo transfer, in which the embryos are placed directly into the uterine cavity approximately 72 hours after fertilization. See also, tubal embryo transfer.

Endometrial biopsy: A sample of tissue taken from the endometrium. In egg donation, it is performed on the recipient prior to the donation attempt during a practice cycle. The purpose is to examine the condition of the endometrium and determine its receptivity to an embryo.

Endometriosis: A condition in which nests of cells from the endometrium grow outside of the uterine cavity, most commonly in the abdomen and pelvis, behind the uterus and in the ovaries. It is associated with infertility and may lead to tubal blockage and pelvic pain.

Endometrium: The tissue that lines the interior of the uterus. It grows during estrogen stimulation, becomes receptive to implantation when stimulated by progesterone, and sloughs off during menses.

Epididymis: The location in the male reproductive tract where sperm collect after leaving the testicle.

Estradiol (E2): The most potent of a class of hormones called estrogens, produced by the follicle, corpus luteum, and the placenta.

Estrogen: The female sex hormone that predominates during the first half or follicular phase of the menstrual cycle. This hormone, in addition to assuring female sex characteristics, also interacts with over three hundred tissues in the body, including the bones and the heart. Its levels are greatly diminished after menopause.

Fallopian tube: One of two narrow tubes that carries the egg from the ovary to the uterus. Fertilization of the egg by the sperm takes place at the distal end of this tube. See also *Oviduct.*

Fertilization: Penetration of the egg by the sperm.

Fetus: The stage of human development that follows the embryo; from about 7 to 8 weeks after fertilization until birth.

Fimbriae: The fingerlike projections of the fallopian tubes that pick up the egg as it falls from its follicle after ovulation.

First polar body: A small satellite portion of the egg located within the zona pellucida which is pinched off from the main part of the egg to fertilization. It contains half the chromosomes as a result of the first meiotic division. See also *Second polar body.*

Follicle: The fluid-filled, estrogen-producing sac that encloses the egg inside the ovary. During ovulation, the follicle bursts open, releasing the egg into the peritoneal cavity.

Follicle-stimulating hormone (FSH): The gonadal hormone released by the pituitary gland that acts as a messenger to the ovary or testicle, telling them to ripen one or more follicles in the female and to produce sperm in the male.

Follicular phase: The first half of the female menstrual cycle, driven by the production of FSH by the pituitary and characterized by the release of estrogen from the follicle.

Gamete: The male or female reproductive cell, that is, the sperm or the egg.

Gamete intrafallopian transfer (GIFT): A laparoscopic procedure where the sperm and egg are placed in the fallopian tube together.

Germ cells: The precursors of gametes.

Gestational surrogacy: A pregnancy where a woman other than the mother carries the fetus. This usually occurs in cases where the mother has had a hysterectomy and has no uterus, but may also occur when the mother has an illness that would make labor and delivery too dangerous for her.

Gonadotropin-releasing hormone (GnRH): The hormone released by the hypothalamus that stimulates the pituitary to produce and release the gonadotropins FSH and LH.

Gonadotropins: The hormones FSH and LH which stimulate ovarian function in the female and testicular function in the male.

Gonads: The gamete-producing organs, that is, the ovary in the female and the testis in the male.

Granulosa cells: The helper cells in the follicle that make estrogen and progesterone.

Hatching: The activity of the embryo breaking out of the zona pellucida so that it can implant in the endometrium.

Human chorionic gonadotropin (hCG): A hormone produced by the placenta during pregnancy which is also akin to LH. During an ovulation stimulation cycle, this hormone is given 36 hours before aspiration to prepare the follicles to release their eggs.

Human menopausal gonadotropin (hMG): A preparation of the gonadotropins FSH and LH manufactured from the collected urine of postmenopausal women. After menopause, the ovaries send no feedback signals to the pituitary, which consequently produces large quantities of gonadotropins which are then excreted in the urine. See *Humegon, Pergonal, Repronex.*

Humegon: One of several brands of hMG. This medication is used to stimulate the ovaries to produce multiple, large follicles.

Implantation: The attachment of the embryo to the uterine wall.

In vitro fertilization: (IVF): An ART procedure that involves aspirating eggs from a woman's ovary and combining them in a petri dish with sperm that has been ejaculated into a container and prepared in the laboratory. The resulting embryos are then transferred back into the woman's body, either through her cervix or through the fallopian tubes.

Intracytoplasmic sperm injection (ICSI): A procedure to correct male infertility in which a single sperm is injected into a mature egg so that fertilization can take place in the laboratory.

Intrauterine insemination (IUI): The simplest type of ART, where ejaculated sperm is prepared in the laboratory, and then placed into the uterine cavity at an appropriate time in the woman's cycle.

Isthmus: The part of the fallopian tube closest to the uterus where the embryo must travel before implantation

Laparoscopy: A surgical procedure in which a tiny incision is made near the navel and a telescope-like instrument is inserted in order to examine the internal organs.

Lupron: A brand of leuprolide acetate, the medication given to stop the natural menstrual cycle. It suppresses the pituitary, which suppresses ovarian function, putting the body into a state similar to menopause.

Luteal phase: The second half of the female menstrual cycle, dominated by the LH surge and subsequent production of progesterone by the corpus luteum. It begins with ovulation and ends with menses.

Luteinizing hormone (LH): The gonadal hormone released by the pituitary gland that stimulates hormonal production by the follicle and corpus luteum in the female and the testicle in the male. It is produced in large quantities during the female midcycle LH surge.

LH surge: The release of a great quantity of the hormone LH from the pituitary which triggers ovulation and the resumption of meiosis in the egg.

Meiosis: The process of cell division typical only of gametes. During this process, which means "lessening" in Greek, the cell rids itself of its genetic load by throwing off half the original number of chromosomes.

Menstruation: The sloughing off of the lining of the uterus which marks the end of one female cycle and the beginning of another. It is characterized by low levels of estradiol and a thin endometrium.

Micromanipulation: The use of a powerful microscope and remotely controlled fine instruments to manipulate gametes and embryos, e.g. to inject the sperm inside the egg in the laboratory.

Mitosis: The type of cell division typical of all cells except gametes. The genetic material is duplicated, then partitioned off into two cells. When the cell splits in half, the two daughter cells have exactly the same amount and same copies of the original DNA.

Mitotic spindle: The spindle-shaped array of microtubules which holds the 46-chromosomes (23 pairs) during mitotic division.

Motility: The designation of the quality of sperm movement

Multiple birth: A pregnancy that results in more than one child.

Nucleus: The structure inside each cell that contains the DNA.

Oocyte: The female reproductive cell; an egg.

Oogonia: The germ cell precursors of eggs within fetal ovaries.

Oolemma: The cell membrane of the egg. It is surrounded by the zona pellucida.

Ovary: The female gonad, or reproductive organ, that holds the oocytes and is responsible for the production of estrogen and progesterone.

Ovarian hyperstimulation syndrome: A potentially dangerous condition that can result after ovarian stimulation and ovulation or follicle aspiration in which vasoactive elements from the corpus luteum release fluid from blood vessels into the abdominal cavity. This can result in dehydration, clot formation, or difficulty in breathing.

Ovarian stimulation: The use of medication (an FSH-like drug) to encourage the ovary to produce multiple follicles and eggs in a cycle.

Oviduct: Fallopian tube.

Ovulation: the release of the egg from the follicle.

Pergonal: One of several brands of hMG. This medication is used to stimulate the ovaries to produce multiple, large follicles.

Pituitary gland: The gland at the base of the brain that secretes the gonadotropins and other hormones that control the endocrine system.

Pre-embryo: The term used by ethicists to denote the stage from fertilization to about two weeks after implantation when the fetal plate forms and when the implanted pregnancy can no longer split into more than one individual. (Embryologists commonly refer to all stages beyond fertilization as the "embryo.")

Pregnancy test: A blood or urine test to detect whether levels of hCG (human chorionic gonadotropin) are elevated, indicating that implantation of the embryo has occurred.

Preimplantation diagnosis: Examination of embryonic cells prior to implantation to determine whether the embryo will be genetically normal.

Premature ovarian failure: Aa disorder of the female reproductive system whereby the ovaries stop functioning before the age of 40, also called "premature menopause."

Primary follicle: An early form of the follicle, containing an immature egg in which the surrounding helper cells first start to form a fluid-filled center. See also *Follicle*.

Primordial follicle: The earliest form of the follicle, developed in the fetal ovary, containing an immature egg and a single layer of helper cells. Most follicles in the ovary are of the primordial variety at any given time. They remain in this state until they begin the process toward ovulation by becoming primary follicles. See also *Follicle*.

Progesterone (P4): The hormone produced by the corpus luteum that readies the endometrium to receive an embryo for implantation.

Prolactin: The hormone produced by the pituitary during pregnancy to prepare the mammary glands for lactation.

Pronuclear stage: The stage of embryonic development just after fertilization when the chromosomes from the egg and sperm are bundled separately, and before both sets of genes have co-mingled.

Pronucleus, female and male: A nucleuslike structure that holds either the male or female half of the chromosomes in a fertilized zygote before the genes have comingled. The pronuclei are visible with a microscope 14 to 18 hours after insemination.

Pulse oximeter: The instrument that measures respiration in the donor during follicle aspiration. This device can detect the oxygenation of the blood that flows through a finger. It tells us that the patient is not only breathing normally, but that she is oxygenating well and her circulation is carrying oxygenated blood to all parts of her body.

Repronex: One of several brands of hMG. This medication is used to produce multiple, large follicles.

Retrograde ejaculation: A disorder of the male reproductive system in which the ejaculate flows backwards into the bladder rather than out through the prostatic urethra.

Retrograde menstruation: A condition of the female reproductive system whereby menstrual blood and debris flows back into the pelvic cavity rather than out through the cervix and into the vagina during a menstrual period. A small amount of retrograde menstruation is common and probably normal; in combination with other factors or if extreme, however, it is thought to be responsible for the disease endometriosis.

Scrotal sac: The saclike structure that holds the testes.

Second polar body: The second satellite of the egg which results from the second meiotic division. It contains half the DNA remaining in the egg and a tiny portion of cytoplasm. Since second meiosis is completed only after successful penetration of the egg by a sperm, the presence of a second polar body is evidence of successful fertilization. See also *First polar body.*

Semen: The mixture of sperm and seminal fluid released during ejaculation.

Seminal fluid: The liquid that carries the sperm out of the male reproductive tract.

Sperm: The male reproductive cell.

Sperm aster: The starlike structure that surrounds the decondensed sperm head after fertilization. The formation of the aster is thought to be the sperm's method of moving and organizing the chromosomes prior to and during the 2-pronuclear stage.

Sperm washing: A laboratory technique using a culture medium, a centrifuge or a density gradient in order to separate sperm cells from seminal fluid.

Spermatocyte: An immature sperm cell.

Superovulation: The use of medication (an FSH-like drug) to encourage the ovary to produce multiple follicles and eggs in a cycle. Also known as "controlled ovarian hyperstimulation." See also *Ovarian stimulation.*

Testicle: The male gonad or reproductive organ that holds the sperm and produces the hormone testosterone.

Testosterone: The male sex hormone produced in large quantities in the male and in lesser quantities by the female. It is the chemical precursor of estradiol.

Trophectoderm: the outer layer of cells of the blastocyst.

Trophoblast: The leading cells of the implanting embryo that produce hCG and are destined to become the placenta.

Tubal embryo transfer (TET): An ART technique whereby the embryo, grown in the laboratory, is placed laparoscopically into the fallopian tube. This procedure is often used for women who have had prior uterine surgery or who have abnormally shaped uteri because they were exposed to DES in utero. These conditions would make transcervical embryo transfer difficult or impossible.

Ultrasound: High-frequency sound waves that bounce off tissues and organs in the body in order to make an image on a monitor.

Ultrasound-directed aspiration: The ART technique that uses a vaginal probe and ultrasound to guide a hollow needle to retrieve eggs from follicles in the ovary.

Uterus: The muscular, pear-shaped organ in the female reproductive system that carries the developing fetus. It is lined with a layer of cells called the "endometrium."

Vagina: The portion of the female reproductive system that connects the external sex organs (vulva) with the internal (cervix and uterus).

Vas deferens: The tube in the male reproductive system that connects the epididymis where the sperm are stored, to the prostate, where they pick up the seminal fluid on their way to the penis.

Vasectomy: A method of sterilizing the male by surgically creating an obstruction of the vas deferens. This blocks the passage of sperm so that it cannot leave the testicular area.

Zona pellucida: The human eggshell; the hard protein covering that protects the egg and subsequently the embryo up to the point of implantation.

Zygote: A fertilized egg. After this one-celled entity has gone through several cell divisions, it is usually called the "embryo."

Zygote intrafallopian transfer (ZIFT): The ART technique whereby a fertilized egg is placed into the fallopian tube.

BIBLIOGRAPHY

Blank, Robert H. and Andrea L. Bonnicksen, Eds. *Emerging Issues in Biomedical Policy: An Annual Review, Vol.1.* Columbia University Press, New York, 1992.

Corea, Gena. *The Mother Machine: Reproductive Technologies from Artificial Insemination to Artificial Wombs.* Harper and Row Publishers, New York, 1985.

Domar, Alice D., Ph.D. and Henry Dreher. *Healing Mind, Healthy Woman.* Henry Holt and Company, New York 1996.

Edwards, Robert. *Life Before Birth: Reflections on the Embryo Debate.* Basic Books, New York 1990.

Friedeman, Joyce Sutkamp, Ph.D. *Building Your Family Through Egg Donation.* Jolance Press, Fort Thomas, KY 1996.

Jansen, Robert, M.D. *Overcoming Infertility.* W.H. Freeman, New York, 1997.

Kitzinger, Sheila. *Ourselves as Mothers.* Addison-Wesley Publishing Co., Reading, MA, 1995.

Maranto, Gina. *The Quest for Perfection: The Drive to Breed Better Human Beings.* Scribner, New York, 1996.

Marrs, Richard, and Lisa Friedman Bloch and Kathy Kirtland Silverman. *Dr. Richard Marrs' Fertility Book.* Delacorte Press, New York, 1997.

McGee, Glenn. *The Perfect Baby.* Rowman & Littlefield Publishers, Inc. Lanham, MD 1997.

Morris, Monica. *Last-Chance Children.* Columbia University Press, New York, 1988.

Robertson, John A. *Children of Choice: Freedom and the New Reproductive Technologies.* Princeton University Press, Princeton, NJ, 1994.

Schwartz, Judith D. *The Mother Puzzle: How A New Generation Reckons With Motherhood.* Simon & Schuster, New York, 1993.

Silber, Sherman J. *How To Get Pregnant With the New Technology.* Warner Books, Inc., New York, 1991.

Wisot, Arthur and Meldrum, David. *Conceptions and Misconceptions: A Guide Through the Maze of In-Vitro Fertilization and other Reproductive Techniques.* Hartley & Marx, Point Roberts, WA 1988, 1997.

INDEX